THE 1989 ELECTION OF THE EUROPEAN PARLIAMENT

Also by Juliet Lodge

THE EUROPEAN POLICY OF THE SPD
THE NEW ZEALAND GENERAL ELECTION OF 1975 (*with Stephen Levine*)
THE EUROPEAN PARLIAMENT AND THE EUROPEAN COMMUNITY
   (*with Valentine Herman*)
TERRORISM: a Challenge to the State (*editor*)
THE EUROPEAN COMMUNITY AND NEW ZEALAND
DIRECT ELECTIONS TO THE EUROPEAN PARLIAMENT: a Community
   Perspective (*with Valentine Herman*)
INSTITUTIONS AND POLICIES OF THE EUROPEAN COMMUNITY (*editor*)
THE EUROPEAN COMMUNITY: Bibliographical Excursions (*editor*)
DIRECT ELECTIONS TO THE EUROPEAN PARLIAMENT 1984 (*editor*)
EUROPEAN UNION: the European Community in Search of a Future (*editor*)
THE THREAT OF TERRORISM (*editor*)
THE EUROPEAN COMMUNITY AND THE CHALLENGE OF THE FUTURE
   (*editor*)

The 1989 Election of the European Parliament

Edited by

Juliet Lodge
*Reader in European Community Politics
and Director of the European Community
Research Unit, University of Hull*

St. Martin's Press   New York

Selection and editorial matter © Juliet Lodge 1990
Chapter 1 © Juliet Lodge 1990
Chapter 2 © John Fitzmaurice 1990
Chapter 3 © Alastair H. Thomas 1990
Chapter 4 © Eva Kolinsky1990
Chapter 5 © Kevin Featherstone and Susannah Verney 1990
Chapter 6 © Richard Gillespie 1990
Chapter 7 © Paul Hainsworth 1990
Chapter 8 © Michael Gallagher 1990
Chapter 9 © Philip Daniels 1990
Chapter 10 © Ruud Koole 1990
Chapter 11 © Michael Burgess and Adrian Lee 1990
Chapter 12 © Juliet Lodge 1990

First published in the United States of America in 1990

Printed in Great Britain

ISBN 0-312-04494-1

Library of Congress Cataloging-in-Publication Data

The 1989 Election of the European Parliament/edited by Juliet Lodge.
    p.   cm.
    ISBN 0-312-04494-1
    1. European Parliament—Elections, 1989. I. Lodge, Juliet.
JN36.D55 1990
324.94'0558—dc20
                           89-70326
                              CIP

To Keri-Michèle, David and Christopher

Contents

List of Tables

Preface

The third direct elections to the European Parliament (EP) took place in a climate of some optimism as to the possibilities for further European integration. The political implications of the mere phrase 'a Single European Market' and the magic numerals 1992 (and 1993 in France) remained obscure. There was little sign of the *Angst* that surrounded the implications of the first EP elections in 1979. Equally remarkable was the complacency that greeted the idea of European Union. In both 1979 and 1984, European Union was often spurned as a fanciful federal fantasy. Stemming the accretion of the EP's power, so often seen as necessary to preventing a slide into federalism, had then also commended itself to many governments and parties. Yet in 1989, when the EP had actually gained in influence, little was heard against it. This suggests not only that the EP had become accepted as a legitimate EC institution in its own right but that its pursuit of greater power was no longer easily to be exploited by its opponents and opponents of the EC as an illegitimate aspiration. Furthermore, in none of the states was the desirability of continued EC membership a key issue around which the electorate could be mobilised.

In contrast to the two previous direct elections, when the EC seemed to be drifting in a somewhat directionless manner, the 1989 EP elections took place against a seemingly concrete, pragmatic backcloth. The Single European Market was the goal and few had fathomed its implications, costs and benefits. Fewer made much of them in the elections themselves. Instead, in each member state, the EP elections became another occasion for domestic political jousting. At the same time, as each of the following case studies show, the Euro-dimension to the elections was not to be completely eclipsed.

This book aims to provide a brief overview of the 1989 EP elections in each of the member states. Each case study addresses a common set of issues. Each is designed to be intelligible to non-specialists and to those unfamiliar with the state in question. An introductory chapter surveys the EP's development over the past decade. While progress can be recorded in respect of two of the outstanding issues of the 1979 and 1984 EP elections (the EP's seat and its role in the EC's legislative process) resolution of the third (the uniform electoral procedure) remains elusive. Space limitations preclude the inclusion of a comprehensive bibliography. However, a great deal of material on the 1979 and 1984 EP elections and on the EP itself is now available in English as well as other EC languages.

We thank the EP's Press and Information Offices throughout the EC, the EP party groups, the transnational federations, national parties, EP officials, MEPs and EP candidates for their forbearance in answering our questions. Editing the volume was facilitated by the good-humoured cooperation of the contributors, the eagle-eye of my husband, and the consumer-testing of election stickers and novelties by my children: Luxembourg Euro-lollies, the Belgian EP elections dove logo, and the Socialist Group badge won hands down.

Hull, July 1989   JULIET LODGE

List of Abbreviations

ABC	Atomic, Bacteriological, Chemical
AGALEV	Anders Gaan Leven
AP	Alianza Popular
BRT	Belgian Radio/TV (Flemish)
CD	Centrum-Demokraterne
CDA	Christen Demokratisch Appèl
CDS	Centre des Démocrates Sociaux
CDS	Centro Democrático y Social
CDS	Partido do Centro Democrático Social
CDU	Christlich-Demokratische Union
CDU	Coligação Democrática Unitária
CGT	Confédération générale des travailleurs
CiU	Convergència i Unió
CN	Coalición Nacionalista
COM	Communist and Allies Group
COMECON	Council for Mutual Economic Assistance
CONS	Conservative and Unionist Party
CPN	Communistische Partij Nederland
CSP	Confederation of Socialist Parties of the EC
CSU	Christlich-Soziale Union
CSV	Chreschtlech Sozial Volekspartei
CVP	Christelijke Volkspartij
DC	Democrazia Cristiana
DI.ANA	Dimokratikí Ananéosi
DKP	Danmarks Kommunistiske Parti
DM	Deutsch Mark
DP	Democrazia Proletaria
DP	Demokratesch Partei
DR	Denmarks Retsforbundet
DS	Dansk Samling
D'66	Demokraten 66
DUP	Democratic Unionist Party
DVU	Deutsche Volksunion
EC	European Community
ECJ	European Court of Justice
ECOLO	Mouvement 'Ecolo' – 'Les Verts'
ECSC	European Coal and Steel Community

ECU	European Currency Unit
ED	European Democratic Group
EDA	Eniaía Dimokratikí Aristerá
EDA	European Democratic Alliance
EDOK	Ellinikó Dimokratikó Oikologikó Kínima
EDU	European Democratic Union
EE	Euskadiko Ezkerra
EEC	European Economic Community
EFTA	European Free Trade Area
ELD	European Liberals and Democrats
ELDR	European Liberal, Democratic and Reform Parties
EMS	European Monetary System
EMU	Economic and Monetary Union
EP	Coalición por la Europa de los Pueblos
EP	European Parliament
EPC	European Political Cooperation
EPEN	Ethnikí Politikí Ēnossis
EPP	European People's Party
ER	Group of the European Right
ERASMUS	European Community Action Scheme for Mobility of University Students
ERDF	European Regional Development Fund
ERT	Ellinikí Radiofonía Tileórasi
ESF	European Social Fund
ETA	Euskadi Ta Askatasuna
EUL	Group of the European United Left
EURATOM	European Atomic Energy Community
EUREKA	European Research Coordination Agency
EUT	European Union Treaty
EVP	Europese Volkspartij
EVP	Evangelische Volks Partij
FB	Folkebevægelsen mod EF
FDF	Front Démocratique des Francophones
FDF/ERE	Front Démocratique des Francophones/Europe Regions, Ecologie
FDP	Freie Demokratische Partei Deutschlands
FF	Fianna Fail
FF	French Franc
FG	Fine Gael
FN	Front Nationale
FRG	Federal Republic of Germany

FRP	Fremskridtspartiet
GAL	Grupos Antiterroristas de Liberación
GAP	Greng Alternativ Partei
GDP	Gross Domestic Product
GLEI	Greng Lëscht fir Ecologesch Initiativ
GMO	God Met Ons
GPV	Gereformeerd Politiek Verbond
GRAEL	Grüne Alternativ Allianz
GRAL	Greng Alternativ Allianz
HB	Herri Batasuna
IAC	EP Committee on Institutional Affairs
IDE	Initiative for European Democracy
IGC	Inter-governmental Conference
IND	'Non-attached' MEPs
INF	Intermediate-range Nuclear Forces
IP	Izquierda de los Pueblos
IRA	Irish Republican Army
IU	Izquierda Unida
KAP	Kommunistiske Arbejderparti
KF	Det Konservative Folkeparti
KKE	Kommounistiko Komma tis Elladas
KKE-es	Kommounistiko Komma tis Elladas esoterikou
KODISO	Komma Dimokratikou Sosialismou
KPL	Kommunistesch Partei Letzëburg
KRF	Kristeligt Folkeparti
LAB	Labour Party
LDR	Liberal and Democratic Reformist Group
LO	Landsorganisationen
LSAP	Letzeburger Sozialistisch Arbechterpartei
LU	Left Unity
MEP	Member of the European Parliament
MRC	Movement of Communist Renovators
MRG	Mouvement des Radicaux de Gauche
MSI–DN	Movimento Sociale Italiano–Destra Nazionale
NATO	North Atlantic Treaty Organisation
NB	National Bewegong
ND	Nea Dimokratia
NF	Nordisk Folkeparti
NOP	National Opinion Poll
NPD	Nationaldemokratische Partei Deutschlands
ÖDP	Ökologisch-Demokratische Partei

OIK.ENAL	Oikológoi Enallaktikoí
OI.KI.P.AN	Oikologikó Kínima Politikí Anagénnisi
OJ	Official Journal
OUP	Official Unionist Party
PA	Partido Andalucista
PAC	EP Political Affairs Committee
PASOK	Panellinio Sosialistiko Kinima
PCE	Partido Comunista España
PCF	Parti Communiste Français
PCI	Partito Communista Italiano
PCP	Partido Comunista Português
PDS	Progressive Democrats
PLI	Partito Liberale Italiano
PNV	Partido Nacionalista Vasco
POS	Parti Ouvrier Socialist
PP	Partido Popular
PPR	Politieke Partij Radikalen
PR	Parti Républicain
PR	Partito Radical
PR	Proportional Representation
PRD	Partido Renovador Democrático
PRI	Partito Repubblicano Italiano
PRL	Parti Réformateur Libéral
PS	Partido Socialista
PS	Parti Socialiste
PSC	Parti Social Chrétien
PSD	Partido Social Democrata
PSDI	Partito Socialista Democratico Italiano
PSI	Partito Socialista Italiano
PSOE	Partido Socialista Obrero Español
PSP	Pacifistisch Socialistische Partij
PTB	Parti des Travailleurs Belges
PTE	Partido de los Trabajadores de España
PvdA	Partij van de Arbeid
PvdA	Partij von de Arbijd
PVV	Partij voor Vrijheid en Vooruitgang
RAI	Radiotelevisione Italiana
RBW	Rainbow Group
REP	Die Republikaner
RPF	Reformatorisch Politieke Federatie
RPR	Rassemblement pour la République

RTE	Radio Telefis Eireann
RTFB	Belgian Radio/TV (Francophone)
RV	Radikale Venstre
S	Socialdemokratiet
SDLP	Social Democratic and Labour Party
SDP	Social Democratic Party
SEA	Single European Act
SEM	Single European Market
SF	Socialistisk Folkeparti
SGP	Staatkundig Gereformeerde Partij
SLD	Social and Liberal Democratic Party
SNP	Scottish National Party
SOC	Socialist Group
SP	Socialistische Partij
SPD	Sozialdemokratische Partei Deutschlands
STOA	Scientific and Technical Operations Assessment
STV	Single Transferable Vote
SVP	Südtiroler Volkspartei
TD	Teachta Dala
The Nine	Members of the EC after the first enlargement (Six plus Denmark, Ireland and UK)
The Six	Members of the EC before enlargement (France, Italy, FRG, Belgium, Luxembourg and the Netherlands)
The Ten	Members of the EC after the second enlargement (Nine plus Greece)
The Twelve	Members of the EC after the third enlargement (Ten plus Portugal and Spain)
TUC	Trades Union Congress
UCD	Unión del Centro Democrático
UDC	Union de Centre
UDF	Union pour la Démocratie Française
UEP	Uniform Electoral Procedure
UGT	União Geral dos Trabalhadores
UGT	Union General de Trabajadores
UK	United Kingdom
UN	United Nations
USA	United States of America
USSR	Union of Soviet Socialist Republics
V	Venstre, Danmarks Liberale Parti
VAT	Value Added Tax

VEGA	Verts et Gauche Alternative
VS	Venstre Socialisterne
VU	Volksunie
VVD	Volkspartij voor Vrijheid en Democr
WWF	World Wildlife Fund
YES	Youth Exchange Scheme

Notes on the Contributors

Michael Burgess is a Senior Lecturer in Politics at Polytechnic South West. He is the author of *Federalism and European Union: Political Ideas, Influences and Strategies in the European Community, 1972–1987*.

Philip Daniels is a Lecturer in Politics at the University of Newcastle-upon-Tyne. He is the author of numerous articles on Italian politics.

Kevin Featherstone is a Lecturer in the Department of European Studies at the University of Bradford. He is the author of *Socialist Parties and European Integration: A Comparative History* and co-editor of *Political Change in Greece: Before and After the Colonels*.

John Fitzmaurice works for the Commission of the European Communities in Brussels. He is the author of *The Party Groups in the European Parliament, The European Parliament, Politics in Belgium* and *Politics in Denmark*, and co-author of *The European Parliament: a Guide to Direct Elections*. He has just completed *In Defence of Austria*.

Michael Gallagher is a Lecturer in Politics at Trinity College, Dublin. He is the author of *The Irish Labour Party in Transition, Political Parties in the Republic of Ireland*, and co-editor of *Candidate Selection in Comparative Perspective: the Secret Garden of Politics*.

Richard Gillespie is Lecturer in the Politics of Mediterranean Europe at the University of Warwick. He is the author of *The Spanish Socialist Party*.

Paul Hainsworth is a Lecturer in Politics at the University of Ulster at Jordanstown. He is the co-author of *Decentralisation and Change in Contemporary France* and *Northern Ireland and the European Community: An Economic and Political Perspective*.

Eva Kolinsky is Professor of German at the University of Bath. She is the author of *Engagierter Expressionismus, Literatur zwischen Weltkrieg und Politik, Parties, Opposition and Society in West Germany*, and editor of *Opposition in Western Europe*.

Ruud A. Koole is a Lecturer in Political Science at the University of Leiden. He is the author of various volumes and numerous articles on Dutch politics.

Adrian Lee is Head of the Department of Social and Political Studies at Polytechnic South West. His research interests are in territorial politics and electoral behaviour.

Juliet Lodge is Reader in European Community Politics and Director of the European Community Research Unit at the University of Hull. She is the author and editor of books on the European Community, including *The European Community and New Zealand, Institutions and Policies of the European Community, Direct Elections to the European Parliament 1984, European Union: The European Community in Search of a Future, The Threat of Terrorism* and *The European Community and the Challenge of the Future*, and co-author of *The European Parliament and the European Community* and *Direct Elections to the European Parliament: A Community Perspective*.

Alastair H. Thomas is Principal Lecturer in Political Science at Lancashire Polytechnic in Preston. He is the co-author of *The Consensual Democracies? The Government and Politics of the Scandinavian States* and *The Future of Social Democracy*: *Problems and Prospects of Social Democratic Parties in Western Europe*.

Susannah Verney is an Associate of the Centre for Development Studies, Research and Management (KAMEO) in Athens. She is the author of a number of articles on Greek–EC relations and other aspects of contemporary Greek politics.

1 Ten Years of an Elected European Parliament

JULIET LODGE

Vilified as impotent, irrelevant and a waste of time and money, the European Parliament receives arguably the worst press of all parliaments within the boundaries of the European Community. Negative and undeserved as its poor image is in many states, the third elections to the European Parliament held on 15 and 18 June 1989 overturned popular media portrayals and expectations of the European Parliament overnight. In Britain, in particular (where turnout was only a few percentage points above the 1984 and 1979 levels and where it remained the lowest of any EC state), the transformation in expectations of the widely misrepresented EP was astounding. Moreover, there were hints of a similar transformation of expectations even in countries where turnout had fallen below the 1984 levels and in which such decline was partly attributed to the relatively weak powers conferred on the EP. Ten years after its first direct election the EP had come of age. But why had it taken so long for its potential to be recognised? Why, moreover, after ten years of pundits insisting that Euro-elections were little more than second-order national elections did the EP acquire a clear 'European' image when its Members (MEPs) almost without exception had been elected on platforms in campaigns fought predominantly on national issues?

This is the supreme irony. The 1989 Euro-elections were portrayed almost everywhere throughout the EC as referenda on national governments' records. In the Netherlands, they were seen as a prelude to the summer general election; in the FRG they were seen as a test of Chancellor Kohl's standing with the electorate; in Greece, Ireland and (as is usual in) Luxembourg simultaneous general elections occurred. In the latter, the fear that electorates and candidates might both confuse and/or fail to differentiate national and Euro-issues seemed to be realised. In them, keener interest in the campaigns was observed (at least for some of the time). Turnout was relatively high (not least because voting was compulsory!). But it must not be assumed that the diagnosis of national-issue dominance meant that that is all the 1989 elections were about. It is true that keen interest in and disagreement over national issues were at the heart of the campaigns in the member states but there has been an almost imperceptible change in the EP's stature over the past decade. The 1989 elections also publicly legitimated the 1992 debate.

It is certainly true that national issues seemed to be to the fore. Government parties and opposition parties clashed more vividly than in past EP election campaigns. However, they clashed not so much on the traditional lines of schism or on pro- or anti-Europeanism (e.g. in such states as Denmark, the UK and Greece). Rather, they clashed over the fare of typical national campaigns: over redistributive policy issues that characterise domestic politics. Everywhere, there was concern about social policy, economic and environmental issues. In past EP election campaigns these issues have been raised *de rigueur* by each of the parties. In none, however, have the parties managed convincingly to suggest that they differed fundamentally from one another in their policy prescriptions, all of which have seemed anodyne and platitudinous compared with the cut-and-thrust of 'domestic' electoral debates over the same broad territory.

In 1989 all was changed utterly. The somewhat artificial distinction between things 'European' and things 'national' was subsumed in a battle for the ideological high ground. For the first time in the EC's history, it was made clear that the political priorities of competing parties differed sharply. Moreover, they were presented in a way familiar to the electorate. Voters were given a choice. The parties did not try to present a picture of what they stood for on a wide range of issues. Instead, they simplified the electoral agenda. They made it visible and intelligible. They outlined a range of alternative *future* scenarios and suggested that tangible outcomes would flow from opting for one set of priorities over another. That they were able to do so may be explained in terms of the Europeanisation of national, domestic politics. But such an explanation, while suggestive, oversimplifies and overlooks many factors. Like the previous thesis of the nationalisation of European issues, it fails to take due account of the context within which the EP elections took place.

THE POLITICO-ECONOMIC CONTEXT

The background to the 1989 EP elections can be probed from many perspectives. The internal party political processes and determination of the campaigns provide fascinating fodder for researchers. Parties' interaction with transnational federations (where relevant) and cross-national links are also interesting. However, for the purposes of this very brief overview of the elections, the discussion will focus on macro-level developments. The selection of this perspective can be justified in terms of a critical factor to the 1989 EP elections: the Single European Market (SEM). The 1989 EP elections, though fought by national parties on national issues, nevertheless had a distinctly European flavour.

The high profile given to the SEM's completion since 1985 created public awareness of the EC dimension to politico-economic life. The EC Commission (possibly consciously) and the member states' heads of government, sometimes deliberately, sometimes unconsciously, set the agenda of the 1989 Euro-elections. From the time of the furore at the Milan European Council to the belated implementation of the Single European Act (SEA), the ground was prepared for a political debate on the EC's future. That it should have had an inward-looking focus is not altogether surprising. National elections are rarely fought on international issues. That the EP, the EP's party groups and the national parties should have chosen to contest the 1989 EP elections on a predetermined agenda is interesting. That voters should have responded to them and now anticipate further change of a partisan nature in terms of policy outcomes is even more surprising and places a considerable burden on the EP to deliver. The system transformation within the EC that has taken place over the past decade is incomplete. MEPs are expected to deliver on their promises. They can only do so if further change occurs.

In order to appreciate how much change has taken place since the 1979 EP elections and how much potential there is for the EP to prove that it has come of age in the 1990s, it is necessary to examine the EP's record and the contextual changes to EP elections of the past decade. To this end, this chapter divides into three parts. The first looks at the background, facilitative, environmental conditions of change; the second scrutinises the instruments of change; and the third explores how these have opened new possibilities for replacing the negative image of the EP as an anodyne, static and supine irrelevance with a positive image of it as the dynamo of future change based on principles of justice and democracy.

I Background conditions

From the time of the first EP elections the covert, even subconscious, agenda of the EC was securing a quantum leap in European integration. This was not clearly articulated until the eve of the 1984 EP elections. Even then, the rhetoric of European Union and the need to avoid overly upsetting national political sensitivities hid the significance of the wave of change gathering momentum throughout the first half of the 1980s.

The 1980s opened with slippage in the EC's relative position in the international political economy. Stagflation, the greater competitiveness of the USA and Japan and the ascendancy of the newly industrialising countries in key economic sectors exacerbated a generalised feeling of anxiety. The EC needed to run fast to stand still. Economists made much of the EC's market fragmentation and the alleged benefits that economies of scale would bring if steps could be taken to encourage appropriate changes in economic strategy in the private and public sectors. Particular attention was paid to the question of realising the internal market and eliminating practices that restricted intra-EC trade and distorted competition. These two phrases potentially were all-embracing. While this cannot be discussed here, what is interesting is that this concern was shared widely. It was apparent within the member states, within those seeking EC entry and in the EC's rump. More importantly, it preoccupied the EC's key institutions.

What is often overlooked is the EP's crucial role in moving the debate along. Arguably without its intervention in the early 1980s through the Albert and Ball report, subsequent endeavours to expedite the realisation of the 'internal market' (soon to be known as the Single European Market (SEM)) would have had a much rougher ride. Before returning to the EP's role in the SEM, it will be useful briefly to outline the role of the Commission (which relied on the EP's reinforcing activity, that benefited them both) and to draw attention to the fact that successive European Councils agitated for action, notably from the time of the 1982 Copenhagen summit to the 1984 Fontainebleau and Dublin summits.

The Commission remained the most visible stimulus behind the moves to realise the SEM. From the time of the Commission's 1980 mandate, it issued a regular series of communications to the Council of Ministers and the European Council suggesting lines of action. It also advanced several specific proposals but, finding progress slow, embarked on a campaign to heighten government awareness of the consequences of further prevarication given the state of the international political economy. Through its various communications and its now-famous June 1985 White Paper on the completion of the internal market, it let the member states see the future.[1]

The underlying assumption was that the removal of physical, fiscal and technical barriers to intra-EC trade would realise the four freedoms and help significantly to create the conditions for economic prosperity and the EC's economic revival in the international market-place. It is often wrongly assumed that the Commission accordingly introduced a package of some 300 completely *new* proposals (subsequently cut to 286). Yet, some had been on the table for some time. Deadlock had delayed their progress. The introduction of a tight schedule and the deadline of the end of 1992 was designed to break the deadlock. However, as the EP had argued for years, this could not be accomplished without reforming both the EC's ossified and inappropriate institutional arrangements and defining the socio-economic and political priorities of the agenda of the late 1980s and early 1990s.

The White Paper divided into three main parts. The first, on the removal of physical barriers to trade, included controls over goods and people. This in turn raised many highly contentious political issues concerning fugitive criminals, terrorists, refugees and many related issues. The second, on removal of technical barriers, included questions relating to the principle of freedom of movement for goods, capital, persons and services. It also embraced the controversial areas of discrimination, market distortion and unfair competition and raised again the difficult matter of industrial relations. The third section related to the removal of fiscal barriers, another fraught arena. Behind the White Paper was the construction of sufficient political and economic momentum to ensure that the EC could surmount its past difficulties. Essential to this were both periodic stocktaking progress reports[2] and a 1992 campaign orchestrated by the Commission and commitment from highly-visible, high-profile Commission personnel (notably Commission President Delors and Lord Cockfield, Commissioner with special responsibility for the Internal Market in the Delors Mk 1 Commission). Indeed, by June 1988 Delors could credibly claim that the push for the creation of the Single European Market had reached the point of no return. The Commission had not been able to advance the SEM by itself, however. Commission President Delors was quite right to state that without the EUT, the Single European Act (upon which the SEM rests) would not have come into being. There can be little doubt that the report prepared, at Lord Cockfield's request, by Commission adviser Paolo Cecchini[3] on the likely economic effects of implementing the 1985 White Paper stimulated interest and a wider debate.[4] He had estimated that the cost of maintaining a fragmented market was quadruple the EC's budget; that is, around 200 billion ECU a year.

While this report highlighted the costs to the EC of not implementing the White Paper, the EP had for some years been investigating the 'costs of non-Europe' and had reached similar conclusions. It had issued at least ten significant reports and resolutions on the completion of the customs union (later internal market) before the White Paper saw the light of day [5] and it had consistently emphasised that the completion of the internal market was essential to recovery. The Albert and Ball report was germane to this.[6] MEPs had not only analysed the causes of weakness but isolated steps to recovery. Central to this was, in their view, the need for EC states (whether relatively prosperous or poor) to cooperate with one another in promoting economic growth in the name of the common interest. They argued that even the prosperous would fail in the medium-to-long term if they did not adopt such a strategy.

Following the issue of the Albert and Ball report, the EP set up a special committee to present a plan for European economic recovery. This was adopted in 1984 with four main headings: strengthening the means of EC action (including the realisation of the internal market); coordination of national economic policies; steps to support development at national and EC level; and international cooperation. From here on, the theme of 'the costs of non-Europe' became increasingly dominant. While recognising the economic costs of non-Europe, the EP was to show that there were costs, too, in the absence of institutional mechanisms to manage the policy environment for the SEM.

The Role of the EP

The EP assumed not only a major role in agitating for change but from the outset its view was less lopsided than many of the Council Presidencies who somewhat uncritically endorsed the SEM without setting it into its political context. Indeed, given the linkage between the EUT and the SEM's birth, it is not surprising – though it is telling – that the EP should have continued to stress that a SEM could not be implemented in a political vacuum on the assumption that it was devoid of political and institutional implications for the management of the policy environment at the supranational and national levels of government. The EP argued, from the early 1980s onwards, that economic deregulation could not be pursued without account being taken of the 'social space'. Thus, well before the issue of the White

Paper, it was clear that the EP would not be satisfied with a very limited economic debate. The EP, therefore, extended it to include the questions of national sovereignty, democratic legitimacy and the rectification of the democratic deficit, Social Europe and a People's Europe.

That the debate became broader and embedded in the push for 1992 owed much to the farsighted intervention of the EP under the guidance of Altiero Spinelli and the Crocodile Club. It was not simply a product of the arguments arising out of the Milan European Council's decision to set up an intergovernmental conference with the aim of reforming the EC treaties, including inter-institutional relations.

The EP took every opportunity to emphasise that economic prosperity could not be an end in itself for the few. Recognition of this was rapidly obtained in the EP, Commission and throughout the member states. Mrs Thatcher's intervention through her infamous Bruges speech was, therefore, singularly inappropriate. Not only did it crudely challenge the desirability of greater economic integration but it denied the legitimacy of the accompanying attempts to ensure that those who took decisions to be implemented throughout the EC be held democratically accountable for them. The spectre of national sovereignty was a smokescreen to obscure deep-seated antagonism to any arrangements, economic or political, that would compromise the ability of the British government to invoke Thatcherism at every turn. Just how damaging this was for Britain was proved when immediately after the 1989 EP elections two EP party groups (notably the EPP) turned down the Conservative MEPs' bid to join them. The EPP's members remained as wary of Conservatives in 1989 as they had the previous decade when alignment with them had not recommended itself as a way of securing numerical superiority over the EP Socialist Group.[7]

However, equally revealing of the degree of change that had occurred in EC policymaking since the Milan European Council is the fact that Mrs Thatcher's speech came at a time when expression was being given to the socio-political implications of the SEM. There was in the air a spirit that greater European integration, greater union, was possible, attainable and unstoppable. The changes that had been introduced both through the SEA and subsequently through the 1988 Brussels budget agreement had begun to bite.

Once more, the EP's guiding hand can be seen to have been at work. Shortly after the first EP elections, it had argued for a link to be made between the budget and EC GDP, between members' actual financial contributions and their GDP. The Brussels European Council accepted this principle as a 'fourth source' of EC financing based on each state's wealth. (The original sources of financing – customs duties, agricultural levies and a percentage of VAT – remained.) In addition, this European Council accepted and entrenched the need for medium-term financial planning through its establishment of a five-year frame of reference for spending. The import of this lay with the increased influence it accorded the EP (which with the Council of Ministers forms the EC's budgetary authority but whose views, in the past, had had little impact).

In other respects, too, the growing indirect influence of the EP in shaping the political agenda could be discerned. Moreover, through the SEA, its ability to be seen to be determining policy outputs was asserted. Thus, on the eve of the SEA's coming into effect, the EP's President was invited (for the first time ever) to present to the European Council, the EP's position on the Commission proposals on 'Making a success of the Single Act, a new frontier for Europe'.[8] Since then, the EP President regularly makes the EP's position known at European Councils.

How then is the increasing role of the EP in EC policymaking and in shaping the policy agenda to be explained? Is it simply chance? An unexpected but welcome side-product of the SEA? The answer must be an emphatic no on both scores. The EP has worked systematically to effect these developments since the governments were prodded into agreeing to direct elections shortly after the UK referendum on EC membership. The first directly-elected EP devised a strategy which has served the EP well and which newly-elected MEPs are unlikely to abandon. Moreover, the EP used its first term of office not only to discover the limits of its own influence under existing treaty provisions but to alter policy priorities through the deft use of the budget. It then proceeded to explore sensitive issues under the guise of the equally sensitive issue of European Union and within that framework to devise a way to build winning coalitions able to pressurise a wavering minority. It began to act politically and to take initiatives on new policy areas. The second term of office consolidated gains and the strategy for change.

II The instruments of change

The chief instrument of change was the Draft Treaty establishing the European Union (EUT) that the EP adopted in February 1984. It was subsequently applauded by six of the EC's national parliaments and two called upon their governments to ensure its ratification. The EUT held the key to the EC's future and it remains a potent document for future change.[9] Shortly before the 1989 EP elections, there were several calls for the EP to be given, through a referendum throughout the Twelve, a constituent role. It was argued that the existing treaties, even with the SEA, were incomplete and that a new constitution for the EC should be drafted by the EP using the EUT as a starting point.

The EUT is in many respects the most critical document to have been debated during the 1980s. Not only did it receive widespread cross-party and cross-national support in the EP but it outlined the parameters of what was broadly acceptable and desirable to the majority of states within the EC. Crucially, it played an instrumental role in securing EC reform and in enhancing the EP's powers. There can be little doubt that without it, and without the political momentum it generated, the SEA would not have got off the ground. While the SEA is disappointing compared to the EUT, it is bolder than any treaty amendment might have been had the EC's governments embarked 'cold' on a process of treaty reform. Past experience attests to the validity of this. Moreover, it is possible to detect the EUT's finger-prints in the SEA. Thus, for example, the clearly federal principle of subsidiarity (whereby the European Union, or in this case the EC, takes on only those issues that the member states cannot deal with effectively alone) outlined by the EUT is implicitly accepted into the SEA. More vitally still, the idea that the EC is but a step on the road to a European Union whose parameters have still to be defined through an ongoing, open debate was established firstly through the EUT process and secondly through the conclusion and implementation of the SEA.

The key instruments of change in the EC are legal instruments: the first, a treaty based on the existing *acquis communautaire* but going beyond it to establish a decentralised, democratic federal union; and the second, a series of amendments to the existing EC treaties that expand its scope and its decisionmaking processes in such a way as to render further reform ineluctable. To understand how far the EP has come in ten years, and to show how astute it has been in maintaining the momentum for reform and in securing further reform through developing further instruments of reform by exploiting existing mechanisms, it will be useful to outline very briefly the strategy behind the EP's endeavours.

EP Strategy for Reform

The EP's strategy for reform is closely linked to the timetable of Euro-elections. There may not have been a conscious linkage but there can be little doubt that the prospect of the elections does impel action. Each outgoing EP has left a legacy to its successor which points the way for future reform. This is a major achievement. Each EP has enhanced its credibility as a responsive, pro-active institution concerned with the EC's future and with defining, or at a minimum influencing, the EC's agenda.

What is surprising is that the EP has managed to assume this position within a relatively short time and irrespective of the fact that its members have not been able to campaign in the elections on a highly visible electoral platform or record of achievement in the same way that national MPs seeking re-election might do. What might have been seen as a major inherent weakness of the EP – the electoral credibility gap – has been turned into a source of strength. The EP has transformed the debate about European integration, about where the EC is going and for what purpose, and has shown itself to be the most vital EC institution in stimulating a debate on many *bêtes noires*.

It has accomplished this not through mobilising the public and the electorate at large. Instead, it has coupled a long-term strategy with a series of short-term tactics that have enabled it to demonstrate its effectiveness and to engineer interest in and support for its ideas among political elites broadly conceived. The long-term strategy rests on the idea that institutional reform in the EC is a precondition to rendering the EC capable of responding effectively and democratically to the changing international politico-economic environment. A change in inter-institutional relations (notably a strengthening of the Commission and the EP) is seen as a necessary but not a sufficient condition for this.

Institutional reform is notoriously difficult to effect, because amendments of the EC treaties require the unanimous approval of the member governments and subsequent ratification in the member states. Nevertheless, throughout the 1970s, recourse was had to Article 235 of the Rome Treaty in order to expand the EC's authority beyond the narrow confines of the existing treaties into areas that in some cases were implicit in the treaties but that in others could not have been envisaged by the treaties' framers. While such endeavours could be evaluated positively in terms of extending the scope of European integration and the EC's relevance to contemporary issues, on the debit side was the fact that any extension by definition meant that even more issues escaped effective parliamentary scrutiny and control. The democratic deficit was being increased, probably unwittingly, at the very time that steps were allegedly being taken to redress it.

The question of the EC's democratic deficit remains relevant. In the mid-1970s, it was construed largely in terms of ensuring that the body with parliamentary pretensions was elected by universal suffrage. This was a very narrow interpretation of the notion of a democratic deficit. By the 1980s, however, the operational aspect of the democratic deficit was recognised. The EP's strategy for institutional reform addressed this issue in a systematic and careful way. The cautious approach to institutional reform assumed a far higher profile after the 1979 elections. However, it originated in the early 1970s and began to be employed in a strategic way once the member states had agreed in 1975 to the EP's direct election.[10] The idea of an alternative, gradualist approach to achieving institutional reform to the EP's advantage commended itself to MEPs who, at that stage, were the non-elected nominees of national parliaments.

Following the decision to elect the EP, candidates were careful not to arouse fears that they would seek to usurp the power of national parliaments and erode the authority of the Council. A mixture of political expedience, diplomacy and conviction led many MEPs to deny that they would seek radical institutional reform. Instead, it was argued that elected MEPs could expect to augment their influence over policymaking by making better use of existing treaty provisions. It was suggested that their ability to do so would be enhanced by dint of their being, for the most part, full-time MEPs. The dual-mandated member has become the exception rather than the rule since 1979.

The first elected EP addressed itself to institutional issues raised by a stocktaking exercise initiated by its predecessor. It looked for, and found, various means of capitalising on its existing powers and increasing its inputs in the decisionmaking process. This tactic, since dubbed the minimalist or gradualist approach to reform, has been assiduously employed since then. It rests on the supposition that anything not explicitly forbidden the EP by the EC treaties is permitted. Its instruments are its own Rules of Procedure which have been deftly amended on several occasions in a highly political and astute manner, and its right to fix its own agenda (something normally determined for parliaments by governments in the member states).

However, in the 1980s, the minimalist tactic would not have had the impact it did, had it not been coupled with a maximalist tactic. This is based on the overt goal of advancing European Union through not merely treaty amendment but the supplanting of the old treaties by a new one, a constitution for the European Union. This may well have encouraged governments to bear with and accept the series of small demands advanced under the guise of the first as the lesser of two evils. Both tactics were mutually reinforcing although it would be wrong to suggest that all MEPs applauded or recognised their complementarity. Some, at least for reasons of domestic political expedience, continued to insist that minimalism was sufficient and to deride visionary, federalist ideals.

1981 was an important year in the EP's development. It was important, too, to minimalism and maximalism. The minimalist tactic bore fruit in the shape of the European Court of Justice's ruling in the EP's favour in the *Isoglucose* case; in the shape of a new set of Rules of Procedure which entrenched a power of delay for the EP (backed by the ECJ ruling) and which set the stage for closer and more productive EP–Commission interaction and cooperation. Crucial in this respect was the growing acceptance by the Commission and later by the Council that the EP's Opinions could no longer be casually ignored. While Commission attention to the EP remained imperfect for several more years, and while the Council had to be forced to heed EP views even after the SEA came into force, it is in the 1981 reforms that the seeds of genuine legislative influence for the EP can be detected.[11]

The EP proved adept at exploiting seemingly slight and nuanced changes in such a way as to legitimise for itself and in the eyes of the Commission an expanding role that was recognisably legislative. Its decision to infer for itself a right of legislative initiative (the role ascribed to the Commission by the treaties) naturally grew from this. While the ensuing 'Own Initiative' reports may be criticised on many grounds and while some were poorly drafted, they served two purposes. Firstly, they provided the EP with a testing ground for refining a means of legislative initiative for itself. While the EP had before the 1979 elections resorted to 'own initiative' reports (e.g. on the special rights of EC citizens in October and November 1977), its members did not make systematic and strategic use of this device until the early 1980s. To heighten the impact of these reports, the EP refined its Rules of Procedure to try to ensure that only the most important and those with operational possibilities came up for plenary discussion. Secondly, these reports enabled the EP to begin to set the political agenda, and policy priorities. The onus was placed on both the EP and the Commission to show that their priorities were realistic and coincided. This was only accomplished by following the SEA's enactment with the agreement to pursue legislative planning in a systematic way.[12] Once again, however, the origins lay with the first elected EP.

The other development that was central to minimalism in the early 1980s was the scrutiny of what might loosely be termed constitutional issues by both the European Council (through the Genscher–Colombo initiative for a Draft European Act) and by the EP itself. The EP had shelved its own pre-electoral investigation of inter-institutional matters and the enhancement of its own powers to avoid endangering the elections themselves.[13] However, thereafter, in October 1979 it gave a sub-committee of the Political Affairs Committee the task of dealing with institutional matters within the framework of the existing treaties. The committee's eight *rapporteurs* subjected the EP's relations with the other EC institutions to a thorough reappraisal between 1979 and 1981.[14]

The confluence of this with the European Council's sometimes meandering discussions imbued the EP's endeavours with a wider relevance and legitimacy. Moreover, the context in which they arose is worth noting. The EP was systematically challenging the Council and Commission through Question Time; it brought an action against the Council for failure to act;[15] and exploited its budgetary power to the full. Mediterranean enlargement was on the agenda and the various socio-economic and political as well as constitutional problems which such enlargement would pose for the EC as a whole, as well as for the more integrative aims of the Six, were being discussed. Five years had elapsed since the issue of the Tindemans report on European Union. Almost a decade had passed since the Paris 1972 summit which had emphasised the need for European Union. The EP had submitted to Mr Tindemans its July 1975 resolution on European Union. The internal workings of the Commission had been scrutinised and overhauled, following the deliberations of Spierenburg and the 'Three Wise Men' and there were signs of renewed interest in some of the ideas on European Union that had been cursorily set aside in the mid-1970s.

The EP's determination to influence the EC's policy priorities and agenda were to be underscored by the launching of a maximalist strategy for institutional reform derived from the success of minimalist instruments. Less than two years after the first EP elections, the

EP set up a special Committee on Institutional Affairs (IAC) which began work on 27 January 1982. Through the cross-party deliberations of the Crocodile Club and then employing the device of an own initiative report, the EP embarked on a process that culminated in the EUT. It is instructive that the IAC took into account past documents on European Union. These included its own resolutions, the Tindemans report, the Commission's document on the role of EC institutions (which raised the possibility of greater powers for the EP – the Andriessen report), and the London Report (named after the European Council of October 1981 that advocated *inter alia* the EP's enhanced involvement in matters of European political cooperation). In addition, in October 1981 the new French government submitted a memorandum that (though devoid of institutional recommendations) was designed to stimulate EC activity. In short, change was in the air.

If the EP had created the expectation of change, it was to prove that it could deliver too. Its success in this respect owed much to the strategy developed under the guidance of Altiero Spinelli who was the catalyst behind the maximalist approach. In June 1980 he had sent a letter to all MEPs setting out his ideas for an EP initiative. From this ensued the Crocodile Club, its *Newsletter* and eventually the all-important Crocodile Draft Resolution which was adopted on 9 July 1981 by 164 votes to 24 with 12 abstentions. Spinelli had welded together a majority and had kept it together in the face of formidable countervailing forces.[16]

Past experience having proved the weakness of an approach to reform based on amending the existing treaties and subjecting any amendments to destructive national emasculation, Spinelli's strategy for European Union was based on building up consensus for the EP's proposals and trying to secure the adoption of a new treaty based on the *acquis communautaire*. The IAC duly followed suit. It avoided the pitfall of employing the potentially explosive language bound to inflame governments (federalism, intergovernmentalism and so on). It avoided alienating political groups that forwarded proposals on European Union to it, and initially retained a fairly open mind as to the possibility of advancing European Union along minimalist lines. However, once the IAC set down its guidelines, it became clear that a new treaty was necessary to go beyond the existing treaties to look at general economic policy, sectoral policies, commercial policy, monetary policy, a policy for society, development aid and the gradual development of a common policy in respect of international relations and security.[17] It is striking that the SEA adhered to many of these *domaines*. In addition, the IAC set out the need for institutional reform in accordance with the principles of the separation of powers, democratic legitimacy, operational efficiency and the participation of the member states.

This is not the place to delve into the intricacies of the EUT. Suffice it to note that, crucially, the changes foreseen for the EP in a new European Union reflected post-1979 developments and hinged on the EP's transformation into a genuine legislature. Many earlier ideas advanced by the EP during the 1970s on European Union and inter-institutional relations reappear. Crucial, however, is the affirmation of the principle of subsidiarity; the idea of a legislative procedure based on two readings and majority voting, as well as deadlines; and the idea of a bicameral legislature comprising the Council and the EP.

The EUT was not only the first elected EP's most significant legacy to its successor but was to prove the most potent vehicle for EC reform. There was some discussion of the EUT being put to the people and of it being publicly debated in the course of the second Euro-election campaign. The issue of European Union did not get off the ground in all the member states before voting took place; however, it did take hold in some states, notably Italy.[18] Moreover, between the EUT's adoption and the 1984 elections, Spinelli had persuaded President Mitterrand to seize the initiative. In May 1984, Mitterrand addressed the EP and suggested preparatory consultations on a new treaty arrangement based on the 1983 Solemn Declaration on European Union and the EUT. In June 1984, he went further. Accordingly, the Fontainebleau European Council set up two committees to advance the idea of European Union. One, the Adonnino Committee, focused on questions relating to the establishment of a People's Europe. The other, known variously as the Dooge Committee or the Spaak II Committee, and increasingly as the Ad Hoc Committee for Institutional Affairs, was entrusted with making proposals for improving European cooperation in both the Community field and that of political, or any other, cooperation.

The Dooge Committee's report was on the table in time for the Brussels European Council in March 1985. Its work had been guided by the spirit of the EUT as intended, and there were some notable parallels between its recommendations on the EC's objectives and policy priorities, and on institutional reform (which the Committee conceded was essential to the enterprise).[19] The report called for an **intergovernmental** conference (IGC) to negotiate a draft treaty on

European Union. This highly contentious proposal was not only vehemently opposed by some member states (notably the UK) but was seen as having extraordinary political significance since an IGC was construed as the 'initial act of European Union'.[20]

A year after the second EP elections, an IGC was agreed on by majority vote at the Milan European Council. Italy's audacity in putting such a controversial issue to a majority vote was unprecedented and provoked heated argument not least because the convening of the IGC meant that governments would not be able to procrastinate interminably over the dilution of treaty amendments which, in the past (as with budgetary reforms), had been negotiated within the Council of Ministers. Milan set the seal on a process of reform that concluded with the signing in Luxembourg of what was to become the Single European Act.[21]

Again, it is important to recall the environmental conditions that assisted the successful outcome of the process. Milan had also sanctioned work on EUREKA in a separate intergovernmental framework that involved the EC but in which the EC did not assume centre stage. In addition, it had considered the European Council's request that the Council examine the institutional conditions not needing treaty amendment necessary to complete the SEM within the deadline. The EP had to fight for its views to be heard. A special procedure was set up to allow the EP President to forward to the IGC the comments of the EP's IAC which was entrusted with monitoring the IGC's work. In addition, the EP lobbied member governments discreetly, and other actors were active.

The SEA did not go as far as the EP would have liked. But it did initiate a formula for institutional change that proved far more promising than a first glimpse may have suggested. The cooperation procedure established a system of two readings for draft legislation over a limited range of issues covered by ten articles of the existing treaties. This procedure ensured that the Council and the EP acted as the two arms of a bicephalous legislature but stopped short of calling them the two chambers of the EC's legislature.

The institutional conditions for completing the SEM were only partially met by the SEA's reforms. Consequently, when the SEA came into effect in July 1987, some twenty-three months before the third EP elections, the EP was faced with the need to rethink and continue its dual-pronged strategy for change and European Union. Conceived as strategies for the first legislature, minimalism and maximalism survived the second EP elections and have become entrenched in the third. Thus, constitutional reform (the high point of maximalism) remains on the agenda. At the day-to-day level, however, minimalism has been pursued astutely to capitalise on the new authority which the EP secured in the SEA and to expand the scope of its influence.

The SEA became the single most important instrument for change in the second half of the second elected EP's term of office. A lot of energy went into exploiting its provisions; reforming the EP's Rules of Procedure again to improve its ability both to manage its own business, to define its own political priorities, to increase and refine its links with the Commission, to develop legislative planning with the Commission, and to encourage the Council to play a genuine co-decisional role with the EP in the legislative process.

While very little attention was paid to the EUT during this period, the EUT could not be dismissed as an irrelevance. On the contrary, it remained the yardstick by which EP steps forward in the performance of a genuinely legislative role were measured. It also remained the benchmark for all discussions on where the EC was going in terms of further integration, what its *raison d'être* was, and what the proper scope of its concerns and activities should be. However, from 1987 to mid-1989 it was imperative that the EP give the SEA a far higher profile and priority than the EUT. Rather as in 1977–9, over-emphasis on anything likely to unsettle member governments wary of EP encroachment on national sovereignty could have proved counter-productive. At the same time, it was imperative that the EP did not relinquish its 'motor' role in the integration process. The momentum for European Union and for the successful implementation of the SEA depended in no small measure on the way in which the EP conducted itself.

The SEA as an instrument of reform

The SEA did not constitute the qualitative great leap forward in European integration that the EUT did. However, it provided the EP with the chance to reapply to good effect its minimalist strategy for entrenching and consolidating small but significant changes with a view to subsequent reform of a more far-reaching nature. The latter half of the second elected EP's term in office was preoccupied with showing that the EP, having been given some legislative power under the cooperation procedure, was able to use it effectively and responsibly. This was a time for the EP to establish its credentials as a legislature.

This meant, above all, fully exploiting the cooperation procedure and setting out precedents on which further institutional reform could be based. This was essential, since the SEA otherwise provides for only a modest accretion of the EP's powers. Thus, the EP's assent to enlargement (Articles 99 and 237) and to association agreements (238) is required and there is scope for argument over the financial protocols attached to such agreements[22] and the possibility of some greater influence through the Luns–Westerterp procedures.[23] When these reforms were considered, it was no doubt thought that they offered but a minor increase in the possibilities for EP influence. In fact, given the spate of anticipated bids for EC accession during the 1990s, the EP has important clout in this arena. Indeed, it showed immediately that an expansive interpretation of the provisions gave it further opportunities for influence. In March 1988, it blocked agreement on three protocols to the EC–Israel agreement pending the accommodation of its wishes.[24]

It is through the cooperation procedure that the EP has interlocked the key institutions. This is a major achievement, given that the cooperation procedure applies to only ten articles of the Rome Treaty: Articles 7 – prohibition of discrimination on grounds of nationality; 49 – progressive realisation of freedom of movement for workers; 54(2) – abolition of existing restrictions on freedom of establishment; 56(2) – coordination of provisions on special treatment of foreign nationals on grounds of public policy, public security or public health; 57 – mutual recognition of diplomas, etc. to facilitate work by the self-employed; 100A and 100B – approximation of provisions having as their goal the establishment and functioning of the internal market; 118A – social policy, working environment, health and safety of workers; 130E – economic and social cohesion; and 130(Q) – research and technological development. Two-thirds of the Commission's 1985 White Paper proposals fell under the cooperation procedure.

Given the centrality of legislation aiming at the SEM's realisation, the EP had a chance to participate regularly in the ensuing legislative process. To do so, it had to reform and streamline its internal management and working practices; to ensure the responsiveness of the Commission and the Council to its requests for information and effective consultation; and to prioritise and concentrate its activities on areas susceptible to EP influence. The EP accomplished this quickly, and equally swiftly pressed the Council into following the Commission's example of treating the EP, under the cooperation procedure, as co-legislator.[25]

However, the Council had to be pushed into fulfilling its obligations
under the cooperation procedure provisions which require it to
explain why it wishes to amend or deviate from the Commission
proposal (which the EP has, in all probability, already amended). To
do this, the Council has to examine the EP's amendments. It cannot
simply choose to say nothing. Nor may it simply refer to the preamble
of the proposal. When it resorted to this course, the EP threatened
the Council with legal action on the grounds that it had infringed
essential requirements.[26] Unlike under the traditional procedure
where it could ignore the EP's Opinion, it is bound to scrutinise and
comment upon it. It is also bound to adhere to the substance of the
proposal and may not exercise its power of amendment in what might
be termed an extensive way. However, the EP is in a stronger
position to do this during the first reading and the Commission retains
the right (theoretically at least) to alter proposals at any time. The EP
certainly has a case for being reconsulted in first reading if major
amendments are made. In practice, the Council has come to appreciate the need for cooperation both with the EP and with the Commission (not least since it failed to notice that the Commission had
tabled a proposal under the cooperation procedure when this was not
prescribed).[27] It has genuinely to examine the EP's amendments and
work with it. This remains true even though ultimately the Council
might be said to have the upper hand in that it can adopt a common
position rejected by the EP providing that it is unanimous. It has done so
only once in respect of the fifth directive on the protection of workers.

Whereas the Council adopted a minimalist position, the Commission capitalised on the EP's right to control its own agenda and
timetable. As a result there was EP–Commission agreement on a
legislative programme and planning. Although initially wary of the
EP, the Commission began to see the advantage of working reasonably closely with the EP (but not so closely that it alienated the
Council).

EP–Commission cooperation and even collusion is necessary
throughout the cooperation procedure and not only during the course
of the first and second readings. Indeed, it is vital at the pre-
legislative stage when the EP has the opportunity to try and persuade
the Commission to table as many proposals as possible under articles
subject to the cooperation procedure. This is no easy matter, since
redistributive policy goals cannot be implemented without reference
to both the structural funds (subject to the budget procedure) and
to the more focused aims of the economic and social cohesion

(convergence) programmes (subject to the cooperation procedure). Moreover, the EP examines proposals to see whether they should come under 100A (requiring Council action by qualified majority and the cooperation procedure) or under traditional decisionmaking rules (where the EP is marginalised) or under articles, like 130S on environmental matters, that prescribe Council unanimity.

The EP has not always been successful in pushing for proposals to be tabled under articles subject to the cooperation procedure. After Chernobyl, the Commission used Article 31 EURATOM to fix maximum permitted radio-activity levels for foodstuffs, and so excluded EP intervention as the article provides merely for the EP to be consulted.[28] The EP challenged but failed to get the legal base changed. The Council, too, has successfully excluded the EP by amending a proposal from 100A to Article 235, thus avoiding the second reading. On the other hand, the EP, by judiciously exploiting deadlines, has managed to push the Council into accepting amendments that it had previously rejected. As early as October 1987, it persuaded the Council to accept amendments to its Medical Research Programme. Later, through the channels of the inter-institutional dialogue the EP had itself engineered, the Council and EP agreed on a compromise on a proposal on exhaust emissions, even though, theoretically, Denmark could have vetoed it. Moreover, the EP has used to good effect its right, at second reading, to reject a proposal providing it can muster the 260 votes needed (both for amendments and for rejection). Contrary to expectations, the EP has been able to mobilise these votes and in October 1988, for the first time since the introduction of the SEA, it rejected a common position agreed by the Council in a second reading vote on the 'benzene directive' by 274 votes to 47 with 3 abstentions.[29] In this case, the Commission felt unable to adopt the EP's second reading amendments which it felt would fail to secure qualified majority support in the Council. But EP rejection of the proposal meant that the Council had to be unanimous to overrule it. This was not possible and in April 1989 the Commission took on the tougher EP amendments (favoured by Denmark). This encouraged the Council to reconsider its views. It also highlighted the EP's bargaining power and the opportunities it has to build or thwart the attainment of the requisite Council majorities, and to insist on steps being taken in the public interest as defined by the EP rather than by competing national interests.

The experience of the cooperation procedure up to June 1989 showed the importance of inter-institutional dialogue and contact. In

July, rather than see a contentious proposal on cross-frontier broad-casting lapse altogether, the Council sought a month's extension to reconsider its position following EP amendments in view of Council's common position adopted on a majority vote. While the cooperation procedure has been wanting in that by the end of the second reading, less than 50 per cent of the EP's original amendments are intact, it is a vast improvement on the *status quo ante* when EP views could be ignored with impunity. They no longer can. On a first reading, the Commission has taken up some 78 per cent of EP amendments of which the Council has accepted just over half. At second reading, the EP has approved just over 50 per cent of common positions adopted by the Council and has tried to re-amend the rest. The Council, by contrast, has deleted some 50 per cent of second reading amendments adopted by the Commission.[30]

The way in which the cooperation procedure and other provisions of the SEA can be successfully exploited was the second elected EP's most crucial legacy to the third elected EP. However, it would be wrong to infer that the preoccupation with testing the limits of the cooperation procedure had necessitated the abandonment of the maximalist strategy based on the EUT. Rather, this slipped into the background. It resurfaced again on the eve of the elections as the EP tried to set the next EP's agenda and priorities.

The IAC, which had advanced the EUT, assumed the role of the EP's conscience on European Union. While MEPs had periodically voiced the need for further integration and while an inter-party group for a federal Europe had been set up, the IAC had desisted from pressing the case for more treaty reforms pending a preliminary exploitation and assessment of the operation of the cooperation procedure. This did not mean that it had been idle, however. A few months after the SEA came into effect, it issued a report on the institutional consequences of non-Europe (known as the Catherwood report after its *rapporteur*). The report was 'limited to showing both the magnitude of the gains from a change in the decisionmaking process and the possibility of making the major shifts needed without either demanding many more powers for the Parliament or unduly altering the Treaty'.[31] It stressed the need for a proper recognition of the actual responsibilities and role of the EP and for it to have a single seat. It also called for a second phase of reform where the EP's proposed amendments would become the final decision by default if the Council could not decide against them by a simple majority (as Delors and Tindemans had both proposed to the IGC in 1985).

The Catherwood report was paralleled by reports by von Stauffenberg and Herman, and shortly followed in January 1989 by the Prag report on the conciliation procedure.[32] The Herman report set out the EP's dual-pronged strategy for the future, while the Prag Report, using the minimalist tactic, sought ways to introduce the conciliation procedure into the cooperation procedure. The Herman report, however, also noted ways in which the EP could capitalise on existing SEA provisions using the tried and tested method of exploiting to the limit all existing measures. It stressed the need for the EP to be seen by the public as acting responsibly and positively and, where necessary, as a referee in and resolver of deadlocks. It suggested that the EP concentrate on the following priority areas:

– the internal market and fiscal harmonisation
– political cooperation and security
– environmental protection
– research and the new technologies
– monetary integration and the role of the ECU and a European federal bank
– solidarity and convergence
– the budget and own resources.

It argued that any progress in these areas would 'bring the Community nearer to Union', but that EP intervention was necessary given the deficiencies of the SEA, decisionmaking, EC jurisdiction and the democratic deficit. Without intervention, it argued, 1992 would not be realised. Consequently, it fell to the EP to prepare for the transition from the SEA to European Union; to maintain and strengthen the momentum for European Union; and to ensure that any development or transformation be initiated by the EC's institutions in accordance with its dual legitimacy (i.e. that held by national parliaments and delegated to their governments in the Council, and that held at EC level by the EP).

This report confirmed the EP's intention to seek a constituent role for itself to draft reforms using either the Art.236EEC or Art.82EUT procedure. In either case, the EUT was to remain the basis of the EP's endeavours. Its draft constitution would, accordingly, have to respect the following principles:

– subsidiarity
– a territorial division of powers: sole, concurrent and potential
– flexibility and open-endedness

– the supremacy of Union law
– democratic legitimacy.

While the report did not advocate the EP acquiring a constituent role by means of a referendum throughout the EC on the occasion of the third elections, this idea was widely canvassed and applauded by many. However, only Italy held a referendum. Other states shied away from the idea for a variety of reasons. Anticipating this possibility, the report did, however, stress the importance to the EP of forging multi-layered alliances with, for example, the Commission, the transnational party federations, national representative bodies, national parliaments, the two sides of industry, intellectuals, media, local and regional authorities, and the pro-EP members of the Council.

Awareness of the need for MEPs to interact with such elites matched recognition by outside groups of the mutually beneficial gains interaction might bring. This implied a change in the EP's role conception and self-perception as a legislative body within the EC. It also reflected the growth in the EP's self-esteem and self-image. The success of the EP's quest for European Union (even the first stage of a Union along the SEA's lines) had given the EP a confidence previously lacking. This had been bolstered by its increased impact on the domestic political agenda. It had also been fed by growing international recognition of the EP and the usefulness of its work in this arena (in spite of its very limited powers and role *vis-à-vis* EPC).

The EP's record

From the time of the first elections, it was argued that if the EP were to increase its democratic legitimacy (and that of the EC, which seemed inextricably linked to it) and if it were to become credible as a legislature, it needed both to boost turnout at the elections and to be in a position to campaign on a record of achievement.

At each of the EP elections so far, the campaign issues have largely been determined by national political elites. They have often reflected domestic concerns and politics. They have never assumed the intensity of domestic general elections and in states where voting is not compulsory they have failed to mobilise turnout levels approximating the average at the former. For these reasons, they have been classified as second-order elections on a par with municipal and regional elections.[33] Such a classification may point to the kind of turnout EP elections attract but may be, in other respects, somewhat misleading. Increasingly, a Euro-element has been injected into the elections. This might be defined as a Europeanisation of national politics or as a politicisation of EC-level politics. Whatever the interpretation, it is clear that EC affairs are no longer only seen as 'out there'. An internalisation has taken place almost imperceptibly.

Today's political agenda is recognisably a European one. The EP has contributed to this. MEPs have systematically raised topical issues of central concern to EC citizens. The latter may not always have perceived the relevance of the EP's work, much less been interested in or aware of it. However, the EP has shaped the political agenda and participated constructively in some of the most public EC issues of the decade. Domestically, this is reflected by the way in which it secured a reform of the budget and successfully defended its role as an arm of the budgetary authority.[34] It continues to demand that monies spent by the EC (e.g. financed by the ECSC levy, the New Community Instrument and the European Development Fund, funded by the member states, and equivalent to 25 per cent of the budget) be included in the general budget. The EC's actual budget, relative to those of the member states, is tiny at around 1.15 per cent of EC GDP or 2.5 per cent of the Twelve's national budgets. EP–Council conflict over the budget has marked this decade, as the EP has tried to give the EC the means to effect its policies partly by diverting expenditure from the CAP to the structural funds, and by increasing the resources at the EC's disposal.

The conditions for budgetary reform were eventually established in 1988, several years after the EP had twice (in 1980 and 1985, i.e. immediately after the respective elections) rejected the budget. The EP had objected to the creative accounting which masked the lack of genuine austerity and the real scope of expenditure needed to cope, for example, with agricultural spending over a full twelve not ten months (as in 1985) and rebates to the FRG and the UK. In 1986, the EP again took the Council to task over its budget which overlooked the new members, Spain and Portugal. Moreover, it was necessary to provide funds to meet previous commitments (the 'burden of the past'). The EP proposed big increases to draft expenditure. Council challenged it before the ECJ. The ECJ first ruled that the budget be executed on the basis of the Council's draft but then in July 1986 backed the EP and required the Council and EP to agree on increases needed for non-obligatory expenditure (e.g. regional, social and R&D spending).

The EP had also repeatedly asked for more resources to fund the increasing range of EC activities. In 1981 it sought a link between the wealth (GDP) of states and their actual contributions. Not until February 1988 did the European Council accept this proposition and add to the traditional sources of EC 'own resources' (customs duties, agricultural levies and a percentage of the VAT intake) a 'fourth resource' – that based on states' GDP. Simultaneously, the European Council agreed to bring CAP spending under control; double the structural funds; and establish a five-year frame of reference of spending up to the critical date of 1992. This was important in allowing the EP to make some informed decisions concerning social and regional spending. It could now expect that funding for these areas would not be cut on an *ad hoc* basis to accommodate swings in CAP spending. This was important if MEPs were to be able to lay claim to having been responsible for programmes of benefit to citizens; to their having, in effect, done something tangible to effect a Social Europe and a People's Europe.

The relative invisibility, intangibility and unintelligibility of the EP's work for the EC's voters has given rise to the illusion that the EP is irrelevant to the nitty-gritty of EC policymaking. It is true that the EP seemed obscure and somewhat invisible until the mid-1980s. Change came as the issue of the EC's future was debated publicly in terms of European Union, at least in some states, and attracted the attention of elites if not always of publics. Arguably since then, the EP's visibility and stature have grown. It is doubtful whether this can be attributed solely to its increasing interventions in matters of direct and tangible relevance to voters. Nor should it be simply ascribed to the cooperation procedure alone. Yet it would be wrong to ignore the EP's continuing pressure, since the early 1980s, for action on unemployment, for example. This eventually led the Council to adopt an action programme for the long-term unemployed in 1987. The EP's damning investigation into the effectiveness of the Social Fund in 1986 was corroborated by the findings of the Court of Auditors. Its recommendations, including those regarding the more focused and coordinated use of all structural instruments, were eventually incorporated in large part into the new Social Fund in 1988.

Other areas where the EP's activities and proposals have had some impact range from the celebrated case in which the EP took the Council to the ECJ for inaction on the transport sector in 1985 to its pressure on monetary union, the ECU, regional development and R&D. In March 1987, the EP set up its STOA (Scientific and Technical Operations Assessment) project (modelled on the US

Congress' counterpart). The aim was to link MEPs with scientific experts to assist in evaluating EC technological programmes, notably on transfrontier chemical pollution, restructuring of telecommunications and fusion research.

The EP's involvement in high-profile issues has ranged from campaigns to combat racism, drug production and trafficking, AIDS and cancer. More vitally, the EP has been active in the environmental field, notably in respect of air pollution, the monitoring of dangerous substances, toxic and dangerous waste and radioactivity. In addition, it is partly due to its sustained action in the education field that the ERASMUS and YES programmes got off the ground. The EP has also pushed with some success for changes to directives on sexual discrimination. Finally, the EP has strengthened the right of petition and set up in 1987 a Committee on Petitions, there having been a 400 per cent rise in the number of petitions to the EP since 1984.

This brief survey shows that MEPs have responded to topical questions and to issues relevant to EC citizens. But they have not necessarily been able to campaign exclusively or mainly on the EP's record. Among the reasons for this are: the determination of the campaigns by national political elites; the scant use on the campaign trail of the transnational federations campaign material; the nature of media coverage of the EP and elections; time-lags between EP pronouncements and action on issues and the uncertain arrival of corresponding EC legislation; and the fact that legislative success is rarely due to the efforts of a single party group. This robs issues of high ideological and conflictual content on many occasions. Nevertheless, SEM issues coupled with the 'greening' of conservative parties in particular during the 1989 EP election campaign did highlight differences between the various candidates for election to the EP and did suggest the possibility of policy outcomes being determined along more recognisable ideological cleavages in the future.

The other arena in which the EP has laid claim to some success concerns foreign affairs. Through its fact-finding missions, external relations and CAP-related work, its urgent and topical debates, and the stream of visits from VIPs, the EP has demonstrated its credibility as a forum to the outside world (which tends to hold it in higher esteem than do its member states). It has also demonstrated its concern with major issues of the day, be they defence and security matters or questions concerning non-EC states' activities (e.g. the declaration of martial law in Poland, the US bombing of Libya, etc.).

The EP has been quick to assume the role of the EC's conscience on the world stage.

The overall effect of all this activity has been to show that the EP is both *au fait* with important contemporary internal and international issues and that its work is of some relevance for the EC's citizens. This relevance has not yet translated itself in the minds of MEPs, national political elites and, most pertinently of all, the public, into a concomitant appreciation and recognition of how the EP could be used not just as the voice but, more, as the defender and promoter of the will of the people.

III   The EP: voice of the people and guarantor of democracy?

Wary governmental and national parliamentary elites anxious about their own role and authority in the post-1992 Community are aware that the EP's aspirations to be a genuine legislature may translate themselves in expectations and realities. A certain uneasiness exists in such circles as to the EP's potential as the people's voice. The cooperation procedure has become the tool, unwittingly given by the states to the EP, by which the EP can exercise 'voice'. It can complain. It can argue. It can debate. It can embarrass. It can throw down the gauntlet. The EP has the tools that enable it legitimately to challenge and, equally importantly, to publicise the contrary positions of any member governments whose views do not coincide with those of the EP's majority.

In the past, governments could rest assured that in most cases their national foibles and prevarications would be obscured by the secrecy of Council deliberations. At worst, there would be leaks to some of the national press and questions might be asked in national parliaments. However, the attendant publicity was relatively low-key except when full-blown confrontations occurred within the European Councils. Disagreements among the member states were contained within the Councils. Member governments could openly challenge the Commission and require an accommodation of their views. Now all has changed utterly.

The Commission has a rival source of legitimacy for its proposals: the EP. The EP is in a position to challenge the Council's will and its views as to what amendments need to be made to Commission proposals. The EP can lay claim to a different legitimacy to that of the Council – the people. While it would be imprudent for the EP to parade this legitimacy as superior to that of the Council, the EP has to be seen to exercise certain functions on behalf of the people. Being their 'voice', a check on the Council, is an important function. It is also one that must be exercised carefully in public if at the next EP elections in 1994 MEPs and their parties wish to retain their seats and majorities by claiming that they have 'done something' positive for the 'ordinary people' that would not have happened without their intervention.

CONCLUSION

The major transformation in the EP's role during the 1980s was the product of a dual-pronged strategy designed to give the EP the necessary instruments for effecting change in its own role and in the agenda of the EC itself. The EP's success owed much to its assuming a proactive rather than reactive role in the EC; to its engineering the necessary preconditions and then capitalising on them. In such circumstances it would be easy to overlook the continuing validity of what might be termed the EP's traditional concerns: the distribution and exercise of political authority in the EC. While the issue of the EC's 'democratic deficit' assumed a much lower profile as the EP advanced the quest for European Union, it was not abandoned. Nor was it merely resurrected for form's sake on the eve of EP elections. Rather, it informed much of the debate about inter-institutional relations both in a European Union and in the interim in the Single European Market.

In 1979 rectifying the EC's democratic deficit and recognising the EP's democratic legitimacy were conceived narrowly in terms of enfranchising EC citizens and holding elections to a common institution purporting to be a parliament but lacking many of the attributes typical of legislatures. By 1989, rectifying the EC's democratic deficit had assumed far wider proportions. It embraced the whole scope of the EC's competences and institutions. That it did so owed much to the European Union debate initiated by Spinelli. He had raised the question of the EP as 'king-maker'. He had stressed the importance of increasing the Commission's authority. He had explained how increases in the EP's powers would benefit the Commission. He had desensitised the question of rectifying the democratic deficit by deflecting attention from enforcing EP control over the Council whose democratic credentials and legitimacy had traditionally been presented as inferior to that of an elected EP.

It is instructive that before the 1989 elections, the question of rectifying the EC's democratic deficit was raised once more but this time in terms that were less threatening to the Council. The EP ceased to be portrayed either as the sole source of the EC's democratic legitimacy or as uniquely democratic among EC institutions. Instead, it was argued that any development or transformation of the EC could be initiated only by EC institutions on the basis of the EC's dual legitimacy. This was presented as resting on the legitimacy at the national level held by national parliaments and delegated to governments in the Council, and on the legitimacy at EC level held by the directly-elected EP.

However, from this was inferred an equal right for the EP to that of the other institutions to prepare a draft treaty for European Union: a right, moreover, which it expects governments to respect. While the EP maintains that a new draft should be prepared with the widest possible participation of national governments, intellectuals, parliaments, parties and so on, it sees the referendum as an option (and one supported by over 70 per cent of respondents in most EC states)[35] for pressurising reluctant states and those in a minority wishing to defer steps wanted by the majority. The EP does not see the possibility of a small minority blocking progress towards European Union indefinitely as just or as a reason to stop the majority from moving ahead. President Mitterrand appears to follow this reasoning.

The EP has also invoked the principles of justice and fairness in other areas. It has inferred, from the principle that new and existing members of the EC must respect and practise parliamentary democracy, the idea that the EC must apply such principles itself in its own legislative process: the EC must not ignore the will of the people as expressed by their representatives. This is certainly thinly-disguised code for asserting the EP's right to control the Council by holding it accountable for its outputs and by ensuring that it respect and accommodate the EP's views. In the 1990s the EP will have to continue to move from being a chamber that asserts principles and laudable goals to one that acts according to the wishes of its majority and that ensures that such action is given tangible expression through EC legislation. This will demand the extension of the cooperation procedure to the whole range of EC activity and further progress towards European Union based on a new draft treaty.

However, it is unlikely that the EP will be able to galvanise and mobilise EC publics on European Union as such even though successive *Eurobarometer* polls point to a high degree of public favourability towards the notion of European Union.[36] The EP must be careful to define clearly what it means by European Union. It must take care not to generate excessive expectations of what either the EC or the EP can deliver in terms of Social Europe and a People's Europe. It must be equally careful to ensure that its own spirited defence of the principles of equality, justice and fairness is not so much hot air. In other words, MEPs who gained their seats at least in part because they presented a vision for the future that accorded with the wishes of a majority of the EP's voters must ensure that the vision is translated in a recognisable way through the legislative programmes introduced by the Commission and adopted by the EP and the Council.

The preoccupation with realising the SEM during the current legislature's term of office means that the 'red-green' majority that purports to value social and environmental as well as redistributive policy goals above the creation of a bigger and better rich man's club will have to act accordingly, to ensure that appropriate legislation is drafted and passed. Thus the political choices set out during the election will have to have some corresponding legislative counter-parts. There is nothing to stop the EP from developing framework programmes for discussion over a range of issues. Indeed, it must stimulate well-informed discussion of both existing programmes and initiatives relating to 1992 and of alternative and additional measures that are desirable to complement them. Agenda-setting for the EC rather than simply for itself must assume greater importance, notably in those areas (such as economic and monetary union and defence and security) that will demand an EC response before the 'magic' deadline of 1993.

Does all this mean that the EP has undergone such a fundamental change that it can be said to approximate more readily existing 'types' of parliament? The answer must be probably not. The EP does not have any particular role model. It is true that the German *Bundestag* and *Bundesrat* might be seen as an appropriate bicameral model legislature for a European Union. However, too close an approx-imation to existing national parliamentary arrangements is unlikely to commend itself. The EP is, therefore, eclectic in scrutinising existing parliamentary practices elsewhere and in adopting and adapting those that seem to meet the needs of any functions or roles it wishes to exercise itself. The EP is in a position to innovate. It is not, therefore, intent on mimicking any particular legislature. Rather, it seeks to establish both the legitimacy of its case for, and by actual practice the utility of, a relatively strong supranational legislature: strong by comparison with national parliaments whose influence and powers appear to have been eroded steadily over the past years.

Measured against the traditional attributes ascribed to legislatures in Western liberal democracies committed to representative government, the EP can be seen to have made substantial gains since 1979. These gains have not been achieved by a corresponding loss in the ranks of national parliaments. They have been won through small steps leading to practical results. While comparisons with national parliaments are interesting, it must be remembered that one is not comparing like with like. But there does exist an inchoate view of the powers and functions of an ideal 'parliament' and this is part of the EP's political and cultural heritage.

Many have tried to list the archetypal functions of legislatures in West European polities. These include the functions of: representation, articulation, communication, participation in the appointment and dismissal of the executive, legislation, recruitment, and control over the executive and expenditure.[37] On the eve of the first elections, the EP could claim to exercise partially only some of these functions. Its role was advisory and supervisory: it could issue Opinions on Commission proposals. It had a financial power to be exercised with the Council and limited control over EC expenditure. It had a limited control over the executive: it could dismiss the Commission; it could question it and the Council and the Council of Foreign Ministers meeting in Political Cooperation. It had the potential for developing information, communication, education, legitimation and representation functions.[38]

Over the past decade, the EP has not only improved the effectiveness of its exercise of its original powers but it has adapted and expanded them.[39] It has also realised, though not yet fully, its potential information, education, communication, legitimation and representation functions. It also participates in the appointment of the executive. It does act as an aggregator of interests and articulates them. Above all, it has a vastly increased role in agenda-setting for the EC as a whole rather than simply for itself; in identifying political priorities; in outlining alternatives and choices; in influencing the content of and expenditure associated with legislative proposals; in controlling Commission and Council outputs; and in transforming the EC system in a way compatible with ideals of parliamentary liberal democracy and representative government. It is proactive in a way that few national parliaments are or can be.

Yet, the idea of the democratic deficit persists. The EP does not exercise sufficiently the above functions to overcome perceived weaknesses in the EC's democratic practices. The Council can still escape effective supervision by either national parliaments or the EP. National parliamentary supervision is likely to remain inadequate, and improvement may only occur if there is far greater cooperation with the EP. As long as the Council is the final arbiter in the legislative process, the democratic deficit will persist. It will continue so long as the EP is in a position of relative or unacceptable weakness *vis-à-vis* the Council. Democratic controls in the legislative process are partial. A democratic deficit exists at national level where national parliaments' scrutiny over directives, for example, leaves much to be desired, as the House of Commons has belatedly realised. At EC-level, controls can be exercised effectively only through the EP. Yet, EC legislation can still be passed in certain areas against the majority wishes of the EP and even without the EP having been fully consulted and given a genuine opportunity to influence it. Even the EP's representative credentials are imperfect given the Council's continuing failure to honour the Rome Treaty and ensure that EP elections occur in accordance with a uniform electoral procedure. This is something the new EP will have to take up.

During its third term, the EP must redress these deficiencies and seek the extension of the cooperation procedure to all EC proposals. As yet, when seeking re-election its members are not in a position to campaign on a highly visible record of achievement that is identified with a particular ideological tendency or party group(s). The sense of occasion that accompanies major elections within the member states is absent from EP elections. The disjunction between elections to a parliament and the fate of a government exacerbates the difficulty of impressing upon the voters the idea that the EP 'matters' in terms of policies pursued. While EP elections are not directly comparable to general elections, MEPs and equally importantly national parties have tried with limited effect to convey the impression that if *x* happens in the elections then *y* follows. MEPs are keen to mobilise the electorate to turn out because the level of turnout is seen as a measure of the EP's legitimacy.

So far, getting the vote out has been mainly the task of national political parties that have been free to use as much or as little of any relevant transnational party federation campaign material and so on as they wish. Turnout has fallen slightly with each election overall, but cannot be trivialised and used to undermine the EP's claims for a greater say in EC policymaking. This implies that the EP has been successful in getting itself established in the public mind as one of the EC's key institutions and one that cannot be dispensed with lightly. What is striking about the third EP elections is the degree of national party political mobilisation behind the campaigns. There was a general belief that in 1989 something policywise was at stake. This was not undermined even though again national issues dominated the campaigns. One can only speculate as to the possible effect of simultaneous EP elections under a uniform procedure. The EP must surely press for this for the 1994 elections.

In the meantime, if the democratic deficit is to be rectified, the EP must continue playing its system-transformative role using its dual-pronged strategy to achieve the necessary changes. The EC's rapidly expanding policy agenda means that an increasing range of issues and legislative proposals is not subject to effective parliamentary scrutiny, supervision, influence or control. This must be checked. Keeping European Union high on the political agenda will create the appropriate context and psychological environment for pursuing change. The EP has established itself as its *animateur*. It must follow through on this. It will not be enough for the EP simply to rely on the Petitions Committee for feedback from the public about EC legislation. Nor should MEPs be tempted to relax their information, education and communication functions *vis-à-vis* the public simply because *Eurobarometer* polls show broad public support for the concept of a European Parliament and for one empowered to draft a new constitution for the EC.

MEPs still have to persuade the public that they are doing a worthwhile job effectively. The EP's credibility remains fragile. It will be tested and must withstand such tests. Gestures that underpin its commitment to political decency and democratic credentials are important. But the real test will come in the ways in which the cooperation procedure is exploited and extended, the ways in which the EP presents political choices to the public and mobilises accordingly behind them, and the commitment it brings to promoting European Union with a social and human face. Much depends on its political groups. The EP has to assert itself during the 1990s.

NOTES AND REFERENCES

1. Key documents on 'Strengthening the internal market' are COM(81)572 final and COM(82)799 final; on 'reactivating the European internal market', COM(82)735 final; on 'assessing the function of the internal market', COM(83)80 final; on 'Internal Market Problems', COM(83)144 final; on 'Consolidating the internal market', COM(84)305 final and COM(84)350 final. The *White Paper on Completing the Internal Market* appeared as COM(85)310 final. See *Bull.EC*, 6/85, p. 18.

2. For the first report on the implementation of the White Paper see COM(86)300 fin; second report COM(87)203 fin; third report COM(88)134 fin.

3. P. Cecchini (ed.), *The European Challenge of 1992: the benefits of a single market* (Aldershot: Gower, 1988).

4. For detailed analysis see the 16 volumes published by the Commission on the 'Cost of Non-Europe'. *Basic Findings*, Luxembourg, 1988. Also see 'The economics of 1992' in *European Economy*, no.35, March 1988.

5. In 1981 there was one important report and two notable resolutions: *PE.DOC* 1–241/81. Report on the 1981 Programme for the achievement of the customs union; *OJ C260* 12.10.81, p. 68. Resolution on the Commission's 1981 programme for the achievement of the customs union; and *OJ C287*, 9.11.81, p. 64. Resolution on the establishment of the internal market. These were followed by further resolutions and reports. See *PE.DOC* 1–32/84; *OJ C117*, 30.4.84; *OJ C315*, 26.11.84, p. 111.

6. 'Towards European economic recovery in the 1980s'. Report presented to the EP by Mr Albert and Professor Ball. *PE.DOC* 1983/84.

7. J. Lodge and V. Herman, *Direct Elections to the European Parliament: A Community Perspective* (London: Macmillan, 1982) especially Chap. 8.

8. COM 100.

9. For details see J. Lodge (ed.), *European Union: the EC in Search of a Future* (London: Macmillan, 1986) and R. Bieber et al., *An Ever Closer Union* (Brussels: EC Commission, 1985).

10. See Council Decision (76/787/ECSC, EEC, Euratom in *OJ L* 278, 8.10.78. The Act concerning the election of the representatives of the European Parliament by direct universal suffrage entered into force on 1 July 1978, several weeks after the initial election date of June 1978. *OJ L* 173, 29.6.78, p. 30.

11. See J. Lodge, 'The European Parliament – from 'assembly' to co-legislature: changing the institutional dynamics', in J. Lodge (ed.), *The European Community and the Challenge of the Future* (London: Pinter, 1989) pp. 58–81.

12. J. Lodge, 'The European Parliament after Direct Elections: Talking-Shop or Putative Legislature?', *Journal of European Integration*, 5 (1982) 259–84; M. Palmer, 'The development of the European Parliament's Institutional Role within the European Community, 1974–83',

JEI, 5 (1982) 183–202; S. Steppat, 'Execution of Functions by the European Parliament in its first electoral period', *JEI*, 12 (1989) 5–34.

13. Notably the Kirk-Reay report. *PE.DOC* 148/78.
14. See *PE.DOC* 1–207/81 (van Miert); 1–216/81 (Hänsch); 1–206/81 (Diligent); 1–335/81 (Elles); 1–946/82 (Haagerup); 1–70/80 (Rey); 1–226/81 (Baduel Glorioso); 1–739/81 (Antoniozzi) and 1–685/81 (Blumenfeld).
15. The ECJ took two years to announce that the Council had violated the treaty. For details of the proceedings leading up to this see *OJ C* 267, 1982, p. 62; *C* 49, 1983, p. 9; *C* 144, 1985, p. 4.
16. R. Cardozo and R. Corbett, 'The Crocodile initiative', in J. Lodge (ed.), *European Union: the EC in Search of a Future* (London: Macmillan, 1986) pp. 15–46.
17. *PE* 86.303, para. 120. IAC, Selection of Texts concerning institutional matters of the Community from 1950–1982 (Luxembourg, 1983).
18. J. Lodge (ed.), *Direct Elections to the European Parliament 1984* (London: Macmillan, 1986).
19. See Ad Hoc Committee for Institutional Affairs, Report to the European Council (Brussels, 29–30 March 1985).
20. Ibid., part II.
21. For details see R. Corbett, 'The 1985 Intergovernmental Conference and the Single European Act', in R. Pryce (ed.), *The Dynamics of European Union* (Beckenham: Croom Helm, 1987) pp. 238–72.
22. W. Nicoll, 'La procedure de concertation entre le Parlement européen et le Conseil', *Revue du Marché Commun*, no. 293, 1986, 3–10.
23. W. Nicoll, 'Les procedures Luns–Westerterp pour l'information du parlement européen', *Revue du Marché Commun*, no. 300, 475–6.
24. *PE. DOC* A2–144/88; A2–145/88; A1–146/88.
25. For details see J. Lodge in J. Lodge (ed.), *The European Community and the Challenge of the Future* (London: Pinter, 1989), op.cit.
26. This concerned with common position on diesel vehicles of 15.9.87, *EP DOC* C2–141/87. See too Lord Plumb's declaration in *OJ C318/41* of 28.10.87; and on the threatened legal action OJ C345/59. 1987 EP *Rules of Procedure*, 36(3).
27. See R. Bieber, 'Legislative Procedure for the establishment of the Single Market', *Common Market Law Review*, 25 (1988) p. 716.
28. *OJ C* 125 L371, 30.12.87.
29. *PE. DOC* A2–186/88 and A2–189/88.
30. J. Lodge, 'The European Parliament in Election Year', *European Access*, 1989: 2, 10.
31. Draft Report on the Institutional Consequences of the costs of non-Europe, Explanatory Statement, 1987, PE.118.040/corr.en. and chapter by F. Dehousse, in R. Bieber et al., (eds) *1992: One European Market?* (Baden-Baden: Nomos, 1988).
32. Prag Report, *PE.DOC* A 2–0351/88. Herman Report, A 2–322/88.
33. K. H. Reif (ed.), *European Elections 1979/81 and 1984* (Berlin: Quorum, 1984).
34. See M. Shackleton, 'The Budget of the European Community', in

J. Lodge (ed.), *The European Community and the Challenge of the Future* (London and New York: Pinter and St. Martin's, 1989).

35.   *Eurobarometer*, 29, 6/1988, A18.

36.   *Eurobarometer*, 30, 12/1988, A18.

37.   See G. Loewenberg (ed.), *Modern Parliaments: Change or Decline?* (New York: Aldine–Atherton, 1971); A. Kornberg and L. D. Musolf (eds). *Legislatures in Developmental Perspective* (Durham: Duke University Press, 1970); L. Mezey, *Comparative Legislatures* (Durham: Duke University Press, 1979).

38.   V. Herman and J. Lodge, *The European Parliament and the European Community* (London and New York: Macmillan and St. Martin's, 1978).

39.   For a detailed survey of the 1979–84 period see E. Grabitz, et al., *Direktwahl und Demokratisierung* (Bonn: Europa Union Verlag, 1988).

2 Belgium and Luxembourg
JOHN FITZMAURICE

BELGIUM

The European election campaign in Belgium was conducted in parallel with the first election of the Brussels Regional Council, the last major piece in the jigsaw of the reform of the state, which transformed Belgium into an effective federal system. As a result of the EC 'pacification', Belgium had entered a period of greater political calm. The campaign was therefore rather dull and uncontroversial, raising few ripples on the becalmed pond of Belgian political life. The results were also predictable and conformed with the general trend elsewhere in the EC, though the anti-government swing in Belgium was very limited and benign. Turnout was 92.1 per cent, almost identical with the 1984 figure, but it should be remembered that voting is compulsory for voters under the age of 70.

The 1989 EP elections took place in an almost totally different climate from 1984. This is true of the international, European and domestic political climate. 1984 was still the pre-Gorbachev era. It was the ice-age of superpower relations. The 'evil empire' was still on the agenda. The INF missiles were in the process of deployment and Belgium was to receive 48 at Florennes. The perspectives for an improvement of East/West relations in Europe and thereby EC/COMECON relations remained dismal. By 1989, the INF Treaty had been signed and ratified. There had been significant progress on chemical weapons and a new and more hopeful round of conventional arms reduction talks had opened in Vienna with a real sense of purpose. Soviet forces left Afghanistan in February 1989 and superpower cooperation on the resolution of various regional conflicts had replaced competition. In Eastern Europe and the USSR itself, the Gorbachev revolution of *perestroika* was bringing real change and unhoped for perspectives for change and cooperation. The more European Soviet Republics were showing signs of real independence and various forms of multiparty developments were emerging in several central European countries such as Hungary, Poland and Yugoslavia. German MEP and ex-heir to the Hapsburg Empire, Otto Von Hapsburg was received with full honours in Budapest in early March, where he declared that Hungary would eventually join the

37

EC. That did not please his hosts! That is just one example of the ground covered. As a result, the EC has been able to sign a Joint Declaration with COMECON and agreements have been signed with several COMECON member states. All now seems possible. International relations have gone from deep pessimism to a new optimism.

The EC itself has also undergone a sea change in the last five years. Here too, 1984 was a period of deep pessimism about the future. The EC seemed to have stagnated and to lack any broad political and strategic goal. It was dominated by the UK rebate issue and the associated problems of financing of EC policies and control of the spiralling cost of the CAP. The ambitious European Union Treaty drawn up by the EP in early 1984 seemed utopian. The issue was less progress than mere survival. There was in Belgium an inchoate concern on all these fronts. There has always been a strong passive consensus in favour of the EC in Belgium and at least a realisation that Belgium has much to lose from any disintegration of the EC. By 1989, the EC had turned itself round. It had developed a new sense of purpose and new and ambitious objectives in the 1992 market. The problems of financing and the control of CAP expenditure have been resolved at least until 1992. The EC and its institutions have developed a new sense of purpose and a more positive image. EFTA states have been forced to re-evaluate their relations with the EC and some, such as Austria and Norway, are seriously considering full membership. The SEA has been signed and ratified. The SEA is certainly not European Union, but it does represent both significant and substantive progress and a change in the way the EC makes decisions. This is particularly welcome in Belgium, as there has always been strong support for greater use of majority voting and a stronger role for the EP and above all a fear of stagnation or disintegration. For the first time, the EP can effectively run both on its own record as an institution and on the record of the EC as a whole.

The international climate had moved through almost 180 degrees. In 1984, the USSR was leaderless and the standard US position was based on the 'evil empire' syndrome. NATO was split and the postwar consensus over defence had broken down in many NATO countries such as Norway, Denmark, the Netherlands, Britain, Germany and Belgium over the deployment of Cruise and Pershing INFs, in accordance with the 1979 Twin Track decision. Belgium had seen a series of massive disarmament marches, the SP had radicalised its position so far on this issue that, whilst it might garner votes, it was no longer a potential coalition partner in any likely combination. It was even out of step with the PS, which attached less weight to this issue. By 1989, the superpowers had signed and begun to implement the INF Treaty, agreed to significant reductions in strategic arms and set up new talks on conventional weapons and on ABC weapons. Europe seemed a much safer place. The Soviet threat had receded and radical developments towards forms of pluralism were underway in Eastern Europe. The EC had signed a framework agreement with COMECON and was discussing significant agreements with most COMECON members. Here the EC was seen as having an innovative and original role to play. It too was part of the EC's more positive and dynamic image.

In 1984, the domestic political situation was turbulent and the opposition sought to use the EP elections as a weapon against the centre right CVP/PSC–PVV/PRL coalition that had come to power in 1982. In Flanders, the SP was able to mobilise opinion against the deployment of INFs in Belgium and other NATO countries under the controversial and increasingly contested 1979 Twin Track decision. In Wallonia, the PS completed its transformation into a Walloon federalist party, espousing the symbolic cause of José Happart, Mayor of the Fourons, who had not hitherto been identified with the PS, but was given an electable position on the PS list. He was probably worth an additional seat to the PS. By the time of the 1989 elections, Belgian domestic politics had entered one of its calmest periods in recent history. The 1987 election had seen the fall of the centre right (CVP/PSC–PVV/PRL) coalition and its replacement by the more usual centre left (CVP/PSC–PS/SP) alternative, augmented with the VU in order to broaden support in Flanders for a new phase of reform of the state. The new government's programme was carefully negotiated by Jean-Luc Dehaene (CVP) as *formateur*, who then made way for Mr Martens with the necessary prestige to bind the CVP into the coalition. After a year in office, the coalition had achieved considerable success, with the carrying through of a new slice of devolution, including education; a new financing arrangement for the devolved Regions and Communities; a tax reform; a continuation of the reform of government finances; a new social dimension to economic policy; and an agreement among the coalition parties on NATO modernisation of short-range nuclear weapons. Indeed, as the October 1988 municipal elections had shown, there was little potential for the opposition, especially the liberals, to exploit the EP elections as a classic mid-term test of government (un)popularity.

This then was the broad political background to the elections: a new dynamism in the EC; domestic political calm and an optimistic international environment. The more immediate national, or more accurately regional political environment was the combination of the EP elections with the Brussels Regional elections. As part of the major reform of the state package carried through in 1988 and early 1989, distinct and independent Brussels regional institutions were created. Brussels was to be the first Region or Community (apart from the small German-speaking Community) to have its own directly elected Assembly, to which its Executive is responsible. Thus, in addition to electing its MEPs, the Brussels electorate also elected 75 members of the Brussels Regional Council.

There was no change in the electoral system or the distribution of seats in the Belgian contingent of 24 MEPs between the two linguistic regions. The matter was discussed in the cabinet and the VU argued for a more favourable distribution for Flanders, such as 14:10, but it was not possible to reach any agreement and the *status quo* was retained, with a commitment to review the matter in the framework of the third phase of the\ reform of the state. Thus the present distribution of 11 French speakers and 13 Dutch speakers was retained. As in 1984, there was a legal incompatibility between the position of MEP and national MP, to avoid 'cumulation' of political offices. The 'cumul' of the posts of Mayor or *échevin* of a municipality with over 50 000 inhabitants, member of a Regional or Community Executive (cabinet) or member of the Provincial Executives (*Députations Permanentes*) is also forbidden by law. The Law establishing the Brussels Regional Council and the Law of 23 March 1989 on the EP elections does not make membership of the Regional Council and the EP impossible and indeed, several candidates stood for both at the same time.

The electoral system remains as it was in 1979. The country is divided into a Flemish electoral district, to which 13 seats are allocated and a Walloon/German Community electoral district, to which 11 seats are allocated. The country is also divided into three voting districts. In the Flemish district, voters may only vote for unilingual Flemish lists (except voters in the Fourons, who may register in a French-speaking municipality, if they wish). In the Walloon voting district, voters must vote for a Francophone list. In the third district, covering Brussels, voters receive a ballot paper with the Flemish lists on one side and the Francophone lists on the other side. They may thus vote for either a Flemish list or a Francophone list. Their votes are then counted in the allocation of seats in their chosen linguistic electoral district. Voters may vote for a list as a whole, or for an individual on a list, to whom the voter wishes to give his preference. Seats are allocated to lists by the D'Hondt divisor method. Once the number of seats for each list has been determined, the candidates actually elected are determined by a complex system that applies a mixture of the 'list votes' and the preference votes. In theory, the order of the list, fixed by the party, can be modified by the electorate through the preference vote system, but it is quite rare in national elections, where the number of preference votes needed would be very large.

There are few rules governing election campaigns in Belgium. There are at present no legal rules governing campaign expenditure, though a new law has recently been enacted and will be in force in future elections. There is, however, a voluntary agreement between the parties, to limit expenditure, which was getting out of hand. Many candidates have financed a personal campaign, as distinct from party campaigns. There are no official 'European party political broadcasts' but both the French-speaking RTFB and the Flemish BRT public service channels have held a small number of inter-party debates. Parties were, of course, free to devote part of their normal periodic allocations of free air-time to European issues. Opinion polls are banned in the month preceding the election.

What was the immediate political context of the campaign and what was the record of the parties that had been represented in the 1984–89 legislature and of the Belgian MEPs as individuals? The Martens VIII coalition was one year old as the campaign opened and had shown an unexpectedly strong capacity to follow through on its programme, seemed to work well as a team and had survived the October 1988 municipal elections without difficulty, as these had given no clear national political signals. The final polls before the legal campaign blackout, though neither conclusive, nor consistent, did suggest that government parties as a whole would not fare badly for what was essentially a mid-term test. The PS was expected to make gains or at least achieve a 'status quo' result. The others were expected to lose, though one poll suggested a 0.2 per cent gain for the SP as well. Significant (in Belgian terms) losses were expected for the VU and less for the CVP. The Greens (ECOLO and AGALEV) were also expected to gain, but not the Liberal opposition. The predicted losses for the government parties taken together were about 3.5 per cent. These results suggested real political problems only for the VU. Little headway appeared to have been made by the PVV and PRL in its campaign to turn the elections into an anti-government mid-term protest. This was also confirmed by the relative calm of the campaign.

The key event in the EC in the immediate pre-campaign period was the debate opened up by Mrs Thatcher's Bruges speech, which was itself a reaction to a speech by Commission President Jacques Delors to the EP in July 1988 when, reflecting the new 'Europhoria', he predicted that by the end of the century, some 80 per cent of economic, social and perhaps even fiscal legislation would be of EC origin. At the same time, the discussion about monetary union was relaunched by the establishment of the Delors committee. The debate launched by Mrs Thatcher about the EC's future shape was a real one that could not be ignored, even if her views were widely rejected outside the United Kingdom. The debate led to a sense that the EC now faced hard choices about its future, as to whether it should drive towards a monetary union, a social dimension and perhaps full European Union and could as a result no longer fudge the issue of sovereignty. Where Mrs Thatcher clearly answered 'No' to these questions, almost all Belgian parties answered 'Yes' and rejected the Thatcherite vision of pure market EC. There was general agreement about the broad canvas. The campaign was therefore not very controversial. It was about nuances, about credibility and competence, about method and approach, rather than substantive differences, which were actually rather few.

Each party and candidate tried to demonstrate special credibility and competence to deal with EC issues. From that point of view, developments since 1984 had been helpful, in that the EP had greatly enhanced both its image and effectiveness since then. Its use of its new powers under the SEA had shown that it could exercise a constructive and meaningful influence. This new credibility strengthens the argument for more powers for the EP to fill the democratic deficit that the new dynamism of the EC is opening up, as the EC gathers power to the centre in Brussels, without a corresponding increase in the powers of democratic control by the EP. Belgian MEPs have been active in this institutional debate during the last legislature.

Among Belgian MEPs, as a recent survey shows, Mr Herman (PSC) was undoubtedly the most active. He was the *rapporteur* for nine reports and nine opinions, well ahead of his nearest rival, Mr Glinne (PS), with two reports and six Opinions. Mr Herman has become the successor to Altiero Spinelli as the EP's institutional strategist, as the author of the EP's new European Union strategy report. He also drew up reports on a wide variety of economic topics, such as telecommunications and public procurement. Among his more original proposals was the idea of an 'individual' motion of censure against specific members of the Commission, which has not yet been adopted. Mr Herman was active in the Institutional Affairs, Rules, Economic and Monetary, and Industrial Affairs Committees. Mr Glinne was active in the Political Affairs Committee on matters relating to human rights in central and south America and southern Africa. He has drawn up several reports on central America. Mr Roelants du Vivier, elected in 1984 on the ECOLO list, has had a stormy passage. He has been active in the Environment Committee, but broke with ECOLO as it moved to the left. He was then briefly in the PSC, but contested the elections on a list with the FDF. Mr Luc Beyer (elected as PRL) was 'deselected' probably for his strongly pro-Arab views in relation to the Middle East and his generally very right-wing views. For example, he refused to join in a minute's silence for victims of Pinochet in Chile, strongly supported the Maronites in Lebanon and the Turkish cause. Mr Happart has not been active in the EP. He sits on the Agriculture Committee. Mrs Lizin (PS), Mr Ducarme (PRL) and Mr Van Miert (SP), three of the more colourful and active MEPs, left during the term to take up national political positions, showing again that in Belgium the EP is a valuable springboard for national office. Among the other Flemish MEPs, Mr Croux (CVP) was very active in the Institutional Affairs Committee. Mr De Gucht (PVV) drew up the EP's Charter of Rights to go alongside the European Union Treaty. Mr Chanterie (CVP) was the only Belgian Committee Chairman. He did much to put the new Petitions Committee, created in 1987, on the map.

The banning of the dual mandate has meant that Belgian parties and individual politicians have been forced to make difficult choices between Europe and national politics when drawing up lists. It has become impossible to ride both horses at once, though of course politicians can and do move backwards and forwards: for example, Mr Tindemans, who was in national politics, became an MEP, then went back into national politics as Foreign Minister and has now gone back to the EP. Initially, parties could make the choice after the elections, but this option is becoming less and less credible. The electorate now expects only 'real' candidates to stand. Lists must follow the computer-speak maxim 'WYSIWYG' (What you see is what you get). Juggling between the national and European levels has become very difficult. The key strategic decisions about whether major political figures should get into the European race or not must be taken well before the elections, with no going back.

All the major parties, with both heavyweight national leaders and existing, but much less well-known MEPs, had to make the choice between a list favouring 'heavyweights' or 'experience and competence' in the form of its MEPs. Only the PSC, whose leader Gerard Deprez was already an MEP, did not face this particular choice. What one party does influences another. For example, since PS leader Guy Spitaels declined to lead his party's list or even figure on it at all, it was easy for Jean Gol (PRL) not to head his party's list. National political considerations also played a part. Since the PRL was not going to be able to turn the elections into an anti-government plebiscite, it made little sense for Jean Gol to expose himself. At the same time, it became unnecessary for Guy Spitaels to accept any challenge. He could leave the matter in the hands of the outgoing team that also neatly balanced party factions, including those that he had recently defeated when the government was formed and in the recent PS Congress. Furthermore, he could conveniently avoid measuring his own popularity against that of José Happart, who was defending his record 240 000 personal votes from 1984. For the PVV, the need was for a European elder statesman to face Tindemans. Here, Willy De Clerq, the respected former external relations Commissioner, was the obvious choice. For the smaller parties, the choices were more limited. The VU and AGALEV headed their lists with their outgoing MEPs, but the VU included party President Gabriels and Budget Minister Schilz in non-electable positions on the list. Regional balance played a part too. The PRL, with Mr De Donnéa, the PS with Raymonde Dury, the FDF with Antoinette Spaak all played the Brussels card, which was obviously not unrelated to the parallel electoral battle for the Brussels Regional Council. Lower down the list, but in electable positions, figured most of the various parties' outgoing MEPs. Apart from the PRL, which unceremoniously dumped Luc Beyer, Mme André and Mr Toussaint, all its outgoing MEPs, there is no evidence that there was any tendency to penalise experience. Some candidates were under considerable personal pressure to deliver a strong preference vote. This was true of Mr Herman, who was by no means certain of re-election. It was true of his party leader, Gérard Deprez, who faced a right-wing revolt inside the PSC, which would have ignited had he fallen far under his 1984 result of 90 000. José Happart had to show that he was still a factor in Wallonia and inside his own party and that his recent moderation had not made his star wane.

The Francophone Green scene had seen considerable change since the 1984 elections. Mr Roelants du Vivier had then been elected, as the moderate face of Green politics, on the ECOLO list and had joined the Green Alternative faction (GRAEL) in the EP Rainbow Group after some hesitation. Immediately after the EP's reconstitution for the second half of its term in 1987, he left ECOLO, which he denounced as having shifted to the left. By joining another faction in the Rainbow Group (the Free European Alliance), he was able to remain in the Group and hence obtain generous official funding. The GRAEL retained its links with ECOLO, this time from the left, to form the Verts et Gauche Alternative (VEGA) that clearly announced its 'red-green' character. Paul Lannoye (a former ECOLO deputy) headed the ECOLO list and he was elected, showing that ECOLO had retained the Green vote in Wallonia. Mr Roelants flirted with the PSC, but ended by denouncing its inaction on green issues and eventually stood as an 'Europe-Régions-Ecologie' candidate on the FDF list, in second position, but was not elected.

The political situation as it was when the campaign opened, and the opinion polls, offered little incentive for the parties to mount a vigorous campaign. The campaign was calm and not very intensive. It was traditional in form, with meetings and rallies in the main centres by the *têtes de liste* of the various parties and other political figures. There were a few general positive press articles on the EP and some personal profiles of MEPs. The main TV networks organised a small number of debates. Posters were, as always in Belgian elections, an important element in the campaign. There was little evidence of new campaign methods or approaches and no greater degree of internationalisation of the campaign than in 1984 and 1979. The four main groupings: (Socialists, Christian Democrats, Liberals and Greens) all subscribed to European 'umbrella' programmes. However, apart from providing credibility in a very general way, these programmes did not feature to any great extent in the campaign.

The results

The overall results are shown in Table 2.1. As well as these, the level of personal preference votes has considerable political importance in terms of a politician's general standing and credibility. Reputations are won and lost on the personal vote and, once gained, such

Table 2.1   The results of the 1987 General Election and the 1984 and 1989
Euro-elections in Belgium

Party List	1984		General Election '87	1989	
	%	Seats	%	%	Seats
PS	13.3	5	15.7	14.5	5
PRL	9.5	3	9.4	7.2	2
PSC	7.6	2	8.0	8.1	2
ECOLO	3.9	1	2.6	6.3	2
FDF-ERE	2.5	0	1.2	1.5	0
PTB (ext-left)	0.2	0	0.2	0.2	0
POS (ext-left)	0.2	0	0.2	0.2	0
Others	2.0	0	1.0	0.2	0
CVP	19.8	4	19.5	21.1	5
SP	17.1	4	14.9	12.4	3
PVV	8.6	2	11.5	10.6	2
AGALEV	4.3	1	4.5	7.2	1
VU	8.5	2	8.0	5.4	1
Vlaams Blok	1.3	0	1.9	4.1	1
PVDA (ext-left)	0.5	0	0.8	0.4	0
Regenbog	–	–	–	0.5	0

positions must be defended in future elections, becoming the benchmark against which future performance will be judged. Mr Tindemans
could not expect to match the one million personal votes that he won
in 1979, but he did lead the Flemish field with 433 000. PSC President
Deprez faced an internal party revolt from the right that would
explode unless he won close on his 90 000 votes in 1984. His 78 826
vote was considered sufficient. José Happart (PS), symbol of federalism in the PS, had to come close to his 1984 result of 240 000. He won
308 000, thereby maintaining his credibility and sending a warning to
Guy Spitaels. Mr Herman (PSC) faced a hard battle for re-election
and fought on his activism and competence which won him the very
creditable personal vote of 42 056. In more general terms, study
of personal votes gives an indication of who is up and who is down
and will be examined for many months to come by the political
class.

The results corresponded broadly to predictions and also fitted
trends observed throughout the EC. There was, as almost everywhere else, an anti-government swing, but in Belgium it was very
mild and not sufficient to cause any serious concern. Like elsewhere,
the main opposition – in the Belgian case the Liberals – was not the

real beneficiary of any such trend. It was spread and generally went to previously more marginal and anti-establishment parties. In Belgium, again as elsewhere, this meant gains for the Greens in both Flemish and Walloon regions and for the extreme right-wing nationalist Vlaams Blok, which won one EP seat.

No major national political repercussions are expected to flow from these results. Certainly, two of the Flemish government parties, the SP and the VU, did suffer rather severe, but by no means dramatic losses. For the VU, this confirmed the trend already noted in the Municipal elections of October 1988. The VU appeared to lose votes mainly to the ultra-nationalist Vlaams Blok and to a lesser extent to the CVP. This is a classic problem for the small Community parties when they participate in government. It would be a more serious problem if it were to signal a long-term secular decline, heralding a marginalisation similar to that which has overtaken the French-speaking regionalist parties. For the moment, the VU seems content to remain in the government and gamble on fuller regionalisation guaranteeing it both an electorate and a political role in Flanders. As such, this result was a national result, without European significance. The SP had achieved a high point in the 1984 anti-missile campaign, which already in the 1985 national election, it had not been able to hold. It is at about the level it held before the gains of the early 1980s. It expects to ride out this result and prepare for the next general election. The CVP and PSC are gradually recovering from the heavy losses of the early 1980s. The PS has confirmed its domination of the Walloon political landscape. The Greens made significant progress in both regions, confirming, as in 1984, that EP elections are probably more favourable terrain for them than national elections. The alliance of the dissident moderate ecologist, Mr Roelants du Vivier, elected on the ECOLO list in 1984, with the FDF, did not 'take' and produced a poorer result than the FDF obtained in 1984. However, the FDF is far from dead. It produced a much better result in the Brussels regional elections, where it became the third political force in the Capital and is likely to have one Minister in the Regional Executive. The most disquieting result was the election of an MEP from the far-right Vlaams Blok, already prefigured in the Antwerp Municipal elections in October 1988. This party is ultra-nationalist; opposes foreign immigration and espouses other far-right positions. All in all, the results tend to confirm that Belgium has entered a period of relative political stability.

LUXEMBOURG

As in 1979 and 1984, the 1989 European elections in Luxembourg were held together with a general election, but unlike those earlier elections the outcome of the general election seems unlikely to lead to a change of government in the Grand Duchy. Nor was there any change in the balance of representation of the parties in the European Parliament, which thus remains 3 CSV, 2 LSAP and 1 DP. The turnout was slightly lower in 1989, at 87.4 per cent, against 88.4 per cent in 1984. As in Belgium voting is compulsory.

For the national elections, the country is divided up into four constituencies: the North (9 seats) covering the rural area bordering

Table 2.2   The results of the 1984 and 1989 Euro-elections in Luxembourg

Party	% share of the vote		Seats	(6 total)
	1984	1989	1984	1989
CSV	35.33	34.87	3	3
LSAP	30.28	25.50	2	2
DP	21.15	19.96	1	1
Greng Lëscht	–	6.13	0	0
GAP	–	4.27	0	0
GRAL	–	0.86	0	0
Greng Alternativ	6.13	–	0	–
KPL	4.11	4.70	0	0
NB (right)	–	2.90	0	0
Others	2.87	0.81	0	0

on the Belgian Ardennes; the Centre (21 seats), covering the Capital; the East (7 seats) and the industrial South (23 seats). The total number of seats was reduced from 64 to 60 before the election. For the European elections, the whole country is one single constituency. The electoral system is complex and contains highly personalised elements. Each voter has as many votes as there are seats to be filled (six for the EP) and *panachage* is permitted, which means that a voter may distribute his votes not only within one party list, but between several lists. Seats are allocated to the parties according to the Hagenbach divisor method and then the individual candidates are elected to fill the party quota in order of the number of votes they obtained.

For the EP, the effective threshold is 16 per cent of the total vote. This excludes all but the three major parties, though if they were united the Greens would come close to the necessary share. It is also necessary for there to be a massive swing for any seats to change hands. The national election result was very different, due to the fact that there was an additional single-issue list, the 'Aktiounskomitee $\frac{5}{6}$ Pensioun fir Jiddfereen', which was demanding the same pension rights for all, as civil servants enjoy, that is $\frac{5}{6}$ of their last salary before retirement. This list, which obtained 4 seats and almost 10 per cent of the vote, did not stand in the EP elections. It seems to have taken votes from all the major parties, but most from the DP and the CSV. Indeed, several of its leading figures came from the CSV.

The EP lists were led by the party leaders: Jacques Santer (CSV), Jacques Poos (LSAP), Colette Flesch (DP), René Urbany (KPL), Jup Weber (Greng Lëscht) and Jean Huss (GAP). The members initially elected were: Jacques Santer, Jean-Claude Juncker, Jean Spautz (CSV); Jacques Poos, Mady Delvaux (LSAP) and Colette Flesch (DP). However, as always in Luxembourg, there will be games of musical chairs, as those elected prefer to take up seats in the Chamber and or Ministerial posts. Though the dual mandate is legally permitted, it is in practice rare. Only one of those elected (Colette Flesch for the DP) took her seat. It was particularly difficult for the CSU to fill its three European seats. As in 1979 and 1984, this was a serious problem of credibility, as the strongly personalised voting system had almost no impact on who finally went to sit in Strasbourg.

As it has now become a firm tradition for national and EP elections to be held on the same date and as, in Luxembourg, virtually all major political issues are inevitably also European issues, there is no distinct 'national' and 'European' campaign. That means in practice that there is no European campaign, as the European dimension tends to get drowned out in a national campaign. This tendency is reinforced by the fact that both campaigns are in fact led by the same major national figures and that most EP candidates are also candidates for the Chamber of Deputies as well.

However, European issues were at the centre of the campaign in so far as all Luxembourg political goals can only be realised in the framework of the EC. Indeed, the DP tried to make readiness for 1992 a key campaign issue, accusing the government of failing to ensure the necessary preparedness, but failed to make much headway here, losing as heavily as the coalition parties (−3 seats). Harmonisation of taxation, especially the threatened 15 per cent witholding tax on savings, was a major issue, opposed by all main parties as against the national interest. The LSAP was careful to register a footnote reservation on this issue in the CSP Manifesto adopted in May 1989. Migration in general, a major concern in Luxembourg was excluded from the debate by a gentleman's agreement between all the major parties (CSV,LSAP,DP,KPL). Immigration is objectively a major matter of concern in Luxembourg, where in some areas over 30 per cent of residents are foreigners from other EC countries. Immigration is, unlike in neighbouring France or Germany, mainly from the EC, with Portugal the main country of origin. Thus, Luxembourg obtained a specially long transitional period for the full implementation of the free movement of labour in the Portuguese Adhesion Treaty and a derogation for the first municipal election to take place after the entry into force of the proposed Directive granting the right to vote in municipal elections to residents from other EC states. The issue of the seat of the institutions was raised but did not have the same impact as an issue as in 1984.

The two coalition parties did not conduct a very active campaign. They saw no reason to ruffle the surface in what appeared, at least superficially, to be a period of calm in Luxembourg political life. The situation of the country was seen as being excellent and the motto was 'steady as she goes'. There was no formal prior commitment to that effect, indeed that would not be the tradition in Luxembourg, but the general presumption was that the existing coalition should continue. The DP's campaign was not very active or aggressive. It was mainly directed against the LSAP. The DP's aim was to emerge from the election as the unavoidable coalition partner (either in a CSV/DP or LSAP/DP coalition). As it turned out, the parliamentary arithmetic excluded an LSAP/DP coalition and hence the present coalition continued.

The results, more than an apparently routine campaign, showed that the major parties had underestimated the accumulated concerns of the electorate. Since the major parties had refused to conduct a serious debate about these concerns, it had been left to new and untried parties (a record 16 lists) and a record 546 candidates to enter the lists in order to raise the issues. They did so with a considerable degree of success, imposing losses on all three major parties. They pointed to a number of issues that had been consciously or unconsciously neglected or ignored by the major parties. Some of these issues were of a specific nature, such as the pensions question, whereas others were of a broader nature, affecting the future identity of Luxembourg.

The pension privileges of civil servants in Luxembourg have become a major issue in recent years. The term 'civil servant' is broadly defined, covering teachers and railway staff and represents over 50 per cent of the workforce. Yet there remains a large private sector and in particular the self-employed ('independents'), who do not enjoy the $\frac{5}{6}$ of final salary pension regime. The major parties failed to act on the matter and, indeed, did not take it seriously. As a result, the single-issue 'Aktiounskomitee' was formed, winning four seats in the Chamber of Deputies.

Green issues were already significant in Luxembourg, where the Greng Alternativ had achieved a significant breakthrough in 1984 with 6.13 per cent and two seats. However, its growth had been beset with strategic and personal divisions that had led to two breakaway lists and *liste d'union* in the North constituency only. The Greng Lëscht fir Ecologesch Initiativ (GLEI) split off in protest against the increasingly red/green orientation of the Greng Alternativ Partei (GAP), formed out of the early movement. The GLEI is a pragmatic, moderate Green party. The GAP remains, claiming to be 'the real green party'. At the same time, a left-wing splinter group, the Greng Alternativ Allianz (GRAL) was also formed. Only the GLEI and the GAP achieved a significant electoral following, with two seats each. The KPL, now in long-term decline, lost one of its two remaining seats, though its vote has stabilised. It is no longer a major force except in the industrial south, where it still obtained 7.3 per cent.

Several smaller groupings, in addition to the Greens, raised more existential issues related to the future identity of Luxembourg in Europe. The small, but interesting Firwat Niet (Why Not?) list argued for a multicultural and pluralistic Luxembourg. More danger-ously, the election saw the first evidence of the extreme xenophobic right in Luxembourg, with the National Bewegong (NB), with its evocative use of the traditional patriotic slogan 'Luxembourg for the Luxembourgers'. Its result was modest but disquieting: 2.13 per cent, with a peak of 3.06 per cent in the South constituency. It probably reflects a wider concern at threats to the country's identity and traditions, with its patriotic slogans, used in earlier periods such as the two world wars, having an appeal well beyond the confines of the far right. The emergence of these groups should perhaps be seen as a warning.

Below the surface of a becalmed, routine election campaign lurked issues of national identity. The celebration of 150 years of independ-ence (1839–1989), though less emotive than the 100 years anniversary in 1939, on the eve of the second German occupation, nevertheless crystallised thinking about the national identity. Should Luxembourg accept the changes that multicultural immigration on a large scale brought, as a plus, as a positive element to be blended with her traditions, or should she react against it in order to defend her tradition as unchanging and static? The 1992 programme has brought Luxembourg society face to face with the implacable logic of almost forty years of unthinking allegiance to European integration. Could economic growth and Luxembourg's vocation as a financial centre continue indefinitely? What price solidarity with the wider Europe? At the same time, Luxembourg was becoming more determined in the defence of national interests, even if, as in vital financial services areas and in fiscal harmonisation, this threw her together with Mrs Thatcher's Britain. Was Luxembourg's unswerving European commitment weakening? Should she become as nationalist as other member states in defence of her specific national interests? Or should she accept that Luxembourg's future is firmly within a Europe of the regions? Is there a middle way? All these questions were under the surface in this apparently uninteresting election.

In the mainstream of Luxembourg politics, the three parties assessed their own and the other parties, losses relative to their own. The LSAP had clearly failed to achieve a breakthrough and had become the largest party, with room to manoeuvre, forming a coalition either with the CSV or with the DP and, in either case, claiming as of right the premiership for its leader. On the other hand, the DP had not achieved its goal of dealing the government a severe blow. As it was, five years of opposition had brought a loss of three seats. Only two options remained, and the CSV was central to both: CSV + LSAP or CSV + DP. The game was in its hands. It chose to continue the existing CSV + LSAP coalition. Business as usual, but the broader questions remain.

3 Denmark
ALASTAIR H. THOMAS[*]

BACKGROUND: MAIN POLITICAL EVENTS SINCE 1984

When he entered office in 1982 Poul Schlüter was the first Conservative Prime Minister since 1901, and his party has looked to Britain for inspiration from the only other party in Europe which admits in its name to being Conservative. But not only has he had to work with coalition parties in cabinet: throughout his period in office his minority coalitions have had constantly to seek broader parliamentary support and to evade the consequences of hostile parliamentary resolutions imposing reservations on the government's EC and foreign policy. The two most notable of these precipitated the 1986 referendum on the Single European Act and the 1988 election, in which the conditions of Danish membership of NATO were called into question.

Schlüter's 1982 cabinet included Liberals (Venstre), Centre Democrats (CD), and the Christian People's Party, with support totalling 65 members in the 179-member *Folketing*. The centrally-placed Radical Liberals (RV) gave additional parliamentary support on economic policy. But on many foreign policy, environmental and other issues the Radical Liberals and the Social Democrats (S), with the Socialist People's Party (SF) and (intermittently) the Left Socialists (VS), constituted a parliamentary majority which was able to impose significant reservations on government policy, for example on NATO missile deployments and East–West missile negotiations (while supporting continued NATO membership). The Foreign Minister was frequently compelled by majority parliamentary votes to enter Danish reservations ('footnote-politics') to the decisions of the international organisations which he attended. The relative strengths of the parties was little changed by parliamentary elections in January 1984 and September 1987.

A parliamentary resolution in May 1984 confirmed support for continuing Danish EC membership but made it conditional on the continued right of veto and on continuity of the existing power relationships between the Council of Ministers, the Commission and the European Parliament. Danish public opinion has remained particularly sensitive to incursions into national sovereignty or detractions from high standards of environmental and welfare legislation.

53

The socialist-plus-radical alignment defeated the minority government's attempt to obtain parliamentary support for the Single European Act by 80 votes to 75 in January 1986, even though the Progress Party supported the government parties. The Prime Minister responded by calling not an election but a consultative referendum for 27 February. The government parties, with heavy financial support from the Industry Council, ran a campaign threatening economic chaos and loss of the benefits of EC membership if the country did not accept the reform package. They hinted at higher unemployment. However, since Danish unemployment has been lower than the EC average but higher than their Scandinavian neighbours', this threat was unconvincing. Though S was divided, opposition was concentrated on the left, and included the Popular Movement Against the EC (FB), which was solidly against the reforms.

Opponents sought to limit the campaign to the Single Act and its implications for the environment and the control of pollution. Unlike West Germany, the Green movement in Denmark has expressed itself electorally not as a vote for a Green Party, but in vigorous competition between the other parties. Although green is the Conservative party colour, the Radicals and the SF have the strongest claims to being 'green', while the claim of the agrarian Liberals (*Venstre*) has also attained some credibility. The S and their trade-union supporters in LO argued that they had secured EC agreement to high levels of workplace environmental protection, and feared that majority EC voting under the Single Act might jeopardise these gains. The Danish left and centre have tried to defend the welfare society against the intentions of the Schlüter government and did not want it undermined by closer European integration.

The Popular Movement Against the EC (FB) coordinates some 300 locally based anti-EC groups and runs a joint EP voting list, reflecting opposition to the EC, whether socialist, liberal, bourgeois or green. Since Fitzmaurice's analysis[1] the three radical socialist parties (SF, Left Socialists and Communists) remain prominent, but the Danish Union and the very small Nordic People's Party have been replaced by the Justice Party, the Greens and others. Their MEPs sat with the Rainbow Group. The SF ran a separate list and sat with the Communists and Allies. The Movement campaigned actively in the referendum. A Gallup poll asking: 'At the coming referendum will you vote for or against the European Community reform package?' elicited the responses in Table 3.1.

The poll showed that public opinion was polarised. Over 90 per

Table 3.1   Opinion poll on the Single European Act, Denmark, 1986
(percentages)

	For	Against	Undecided
All respondents	46	33	21
Voters to the left of S	13	76	11
S voters	25	53	22
Voters to the right of S	77	8	15

Source: *Berlingske Tidende* (Copenhagen) 3 February 1986

cent of respondents thought they knew about what they were being asked. The government had largely persuaded its own supporters but had a major task to convince the undecided to support the reform package. Schlüter and his government colleagues widened the referendum campaign into a vote of confidence in themselves, their government record, continuing Danish membership of the EC, and indeed the country's economic survival and prosperity, and managed to leave S and the socialist parties in some disarray.

The referendum result supported the Single European Act package, with 42.0 per cent Yes votes to 32.7 per cent No votes, on a 74.7 per cent turnout. The campaign reduced the commitment of a few voters who had said they would vote 'Yes' in the poll, while those intending to vote 'No' remained steady. The SF improved its standing in public opinion as a result of its referendum campaign, while S, despite having precipitated the referendum, were the principal losers. All the parties except SF (with 21 seats in the *Folketing*) accepted the legitimacy of the consultative referendum.

Advocates of EC membership in 1972 had to persuade a reluctant public that its rational economic interests lay in the EC, despite emotional misgivings. In the 1986 referendum the parliamentary majority opposed the Single European Act but the public favoured it. The pro-EC vote in 1972 was 56.7 per cent, so the 1986 referendum showed a decrease in support for the EC, with no reduction in opposition. Schlüter claimed a vote of confidence for his government and the Foreign Minister, Uffe Ellemann-Jensen, signed the EC agreement without further delay.

EC proponents used the referendum to start a debate which they continued into the 1989 EP election. Non-economic advantages were said to include the continuing importance of the EC in keeping the peace, as a bulwark of democracy in southern Europe, and as a means of combining technological advance with a vision of the future. The Liberal Education Minister, Bertel Haarder, argued that, far from conflicting with Danish loyalties to fellow Scandinavians, both Norway and Sweden valued the presence of Denmark in the EC as their spokesman. EC membership eased many of the problems of Danish export trade by offering a single set of standards to be met, and the Single European Act would help to speed the establishment of the EC internal market. What would count would be the extent to which protectionism and non-tariff barriers could be reduced, the help that could be given towards solving Danish environmental problems, and whether reasonable trading relationships could be retained with the USA and Japan. Japanese and French trade barriers were the most serious concern to Danes.

After the referendum the government still faced a parliamentary majority concerned to maintain the country's environmental defences, critical of losses of sovereignty to the EC, and determined to show its unhappiness with NATO's reliance on nuclear weapons while the USSR was taking increasingly bold unilateral initiatives to reduce armaments. This situation came to a head in a confused and heated parliamentary situation on 14 April 1988: an S resolution was passed drawing attention to the Danish policy, maintained for the previous thirty years, of not allowing nuclear weapons on Danish territory, including harbours, and calling on the government to inform visiting naval vessels of this. NATO allies reacted promptly and adversely, and the Prime Minister called for a parliamentary election for 10 May 1988, only eight months after the last election.

1988 election and government changes

A controversial election campaign produced a parliament in which support for a new government, still less a majority, was not easily discerned. The Progress Party gained most, taking its seats from 9 to 16, but their addition would not take the government parties to a majority, while it would alienate potential support for the coalition from the centre and centre-left. The Social Democrats gained one seat, halting their slide in support at each of the three elections since 1979, but the SF lost three and the socialist bloc was well short of a majority.

Once again the ten Radicals could hold the balance from the centre. Simply adding them to the cabinet would increase the number of parties to five, which was considered unmanageable. Instead the 1968–71 Radical–Liberal–Conservative combination was revived. The Radicals reluctantly agreed to accept Schlüter's leadership. But it remained a minority government, still depending on parliamentary support from the Centre Democrats and the Christian People's Party, a role which the former found hard to accept after their part in the 1982–88 four-party government.

Opinion polls in April 1989 indicated a shift of support to the right, from the Conservatives and the Radicals towards the Progress Party, while S and SF held their ground. Schlüter responded by suggesting another consultative referendum in June on the drastic economic measures needed to reduce the notoriously high Danish tax burden. The package would comprise public sector cuts, payment by consumers for public services, 'rationalisation' of the numerous tax allowances, and reforms of social security benefit payments, partly justified as making it easier to harmonise with EC tax levels in the post-1992 internal market. The referendum idea was soon dropped, but speculation followed about an early election, possibly coinciding with the November 1989 local elections. S offered alternative proposals as the basis of a possible compromise with the government parties, expecting its hand to be strengthened by a successful showing in the June EP election.

THE 1989 EP ELECTION

The highly complex electoral system uses a single national constituency for EP elections and gives closely proportional results and allows electors to vote for a list or a single candidate. A personal vote for a candidate can thus amend the priorities allocated by the party. As in national elections, voters and candidates become eligible at age 18. Dual mandates are legal: some party rules (e.g. CD) allow them but others (e.g. S and Conservatives) do not.

Of the 16 MEPs elected in 1984, all but three served out their full term of five years. Poul Møller withdrew from the Conservative delegation soon after he was elected, and his party colleague Claus Toksvig died after serving for about four years. One member of the Popular Movement Against the EC also retired before the completion of his term of office. They were each replaced by alternates drawn from their respective lists.

Given the breadth of support for the Popular Movement Against the EC, the background of their 16 candidates is worth analysing. Their leading candidate, Jens-Peter Bonde, and one other are Communists. There were also two Left Socialists and one Social

Democrat. Those with non-socialist affiliations include Ib Christensen MEP (Justice Party), Birgit Bjørnvig MEP, one of the two
Radicals, one Liberal, and one Green, who came tenth of the 16.
There were also ten candidates with no declared party affiliation,
including Ulla Sandbæk, elected as the fourth of the FB MEPs.
Although she has deep S roots, she stood for FB because she opposed
'S's positive attitude to the EC'. Three of the non-party candidates
acknowledge links to the youth wings of parties, one each to S, the SF
and the Communists. But the list clearly attempted to balance
socialist and non-socialist, party and non-party opponents of the EC.

Candidates' expectations

Asked whether they expected from opinion polls that their list would
receive more or less support in 1989 than in the 1984 EP election, an
Anti-EC MEP replied: 'Less: not for lack of support for our views, but
because of media silence/smear campaign against the Popular Movement Against the EC'. Two S respondents both expected more, one
naming 'issues in the social dimension' and the other the Single Act as
the issues which would bring increased support. This theme was pursued
by asking: 'How much effect do you expect the Single European Act and
the expansion of European Parliament powers to have on the election
campaign?'. Ib Christensen thought: 'Fairly much influence' regarding
the Common Act (negative experience on the facts and on the
propaganda of its supporters). A retiring S MEP thought: 'Very little'
but a prospective MEP party colleague expected 'a great impact'.

When asked whom they thought they represented, Ib Christensen
saw his role as: 'To speak for Danish sovereignty and for free and
open cooperation between all countries', while the retiring S MEP
replied 'First and foremost the interests of wage-earners' and the
prospective S MEP thought she would: 'mainly speak on behalf of the
Socialist Group in the European Parliament'.

Asked which European issues they and/or their party-list colleagues had been able to influence most effectively since the 1984
European Parliament election, Ib Christensen's broad reply was
'Denmark's EC policy' while the two Social Democrats mentioned
the environment, health and safety at work, the budget, the Third
World, and the internal market. To the question, 'On these issues, do
you consider that your party group has been able to act most
effectively in the EP by working mainly with national (Danish)
colleagues, or by working mainly with party colleagues across

national boundaries?', Christensen replied: 'Neither. We have influenced Danish opinion on various issues', but the two S respondents mentioned cooperation in the Socialist Group in their replies.

Asked how much their party had been helped in preparing for the June 1989 EP election by propaganda material drafted by its European party group, the Rainbow Group had been 'No help whatever. We have prepared our own material', but help from the Socialist Group had also been 'minimal' or 'not much'.

Soon after Denmark first joined the EC, the *Folketing* Market Committee (*markedsudvalget*) came to have an important function to ensure that Ministers did not make greater negotiating concessions than would be supported by Danish public opinion. Asked how, in their opinion, the role of this committee had changed, and would it be able to retain its significance over the next five years (to 1994), Ib Christensen was of the view that 'the Market Committee in practice can no longer keep pace with the number and scope of EC directives', but the S replies stated that 'the Market Committee still plays the same important role, and there is broad agreement in the *Folketing* that it should continue to do so', and 'as long as Denmark has a minority government, the significance remains'.

The campaign was a rather quiet affair, short of electoral razzamatazz and confined largely to the distribution of written publicity material, posters on lamp-posts, relatively thin newspaper coverage, and the customary eve-of-poll television marathon, with time evenly proportioned, as usual, between the party lists.

A very misleading opinion poll shortly before the election indicated 30 per cent support for S, greeted by party-leader Svend Auken as presaging five MEPs, so there was some disappointment in the party when the outcome was only four, a result which Auken linked to the low turnout. Conversely the poll promised the Popular Movement Against the EC only 10 per cent of the vote and a loss of two seats, a depressing prediction which they were pleased to see almost doubled on the day.

Issues: national or EC?

The campaign was overwhelmingly concerned with the projected impact of EC policies on life and work in Denmark and with domestic issues. As we have seen, expanded EC powers were a contentious issue since the 1986 referendum campaign and continued to be throughout the EP election.

The Conservatives put out a bunch of policy leaflets with a common title: *European, Conservative*, which acknowledged the European Democratic Group. Perhaps it was no accident that both they and their British Conservative allies in the Group were heavy losers. Their party newspaper contained an article criticising the S programme for the EP elections for the high tax-burden and the large public sector which it implied. Another article quoted the annual report of the recently-appointed general secretary of the party, John Wagner, regretting the suspicions and internal conflicts in the party, under the heading 'We are losing too much blood'. A leading article commented on the costs to the party of being in government, of being identified with its compromises, and of blurring its identity.

· On the day that the results were declared (19 June), the independent newspaper *Politiken* wrote in a leading article: 'Among the very few uplifting moments in the recent EC election campaign must be counted the marked lack of enthusiasm of the voters to support the Conservative battle-cry to vote down taxes, not only because the theme was misplaced, but especially because all talk of increasing people's disposable income and thus their spending power is quite absurd in the current economic situation'. The article went on to quote approvingly the view lately expressed by the director of the Danish national bank that it was impossible to show from the experience of the previous 15 years that the propensity to save could be influenced by marginal changes in tax rates. These comments were contributions to the revived socialist/bourgeois debate on basic economic policy which started when Nordic social democratic and trade union economists met to evolve a new economic strategy early in 1989, continued during the EP election campaign, and seemed likely to precipitate a premature parliamentary election in late 1989. The Conservative response had been to adopt the slogan: 'Vote taxes down' for their EP campaign. The domestic orientation of this was widely seen to have been a complete failure. By contrast, CD had used 'Reliability in Europe' and had emphasised the EC dimension in its campaign. Their leader, Erhard Jacobsen, felt sure that they had gained many Conservative voters in consequence.

The Liberals sent out packets of cornflower seeds (their blue symbol) with a colourful party newspaper proclaiming that 'The EC's internal market is an historical opportunity'. Another article by Simone Veil proclaimed that 'We have Europe within us', while one on Henning Christoffersen (previously leader of the party) was headlined 'A Dane put fresh air into the EC Commission'. Christoffersen himself rejected the charge of remoteness by emphasising that every Brussels initiative would mean action around people in their own member countries. Foreign Minister Uffe Ellemann-Jensen wrote that the close personal links between EC Foreign Ministers meant much for their cooperation. Another article illustrated the export of Danish fish to the EC with the help of Swedish investment, in answer to those who feared that closer EC links would weaken existing Nordic ones. Pamphlets on specific policies featured leading party figures rather than EC links.

The Social Democrats used the slogan 'Go in the 90s' (*Gang i 90'erne*), promising reduced taxes and customs duties, increased savings, and improving competitiveness through collective effort during 1990–95. A leaflet, printed on recycled paper, set out the aim of 'An Open Europe' and spoke of red/green policies to tackle air and water pollution by collaboration beyond the EC to negotiate international rules with the countries bordering the Baltic and the North Sea. Another spoke of 'Growth in the human condition'. Their lead candidate was promoted strongly through her views rather than by name, and her contribution to an S conference in January 1989 entitled 'Europe: the third way for the third world' was quoted at length.

The SF offered 'Opposition that works!': opposition to the Treaty of Rome, to the Single European Act, and to European Union. Arguing that Europe is wider than the EC, they favoured broad European and Nordic collaboration for secure and safe workplaces, for a clean environment and to safeguard the interests of Danish wage-earners. Their record in the EP was covered via a long review of retiring MEP Bodil Boserup's ten years' experience. There was only small mention of the Communist and Allies Group.

Much the largest range of paper propaganda came from the Popular Movement Against the EC, under the slogans, 'Think a little longer' and 'Yes to the world – no to union. . .'. In greater detail, they wanted collaboration with the whole world at the global, European, *and* Nordic levels, with free trade rather than EC preferences; Danish democracy, with all EC directives subject to consultation with the affected organisations and the continued right of veto. They wanted an independent Danish system of consumer-labelling of the 220 substances which the UN lists as carcinogenic, 'regardless of whether the EC will only allow' this labelling on 32 substances. This would be one aspect of independent Danish partici-pation in international efforts to improve the environment. Instead of

European Union they wanted independent development of the welfare society jointly with the other Nordic countries. Specifically they did not want an EC which could put a stop to environmental decisions made in the *Folketing*, or which could make a Danish law unlawful, or which could negotiate international agreements in secret.

THE 1989 EP ELECTION RESULTS IN DENMARK

The election was fought largely on party lines, and the balance between socialist and bourgeois blocs remained unaltered. Across the other dividing line, between EC supporters and outright opponents, the latter (comprising SF and the Popular Movement Against the EC) lost 2 per cent of the vote in aggregate, and one seat. Most of this loss was attributable to the SF. The Popular Movement Against the EC retained all four of its seats despite the marginal decrease in its vote.

Among the parties supporting the government, loss by the Conservatives of two seats made them the main electoral losers. Perhaps more damaging domestically, they dropped from being the largest group to fourth-largest. There was some compensation for the cabinet parties in the gain of one seat by the Liberals. An obviously disappointed Prime Minister conceded that the Conservative campaign

Table 3.2   Share of votes and seats won, 1984 and 1989, in Denmark

Party/list	Abbreviation	1984 votes	1984 seats	1989 votes	1989 seats
Conservatives	KF	20.8	4	13.3	2
Liberals (Venstre)	V	12.5	2	16.6	3
Progress Party	FRP	3.5	–	5.3	–
Christian People's Party	KRF	2.7	–	2.7	–
Centre Democrats	CD	6.6	1	7.9	2
Radical Liberals	RV	3.1	–	2.8	–
Social Democrats	S	19.5	3	23.3	4
Socialist People's Party	SF	9.2	2	9.1	1
Popular Movement against the EC	FB	20.8	4	18.9	4
Total			16		16
Turnout		52.4		46.1	

Source: European Parliament Information Office, Copenhagen, 19 June 1989

had been mistaken, commenting that their candidates were too little-known, which might give the party reason to consider allowing double mandates. This caused some surprise, however, since it was Schlüter himself who set the final seal on the Conservative television election programme, and there were those who thought *that* was where the problem lay. The Conservative showing in June augured badly for their chances in the local and county elections in November 1989. On the far right, the Progress Party missed any representation: a slightly greater proportion of votes for them could have obtained a seat and deprived the Centre Democrats of their second mandate, but would have been no help to the Conservatives.

In the centre, the Radicals, with 50 191 votes, were some 31 000 short of representation. During the campaign they announced that they had entered into electoral cooperation with the Social Democrats.[2] This was intended as a technical device to increase the chance of Radical representation. While failing to achieve this, the move cost the Conservatives one of their two seats. If, instead, the Radicals had allied with the Conservatives, the latter would have lost one and not two seats, an outcome unlikely to improve relationships in the Conservative–Liberal–Radical cabinet. However, this alliance probably encouraged S to look more favourably on European Union.

Among the socialist parties, the S gained one seat, offset by the SF's loss of one mandate for only a marginal loss of votes. John Iversen originally entered the EP at the point when Greenland withdrew from EC membership and the Siumut mandate passed to the SF: with the retirement of Bodil Boserup in 1989, he was re-elected as the single MEP for SF. He attributed his party's loss of new support to its record of having 'played along' in the EP.

By contrast with results elsewhere, there was no significant Green Party challenge in Denmark. Their one candidate, Eva Damgaard, was listed eighth and came tenth on the Anti-EC list. Nevertheless, as we have seen, green issues were prominent in the campaign.

The provision for electors to cast personal votes made a considerable impact on the results. The founder of the Centre Democrats, Erhard Jacobsen (aged 72) gained the largest personal vote of any candidate, allowing him to continue a membership of the EP which dated back to Danish EC entry in 1973. As an enthusiastic European he repeatedly advocated European Union, preferring to see a Danish role there rather than in the Nordic context. No longer party chairman, he seemed undaunted by the task of combining his EP mandate with his seat in the *Folketing*. His personal electoral popularity contributed to his party's gain of a second EP place for former Communications Minister Frode Nør Christensen.

Kirsten Jensen entered the EP for the first time as the lead candidate for S with the second-largest number of personal votes, and campaigned with the slogan 'Progress in the 90s' for a positive attitude to the EC in place of the divided views previously held by her party. Her party colleague (a former S party secretary) Ejner Hovgaard Christiansen sought a second term as an MEP but was allocated twelfth position by the party. Nevertheless, he attracted the second largest number of personal votes on the S list, assisted by former party leader and Prime Minister Anker Jørgensen, and was re-elected. Two S MEPs, Eva Gredel and Ove Fiche, retired.

Significant personal votes benefited Christian Rovsing, listed seventh by the Conservatives but elected as their second MEP, and Klaus Riskær Pedersen, fifth on Venstre's list and elected as the second of their three MEPs. Otherwise there was substantial continuity at the upper end of the lists of candidates nominated.

EP group membership

All four Anti-EC MEPs (including Jens-Peter Bonde, a member of the DKP) joined the Rainbow Group. John Iversen (SF) joined the European United Left. The two Centre Democrats stayed with the European People's Party (EPP) and Venstre's three MEPs joined the Liberal Democratic and Reformist Group. Before the election the departure of the Spanish contingent to the EPP had thrown the continued existence of the European Democratic Group (ED) into doubt (the two Danish Conservative MEPs are now the sole allies of the 32 British Conservatives in the ED).[3] The four Social Democrats joined the Socialist Group.

CONCLUSIONS

In the complexities of the domestic political situation, the 1989 EP election was not much more than an additional and incidental arena. The main issues had been debated since the referendum for two-and-a-half years and the campaign was lacklustre, without vision or commitment. Turnout, at 46.1 per cent, was even lower than the 52 per cent of 1984 and was the second lowest in the Twelve, ahead of the UK's 37 per cent, though only just behind the 47 per cent of the proverbially pro-European Dutch. Thus one clear result of the election was an increase in the 'democratic deficit' in Denmark, although by not quite so large a margin as elsewhere in the EC. The campaign and results reinforced the impression that Danes are unenthusiastic about the EC, and resent the probably adverse effects it may have on their welfare society, their environment and their relations with Nordic neighbours, although they accept the EC as necessary to their economic survival.

NOTES AND REFERENCES

*   The author would like to thank the following for making time to respond to questions: Ib Christensen, MEP for the People's Movement Against the EC, 1984–89, re-elected 1989 (18.7.89); Henk Hofma, on behalf of Ove Fich, Social Democrat MEP 1984–89 (24.7.89); and Kirsten Jensen, Social Democrat MEP 1989– (4.8.89). Thanks are due also to Grete Edelmann for generous hospitality in the past and for her help in monitoring the EP election campaign in the press.
1.   J. Fitzmaurice, *Politics in Denmark* (London: Hurst & Co., 1981).
2.   *Nordisk Kontakt*, 9/1989, 29–32.
3.   Michael Waller, 'Communist Parties and the Greens in the European Elections of 1989' (draft article); the EP Information Office, Copenhagen, and the EDG Press Office, Strasbourg, 13.9.1989.

4 The Federal Republic of Germany

EVA KOLINSKY

Compared with elections at national, regional or local level, those for the European Parliament have aroused less interest among the West German public.[1] Until shortly before polling day in June 1989, two out of five people stated they knew nothing about them;[2] and by West German standards, turnout has tended to be low (see Table 4.1). It would be misleading to interpret the number of parties who compete for EP seats – twenty-two in 1989 – as evidence of an interest in Europe. The electoral law which governs direct elections is more lenient than its national equivalent in recognising associations and groups as *bona fide* political parties.[3] Moreover, in contrast to other European countries, West German political parties are entitled to a

Table 4.1 Electoral turnout in direct elections to the European Parliament by West German regions, and in comparison with the 1987 federal and the most recent regional elections

Region	Eu.1989	Eu.1984	Eu.1979	Fed.E.1987	Last regional
Schleswig Holstein	58.5	57.5	65.6	84.4	77.4
Hamburg	56.6	58.4	66.4	83.0	79.5
Lower Saxony	63.3	61.0	70.0	85.0	77.3
Bremen	58.7	55.1	66.3	82.7	75.6
North Rhine–Westfalia	62.4	59.4	67.4	85.4	72.5
Hesse	60.2	58.9	66.5	85.7	80.3
Rhineland–Palatinate*	78.0	76.3	78.1	86.7	77.0
Baden–Württemberg	58.4	48.2	59.2	83.1	71.8
Bavaria	61.1	46.2	58.9	81.7	70.1
Saar Region*	78.8	78.4	81.1	87.3	85.0
Berlin**	–	–	–	–	–
Federal Republic without Berlin	62.4	56.8	65.7	84.3	76.9***

*   Local elections were held on the same day as Euro-Elections
** Of the 81 MEPs for West Germany, 3 are delegated from the Berlin parliament (Senate) in accordance with party representation there. Berlin does not hold Euro-elections.
*** Average turnout for the regional elections (Landtagswahlen) listed.
Source: Wirtschaft und Statistik 3, March 1989: 153; Statistisches Bundesamt. Bevölkerung und Erwerbstätigkeit. Fachserie 1 Heft 2: *Vorläufiges Endergebnis, 1989.*

Table 4.2   West Germany: political parties elected to the European
Parliament, 1979–89*

Party	1989		1984		1979	
	%	seats	%	seats	%	seats
CDU/CSU	37.8	31	45.9	39	49.2	40
SPD	37.2	30	37.4	32	40.8	34
FDP	5.6	4	4.8	–	6.0	4
Greens	8.4	8	8.2	7	3.2	–
Republicans	7.1	6	–	–	–	–
Others**	3.7	–	3.7	–	0.8	–

*   In 1979 and 1984, the CDU sent 2, the SPD 1; in 1989, one each of SPD,
CDU and Greens.
**   normally between 14 and 16 parties.

Sources: *Statistisches Jahrbuch 1987 für die Bundesrepublik Deutschland*,
Mainz: Kohlhammer 1987: 86 and *Frankfurter Allgemeine Zeitung*, 20 June
1989.

reimbursement of campaign costs if they poll at least 0.5 per cent of
the vote. It has been alleged that political parties are keen to contest
EP elections in order to replenish their party funds.[4] The 1989 result,
for instance, generated an income of 18 million DM for the Greens,
and 16 million DM for the Republican Party, whose entry to the EP
from the right points to a major change in the party system; but even
parties without electoral prospects, such as Herbert Gruhl's conservative Ecological Democratic Party (ÖDP, 0.7 per cent) or the
neo-Nazi German People's Union (1.6 per cent) won enough votes to
qualify for public funds – three million DM for the People's Union
and about 1.5 million for the Ecology Party.[5]
   When the EP elections legislation was prepared in the mid-
seventies, small parties seemed a feature of the past. Although a
dozen or more parties tended to contest elections at regional or
national level, only three entered parliaments and the remainder
tended to fall below one or two per cent between them.[6] Since then,
electoral politics have become more diversified. Small parties have
increased their share of the vote in all elections. Starting with the
Greens in 1979 and continuing with the Republicans in 1989, new
parties have succeeded in winning parliamentary representation.
They draw on an electorate that is more mobile and less committed to
party loyalties than in the past.[7] They also benefit from a political
environment in which the ability of the major parties to address the

salient issues of the day has become doubtful and new political forces – outside and also inside parliament – have emerged to fulfil the role of issue-based opposition.[8]

In national elections, the potential attractions of small parties and the protest they might voice, tend to be mellowed by voters' interest to elect a stable government based on a parliamentary majority and strong enough to make and execute political decisions in a national and international context.[9] At the European level, elections lack a king-maker function. The EP's composition does not alter the balance of power in Europe.[10] The special status of these elections has made it easier for small parties to win support: voters, hesitant to register a protest vote in a national election, are less inhibited in the European context. By the same token the relatively good chances of small parties to win enough votes to qualify for state funding or, given the low turnout, enter the EP, have mobilised protest voters or voters for marginal parties more fully than voters for established parliamentary parties. In their political function and in voters' perception, EP elections in West Germany resemble British by-elections as a chance to voice political views rather than decide on government or the distribution of power.

Since direct elections enhanced the EP's democratic legitimacy, it has consolidated its political role as monitoring policy processes, extended its powers of political control to veto and initiate decisions, and established itself as a core political institution.[11] Since 1977, a special information office in Bonn has been devoted to promoting the EP and its work, quite apart from the steady stream of publicity materials, reports and documentation from Strasbourg, Luxembourg and Brussels. Yet, West Germans are surprisingly ignorant about an institution which has existed in its present form for a decade. In autumn 1987, 37 per cent of adults professed never to have heard of the EP.[12] Just three months before the third direct elections, the cohort of the uninformed had risen to 55 per cent.[13] Is it that Germans have lost the hunger for political information which had impressed Almond and Verba in the fifties or Edinger in the sixties as a feature of the political culture which set West Germans apart from other democratic, yet less knowledgeable nations?[14] Or do we witness something more in line with the early postwar years when people tended to hide their uncertainties about acceptable democratic answers or their unfamiliarity with answering questions in opinion polls behind a protective screen of don't knows?[15] Not answering, like not voting, could also imply objections and detachment.

Contrary to the popular myth that they had always been enthusiastic Europeans, West Germans in the fifties distrusted a policy which had been imposed from the top and institutions which they could neither fathom nor influence.[16] While postwar generations began to look towards Europe in the sixties and seventies to ensure military security, coordinate economic development and alleviate social and environmental problems,[17] confidence in European solutions which existed a decade ago has been diluted by a new scepticism over whether European ideals serve European institutions and policies. Although most West Germans (90 per cent) are broadly in favour of the EC, specific issues are more controversial. Only half expect improvements from the Single European Market; the others fear an erosion of West German economic standards and achievements.[18] The prospect of creating a European government is less popular in West Germany than in most other European countries.

Two developments in particular have underpinned this lack of enthusiasm for Europe. The first concerns changes in the relationship between citizens and the state; the second, the link between a European and a national consciousness. Traditionally in German political culture, citizens perceived the state, its institutions and leaders as too powerful and too remote to heed the needs of ordinary people or be influenced by their actions or expectations. The educational and occupational mobilisation since the sixties, however, has shaped new generations who feel confident that they can participate in politics and influence their course and who in turn expect political processes to be responsive and transparent.[19] The European setting of multiple institutions, national interests and indirect decision-making process fails to meet these expectations and discourages participation such as turning out to vote.

The second development, the relevance of national consciousness, points to a more recent change in West German political culture: identification with Europe has decreased in the last decade, while identification with West Germany and a more diffuse 'pride in the German fatherland' gained ground.[20] The new sense of nation has blunted the emphatic interest in Europe which seemed to inspire the younger generations. More importantly, it has encouraged a vision that a new age may be dawning from an altogether different direction and with an altogether different role for Germany in the future.[21] The process of political liberalisation and economic restructuring in the USSR, known as *glasnost* and *perestroika*, has given rise to fervent hopes in West Germany that relations with the Eastern bloc and with East Germany in particular may be transformed and unleash a united German nation once again. German unity emerged as a core theme during Chancellor Kohl's visit to Moscow, laced with reprimands about Soviet human rights violations in treating minorities and people who wish to emigrate. Gorbachev's return visit to the FRG on the eve of the EP elections turned into a spectacle of adulation and mass hysteria reminiscent of the Führer cult of yesteryear. What West Germans seemed to be cheering about was not so much the hardheaded reformer of Soviet economic management and political control, but a saviour who would clear the decks, remove the wall and restore a united Germany. It was also mooted that Germany could, as had been the custom in the past, orientate herself to the East and modify the integration with Western democracies which has dominated international relations in the postwar era.

PARTIES AND ISSUES: THE WEST GERMAN CONTEXT

The EC's fading attractions and its promises of political integration and economic advances coloured the issues which dominated the 1989 EP elections. The campaign was essentially non-European, with the spotlight on current affairs and party competition, and it was anti-European from the newcomer on the right, the Republican Party.

The EP elections were awkwardly timed. The mobilisation of electoral choices put a new emphasis on articulating issues and winning support. Before examining how the main political parties tailored their approaches, two further consequences of the mobilised political environment in West Germany should be mentioned. First, the function of elections has changed from an affirmation of existing governments to a contest for power. In the German state tradition governments have been changed through coalition reshuffles retrospectively confirmed by elections.[22] Since the mid-eighties, however, governing parties have been ousted from office through elections as voters are ready to change preferences. Although the EP elections were not designed to determine the composition of government, they were widely interpreted as a test of whether the government in Bonn should or would fall. The second consequence of the new political mobility in West Germany paved the way for this test of government: the Chancellor bonus, a cornerstone of West German electoral stability since Adenauer's days, seemed to fall apart. Although Helmut Kohl has headed the government since October 1982 and had brought the CDU/CSU close to an absolute majority in 1976 when he was leader of the Opposition, he has failed to gain public approval and the above-party adulation which assisted former Chancellors in keeping their position and winning additional votes for their party. Despite winning two national elections as Chancellor, Kohl is among the least popular politicans, much in the shadow of top-rating stars like Rita Süssmuth, the former Minister with special responsibility for women and president of the *Bundestag* since the Jenninger débâcle in November 1988, and of Hans-Dietrich Genscher, the FDP Foreign Minister since 1974.[23] Even if the collapse of the Chancellor bonus has only been caused by Kohl's lack of international flair or political finesse, it has forced the governing CDU/CSU to focus on issues in their electoral appeals.

Since the early seventies, priority issues among West German voters have changed little: the top four places have been held – not always in this order – by environmental protection, employment, peace, economic stability and, jostling for fifth place, health care, pensions, price stability, women's equal opportunities or *détente* with the Eastern bloc. In formulating their 1989 electoral platforms, the parties highlighted the familiar issues, but with a European focus. It provided an additional challenge to the parties that confidence in Europe had decreased for virtually all political, social or economic issues as West Germans looked to their own country, institutions and established, presumably superior, practices. The difficulties of focusing on Europe and persuading the voter of a party's competence, can be illustrated by programmatic statements on the environment, a pot-boiler among priority issues since the early seventies. The CDU presented the issue itself as an international one and pledged to turn it into the hub of European politics altogether: 'Water and air are international – the same goes for their protection. In Europe, increased cross-border environmental protection is urgently required. We therefore want to develop the European Community into an environmental community.'[24] These sentiments were echoed by the Bavarian sister party but with a special rider on the superiority of German approaches: 'The CSU supports the development of the European Community into a responsible environmental community. . . . We want effective, jointly European environmental regulations. The strict German regulations must not be watered down on a European level.'[25] For the SPD, effective European policies appear to consist of effective organisational channels; to advance environmental protection the SPD called for European research programmes and a series of administrative measures: 'We demand environmental taxes which reward environmental protection and energy conservation. We propose to create an independent community agency for environmental inspection' (*Umweltüberwachung*).[26] The FDP adopted a similar institutional view of Europe and envisaged the establishment of an environmental office to encourage and coordinate environmental protection in member countries,[27] while the Greens advocated banning harmful chemicals and imposing – through unspecified agencies or legislative powers – environmental controls on industrial production.

Two approaches characterised policy articulation for the 1989 EP elections: parties with an interest in Europe tended to present themselves as competent to bring about change by defining a new office, institution or agency which would be created to spearhead it. Conventional references to a party's track-record in the previous EP and similar devices to convince the voter that a party can put its programme into practice are unsuitable in the EC context. Not only are national parties normally affiliated to supranational party groups; the decisionmaking practicalities in the EP invite cooperation between political parties and party groups of different political persuasions in common opposition to the EC Commission.[28] At the European level, parties hardly differ and it is against the culture of non-partisan Europeanism to claim that specific policy achievements should be credited to one party or another. The call for new bureaucratic structures has to be seen as an attempt to make one party visible and credible as an initiator of policy change.

With the exception of the Republicans, for whom neither environmentalism nor Europe appear to have been relevant electoral issues, all parties focused on 1992 and the advent of the SEM.[29] All presented variations on the theme of how to create a better, more social, affluent, unpolluted, economically strong Europe. This emphasis was in line with both European policies and the FRG's policy commitments, and with the lower interest in all things European, and fall in public confidence that European solutions could be applied to salient issues. The CDU was seen as the party most earnestly committed to Europe;[30] competence in European affairs, however, could not be a vote-catcher as Europe itself was regarded with suspicion. By the same token, 1992 and the SEM dominated the programme sections on the economy, on social policy and cross-national cooperation, while West Germans had remained doubtful. Doubts were especially widespread among the youngest and the oldest, among the least educated, among potential supporters of the CDU/CSU, the SPD and above all of the Republicans. Supporters of the Greens, who had been anti-European in the past as part and parcel of their left-wing orientation, now look towards Europe more positively; the FDP and its followers have always favoured widening economic collaboration and business opportunities and the party remained pro-European.

Party communications

The uneasy focus on Europe is also evident in the programmatic communications before the EP elections.[31] The CDU aimed for a two-pronged argument: to reassure voters that German economic superiority would not be threatened in a European setting, and that thanks to Chancellor Kohl, the FRG had become one of the leading political powers of the world. As viewers watched a juggernaut meander through the German countryside – 'made in Germany' in giant letters on its side – a political jingle proclaimed: 'We are producing in Germany and exporting to Europe . . . we in Germany live from Europe – create the future here at home and we shall get the best out of Europe' to culminate in the formula: 'The CDU knows about the economy and about Europe'. The second part of the television spot was completely unrelated and showed Kohl as Chancellor *cum* diplomat with virtually every political leader of relevance in a quick succession of publicity shots – an attempt to come as close to the elusive Chancellor bonus as possible.

The dual and uncertain focus reflects the CDU's difficulties in targeting its electorate: not only traditional groups of voters such as the young, women, churchgoers and middle-class people become mobilised as an electorate and willing to support a different party. The backbone of all successful CDU campaigns – conjuring up a crisis and promising salvation – could not be applied this time round. Kohl's public image as incapable of firm leadership made it impossible to cast him in the role of a political St George. Moreover, the economy could not be depicted as crisis-bound, or entry into Europe as fraught with problems, since the party had government responsibility for the first and tried to win backing for the second. Without a negative sting, even the focus on economic issues did not bite, although the CDU continues to be regarded as the most competent party in economic matters.

The problems of policy articulation were even more acute for the

CSU, which organises its own campaign in Bavaria for EP elections. After the death of Franz Josef Strauss it had been left without a prominent leader who could command a personal following. For the first time since the early sixties, when Strauss had become its chairman, the CSU had to find issues and it chose nationalism. As mentioned earlier, German national consciousness and national pride are beginning to gain ground, and the question of a united Germany made the headlines when Kohl visited Moscow, and when Bush and Gorbachev visited the Federal Republic.[32] For the CSU, nation meant the German question, reunification. Europe, for whose parliament voting took place, played a subordinate role. In the CSU's political broadcast, only the last sentence mentioned Europe: 'Bavaria is the homeland, Germany the fatherland, and Europe the future'. The uncertain focus on the German nation between Bavaria and Europe and the sly attempt to avoid referring to Europe in such a way that even anti-Europeans might vote for the CSU did not have the desired effect. The CSU lost over 5 per cent of its vote and with 14.6 per cent the right-wing Republican party obtained regionally its best result in CSU territory (see Table 4.2).

The FDP entered the campaign with an emphatic commitment to the SEM which they interpret as a chance to extend liberal principles and dismantle economic barriers on an international scale.[33] Presenting itself as the 'sensible political force' which would protect individual freedom, keep bureaucracy to a minimum and strengthen the centre at a time when radicals on the left and the right appear to be gaining ground, the FDP pitched its political message to attract its typical voters: the middle class self-employed businessmen or -women, and a clientele whose main concern has been to prevent any of the major parties from gaining political control. Although potential FDP voters are pro-European and the party had little to fear from the recent shift of public sentiments away from European integration, the FDP can only rely on the loyal support of about two per cent of the electorate. In a party system which requires at least five per cent of the vote to ensure parliamentary representation, the FDP has depended on winning voters who endorse the function of the party as a coalition partner, as a moderating force, as a buffer between two main party blocs. The FDP relies largely on the second ballot, the vote cast for the party to enter parliament; it has fielded constituency candidates in compliance with the electoral legislation, but none has been elected to a parliamentary seat since the mid-fifties. While the FDP has been in the *Bundestag* since 1949 and has served in government longer than any other party,[34] it found it increasingly difficult to mobilise support in regional elections and is no longer represented in all *Land* parliaments. The system of electoral lists at EP-level could let in a party which is weak in constituency support; yet, EP elections only allow one vote, and the FDP loses the device of vote-splitting which has tended to sustain it. Despite its pro-European stance, the FDP failed in 1984 to secure enough votes to enter the EP; despite its enthusiasm about the SEM as a chance for liberalism, the same might have happened in 1989 had it not been for the so-called 'Genscher-bonus'.[35] Hans-Dietrich Genscher has been one of the most popular politicians. He has also been the most outspoken advocate of a foreign policy which would preserve West German interests within existing political and military alliances. Genscher's opposition to NATO policies on stationing and modernising nuclear missiles articulated popular fears that NATO policies would make West Germany the nuclear target and battleground in a future war.[36] Sensitised by the peace movement on the dangers of the nuclear armoury on German soil, West Germans across party lines and political orientations have become wary that their country could be used as a pawn in big-power military machinations and deterrent games. Against the backcloth of these fears, the Gorbachev mania signifies a hope for *détente*; Genscher could scoop the publicity bonus and help his party return to the EP.

The SPD entered the EP elections after winning a number of important regional elections, determined to become the largest party and stake its claim to form the next government. It made a clear bid to win pro-European voters: the young, the educated, the socially and environmentally conscious. The SPD slogan 'We are Europe' could not be more pro-European nor more meaningless. In the 1987 federal elections it was already apparent that the SPD shirks defining policy goals. Then it published a dozen or so posters on as many issues, each preceded by the phrase 'majority for'. This time, even these remnants of content disappeared. The television broadcasts were largely devoted to political pop: 'We want to be like the clouds, Nothing stops our flight, Now it is our turn, Because we want a country in which there will be no more wars, Where one loves the victories which are peaceful'. (*Wir wollen wie die Wolken sein. Nichts stoppt unsern Flug. Jetzt sind wir am Zug! Denn wir wollen ein Land, in dem es nie mehr Kriege gibt. In dem man die Siege liebt, die friedlich sind.*) The colloquial 'we' was visually underpinned by groups of young and bouncing people who danced, sang or strode into the sunset, while a brief centre section showed one of the party leaders or the top candidate uttering political nothings such as 'We can create the new Europe' or 'We say yes to Europe' provided it is 'social' and preserves the environment. 'We are Europe' press advertisements were more exclusively geared to the educated reader and tended to camouflage the choice of party as an act of humanity or common sense. *Der Spiegel*, for instance, had a two-page colour photograph of barren rocks with the caption 'Even the Alps would vote SPD'. From a stylishly printed column of white lettering the reader learnt that forests and plants which had grown there since the ice age were being destroyed to create ski *pistes*, cable cars or roads while it would have been sensible to extend to railways – 'and for this we Social Democrats will fight in the European Parliament with all the power you give us'.[37] A full-page advertisement in *Die Zeit* showed Brandt and Schmidt above an open letter to all citizens and signed by the two veteran Chancellors. In its bid to recoup the Chancellor-bonus of old, the SPD argued that the international recognition which the FRG had gained through successful economic and social policies, and through its partnership in Europe may be jeopardised by xenophobia: 'Our country cannot afford to have a shift to the right which wants to replace the openness to the world and good neighbourliness by hostility against foreigners and provincial nationalism. We want to remind you of this when you cast your vote in the European Elections'.[38]

The Greens made their own distinctive contribution to highlight and reject the enmity against foreigners which more than any other theme determined the outcome of the EP elections. To head their party list, the Greens selected a candidate who did not hold a German passport and was, therefore, neither entitled to vote nor be elected.[39] The political gesture had a double purpose: to remind the public of the Nazi persecution suffered by non-German peoples and in particular by the gypsies – the candidate was of gypsy origin – whose fate had not been acknowledged and whose treatment in contemporary societies still smacked of ostracism. The second motive for devoting the top place on their party list to a non-electable candidate was to highlight and contest the xenophobia which has become a major and alarming feature of West German public opinion.

As a political party, the Greens are now firmly positioned to the left of the SPD after initial uncertainities about the political aims of environmentalism. The party also sees itself increasingly as a potential coalition partner of the SPD, a king-maker for the red/green section of the contemporary party spectrum. Since the 1987 federal elections, the Greens have curtailed fundamentalist tendencies in the party organisation and replaced a party leadership who seemed more intent on protest politics than on parliamentarisation and on joining governments. The change of course has also changed the view of Europe: as anti-capitalist remnants of new-left ideologies are obliterated by a new Green political realism, Europe holds the promise of social progress, international ecological cooperation and a better political environment than the Greens expect within the West German political system. Against the backdrop of intensified nationalism, Europe in 1989 seemed to herald an end to the nation state and its anti-democratic legacies. In the 1989 election campaign, Europe and the prospect of a SEM became focal points for the desire to break established political structures and realign political practices which characterised the Green stance from the beginning. Thus, environmental themes, which are commonly linked to the Greens and for which the party is considered the most competent by the West German public, were less important in the Green programme than in the programmes of CDU or SPD, while visions of a new world abounded: a world of social justice as demanded by the trade unions, a world of women's quotas in employment as demanded by the women's movement, a demilitarised world and a world with a new economic order to finally do justice to the Third World. As for the other parties, the Greens' contributions in the EP since 1984 passed without mention as the dreams and scenarios of overall change which had inspired and divided the various factions within the party seemed to fit so neatly under the broad umbrella of creating their kind of Europe. The party adopted the clientele approach of articulating in its programme the demands and aims of the movements, interest factions and groups which constitute the Green *milieu*.[40] The virtually stagnant election result suggests that they reached that *milieu* – and little else.

The Republicans: issues and electorate

The one party to extend its support was the Republican Party. Pre-election surveys have shown that they could attract followers from all political camps, especially from the CDU/CSU and from the silent cohorts of non-voters. In Berlin, where Republicans entered the *Land* parliament in February 1989, gains had been linked to fears of unemployment or socio-economic decline among lower-skilled

working-class people (most of them men) be it through new technologies which might disestablish their jobs or through presumed
competition from foreign workers for increasingly scarce employment and social service provisions.[41] In traditional working-class
districts and among young working-class voters, the Republicans did
particularly well.

At a time when the Greens are trying to groom themselves into a
potential coalition partner and blunt the fervour for system change
which had made them into a vessel for protest voting of the left and
the right, the Republicans again offer a radical anti-system programme:
to leave NATO, to leave the EC and to rid Germany of all
foreigners.[42] In the name of 'preserving the existence of the German
people',[43] the Republicans rank reunification above international
alliances[44] and pledge to keep Germany German: 'As one of the
most densely populated countries in Europe, the Federal Republic of
Germany is not a country of immigration. It has to remain a German
country'.[45]

Two of the Republican's three programmatic 'Nos' articulate
significant facets of contemporary West German public opinion.
While NATO membership has, on the whole, been accepted, Europe
with the impending SEM and the place of foreigners in West
Germany are not. As the only openly anti-European party, the
Republican Party could make some headway among this protest
potential: young people who expect nothing of Europe or any other
aspect of conventional politics, farmers who mistrust the CAP or feel
cheated out of compensation after Chernobyl, and those sections of
the population who perceive modernisation as a threat and feel by-
passed by affluence.[46] Anxiety about modernisation in particular can
explain the strong showing of the Republicans in Bavaria and Baden–
Württemberg, two of the FRG's most affluent regions with the lowest
unemployment figures. Here, the new party gained nearly 15 and 12
per cent respectively and, as we shall see later, reached much higher
figures in some areas.

It is the third Republican 'No' – that against foreigners – which
pinpointed the issue to propel the party into parliamentary representation in local, regional and now EP elections in 1989. On the face of
it, the party only repeated what political parties, factions and action
groups of the extreme right had demanded since the early seventies.
Electoral gains for this kind of political message first became evident
in the early eighties when a group calling itself *Liste Ausländerstopp*
attracted around three per cent of the vote in regional elections, and

when an alliance of NPD and German People's Union won a seat in the Bremen *Landtag*. At extra-parliamentary level, however, verbal attacks and violence against foreigners has been a main focus of right-extremism in the seventies and eighties; criminal acts of this kind shot up by 150 per cent and so did membership in the factionalised extreme right.[47]

The issue to change right-extremism from a National Socialist nostalgia of incorrigible oldtimers into a political force with the makings of challenging the political and social consensus of West German democracy in parliaments is hostility against foreigners, *Ausländerfeindlichkeit*. In the aftermath of the National Socialist violations of human rights, the Basic Law was designed to welcome political refugees: the need for additional manpower during the years of economic expansion persuaded West Germany to recruit foreigners as 'guest workers'. Both policies were out of phase with realities: to escape the political upheavals and socio-economic deprivations in Third World countries millions became refugees; in 1988 alone, over one hundred thousand sought political asylum in the FRG; since 1979, close to 700 000 people arrived in the hope of staying. Although few (around 15 per cent) have been permitted to do so, the state is obliged to provide shelter and food until each case has been decided, and appeals have been heard – a procedure which may take four years to complete. Moreover, one of the consequences of the *Ostpolitik* was the influx of so-called *Aussiedler* (resettlers). These are people who claim to be of German ancestry but have lived in non-German speaking countries and non-German cultural environments, often for generations. Although such resettlers have, in fact, been absorbed into West German society since 1950 – overall 1.6 million between 1950 and 1988 – numbers increased sharply to well over 100 000 per year in the eighties at a time when unemployment and a severe shortage of public housing (*Sozialwohnungen*) made the newcomers' economic and social integration difficult. Their status as German nationals secured them preferential treatment. In everyday life and popular perceptions, the differences in national status between asylum-seekers, guest workers and resettlers have become blurred as West Germans fear for their economic security, their living standards, the financial viability of the state and also harbour prejudices which parties such as the Republican Party can turn into a question of national survival.

In 1988, 4.5 million foreign nationals, some 400 000 asylum-seekers and an estimated 1.6 million resettlers lived in Germany.[48] Contrary to forecasts that the number of foreigners would decline, it has increased by half a million since the late seventies and by nearly one million if asylum-seekers are included.[49] Integration and social acceptance have not followed. On the contrary, since the late seventies, public opinion has turned more hostile. In 1978, 39 per cent demanded that foreigners should return to their country of origin;[50] in 1989, 56 per cent of adults, 66 per cent of CDU voters and over 90 per cent of Republican followers shared the 'foreigners out' point of view.[51]

THE RESULTS – A CRUMBLING OF THE PARTY SYSTEM?

With their low turnout, their low status as a contest of secondary importance and the uncertain focus on Europe by the parties and especially by the public, the 1989 EP elections may be little more than a hiccup in the West German party culture, an articulation of protest and negligible in its possible effects on elections which really matter: those for governments within the FRG. Although the motive of protest articulation has been stressed in the post-election surveys published by the major West German institutes for electoral research, marginal elections have highlighted some longer-term changes in the party system which transcend protest and point to a transformation, a 'crumbling of the party system'.[52] Not since the FRG's founding and the electoral legislation framed which shaped the party system have five parties obtained more than 5 per cent of the vote at national level. Never before in European, federal or regional elections have both big parties – CDU/CSU and SPD – each obtained less than 40 per cent of the total vote. None of the big parties obtained an absolute majority in any of the regions. If the 1989 June elections had been for government, it would have been impossible to form a coalition in which one large and one small party collaborated. To secure a governing majority, a grand coalition or a multi-party coalition would have been required – the former a hindrance to democratic opposition and political diversity; the latter precarious in its resemblance to Weimar instabilities and, given the political differences between the three small parties – Greens, Liberals and Republicans – impossible to install. Never has an election result come so close to conjuring up the spectre of ungovernability which has haunted German politics since the fragmentation of Weimar politics and again since the advent of the Greens in the late seventies. Moreover, the electoral breakthrough of the Republicans (who overtook the FDP and became the fourth largest party in the West German contingent to the EP) confirms that right-extremism continues as a potential political force and that it can be transposed from radicalism into electoral support and parliamentary presence in the FRG.[53]

The north–south divide in West German politics has acquired a new dimension: what appeared as the linkage between Catholicism or a more general Christian observance in southern regions and an absolute majority for the CDU or CSU now reveals itself as a more strident push to the right. In Bavaria and Baden–Württemberg, turnout had been especially low in 1984; in 1989 it was higher than average and rose by 15 and 10 per cent respectively as previous non-voters opted for the anti-European party in the 1989 elections (see Table 4.1).[54] Overall, the Republican Party attracted two million voters, more than half of them (54 per cent) in the two southern states. In Bavaria, the Republicans won 15 per cent, in Baden–Württemberg nine per cent (see Table 4.3). In Hesse, where the local elections in 1989 had already revealed the attractions of the extreme

Table 4.3   West Germany: European election results by region and party, 1989 and 1984

Region	CDU/CSU		SPD		FDP		Greens		Reps*	Others**	
	89 %	84 %	89 %	84 %	89 %	84 %	89 %	84 %	89 %	89 %	84 %
Schleswig–Holstein	36	44	44	39	5	5	7	8	5	2	3
Hamburg	32	37	42	42	6	5	12	13	6	3	4
Lower Saxony	36	43	42	41	6	5	8	8	5	3	3
Bremen	23	31	46	48	7	5	14	12	4	6	5
North Rhine–Westfalia	36	43	44	42	6	4	8	8	4	3	3
Hesse	33	41	41	42	5	5	10	8	7	4	4
Rhineland Palatinate	39	47	40	39	6	5	7	7	5	3	3
Baden–Württemberg	39	51	29	27	7	7	10	10	9	6	5
Bavaria	45	57	24	28	4	4	8	7	15	4	5
Saar Region	35	43	45	44	5	4	6	7	6	3	3
FRG overall	38	46	37	37	6	4.8	8	8	7	4	4

*   The Republicans did not take part in the 1984 elections.
** in 1984: 9 'other' parties. Best results were achieved by the Peace List (1.3%; communist left) and the NPD (0.8%, extreme right); in 1984, 16 'other' parties in addition to the Republicans. Best results were achieved by the German People's Union (1.7%, extreme right) and the Ecological Democratic Party (0.7%, con-servative/right).

Source: Statistisches Bundesamt: Bevölkerung und Erwerbstätigkeit: Vorläufige Ergebnisse.

right and mobilised a potential electorate, the Republicans obtained 6.6 per cent; in other regions, they remained at six per cent or under. The Republicans, it seems, are the electoral and political opposite of the Greens and capable of similar results. While the Greens have been able to score double-figure results – sometimes over 20 per cent in university towns – the Republicans have proved as attractive to voters in small and medium-sized towns in Bavaria where traditional Catholic milieux and the political orientations that went with them have begun to weaken.[55] In Rosenheim, for instance, they won 22 per cent of the vote: in many Bavarian districts, they pushed the SPD into third place.[56]

The SPD's performance shows the other side of the north–south divide. Except in Bavaria and Baden–Württemberg, the SPD emerged as the largest party in all regions and overtook the CDU in habitual strongholds such as Schleswig–Holstein, Lower Saxony and even Rhineland–Palatinate (see Table 4.3). The eighties version of the *Genosse* trend, a gradual rise in the SPD vote, has been camouflaged by the party's apparent stagnation. In fact, between 1984 and 1989, the SPD gained more than one million votes and shifted the balance between the two major parties visibly in its favour. The CDU, for whom the EP elections were to be a test of its future in government, lost nearly one million votes and its hegemony as the dominant party in all but two regions. The CSU, whose percentage score plummeted by 12 per cent, did in fact win 200 000 more votes than in 1984 but they did little to mellow the blow suffered at the hands of the Republicans with their two million voters.

The EP elections revealed not so much a crumbling of the West German party system as a new flexibility. As small parties home in on popular issues and muscle their way into parliaments on the back of anxieties about economic and social stability and a good deal of scepticism as to whether the major parties care for the concerns of ordinary people, the party landscape will be more splintered than in the past. The broad consensus on policies and decisionmaking processes had mellowed partisan conflicts to such an extent that they seemed all but extinct: the emergence of the Republicans has revised political conflicts and shown clearly that the right at least has continued to command an electoral potential and hold a strident political ideology.

Another dimension of the new flexibility concerns the realignment of the political balance between the two big parties and the emergence of the SPD as the dominant force. This is not the first time that the relative importance of the two major parties has changed. The fifties became the era of conservatism as CDU and CSU absorbed the right and destroyed the parliamentary representation of the far and extreme right. For a decade from the mid-sixties, the SPD seemed set to swing the balance and become the dominant political force but was halted through the CDU's political recovery (which had never caved in, in the south) and the rise of the Greens as competitors for the same electorate. The jostling for position between the CDU and SPD today points to the willingness of voters to transfer their preferences from one to the other and the ability of the SPD to gain at the centre. After nearly a decade of losing voters to the Greens, the political boundaries between Greens and SPD have become more defined, while those between SPD and CDU show a new transparency. In this light, the EP elections were indeed a test of government, showing that the SPD could assume that role.

THE EUROPEANS: THE WEST GERMAN MEPS

Against the European trend which brought an increase in the Socialist and Green support and a majority for the left in the EP, West German gains went to the liberal centre and the extreme right, while the SPD and Greens remained nearly level and CDU/CSU lost. As seen earlier, German MEPs are elected from party lists. Voters may know the top candidate or even one or two prominent names. Generally however, in EP elections people vote even more strongly for a party than in federal or regional elections where constituency candidates can build up their own local standing and a personalised clientele. Even the specific contributions of a party or an individual MEP are impossible to distinguish in the general swell of European party groups, cross-party alliances and the joint oppositional stance of parties and EP against the Commission and national governments.

Since the Greens' entry into West German parliamentary politics and the programmatic emphasis on grassroots democracy, the linkage between parliament and people, between elected members and the voters they should represent, has become a more topical issue than in the founding decades of the FRG when citizens assumed the state, its institutions and representatives knew best and would do right. The changes in education, socio-economic mobility and willingness to participate in society and politics have also changed this facet of the political culture: rather than assuming that leaders and elected representatives would do best, West Germans – and the educated young in particular – expect parliaments and their members to represent society as a whole. Given the varied interests and issues, the linkage between political representation and people looks different from different vantage points, and parties have adopted catch-all approaches or, in the case of the Greens and now also of the Republicans – deliberate and factionalised interest politics.

West German parliaments and parties' candidate selection have been measured against a model of fair representation. The most articulate critics of established practices have been women who highlighted the uneven opportunities for female party members and activists to hold parliamentary seats or party offices.[57] Women's associations took a more assertive stand on equal representation after the Greens tended to field equal numbers of men and women for any type of office of electoral function. Since the mid-eighties, parties have moved towards women's quotas; the Greens and the SPD introduced formal quotas of 50 and 40 per cent respectively, while CDU/CSU and FDP pledged to involve women in accordance with their share of the membership in party and parliamentary politics.

At the European level, women had enjoyed electoral chances more freely than in the *Bundestag* or in *Land* parliaments, and in 1984 one in five German MEPs was a woman.[58] For the 1989 elections, parties more than honoured their pledge. Taking all the candidacies together, 47 per cent were held by women.[59] Taking only the top third of the electoral lists, 26 per cent were women, 38 per cent for the SPD, 30 per cent each for CDU, FDP and Republicans, and 17 per cent for the CSU. Since many female candidates tend to be put at the lower end of their party's list, the number of women elected to the EP falls short of the candidacies: 5 (15 per cent) for the CDU/CSU, 10 (33 per cent) for the SPD, 4 (57 per cent) for the Greens, 1 (25 per cent) for the FDP and 1 (16 per cent) for the Republicans.[60] Measured against their policy statements and declared intentions, SPD, FDP and Greens have met their quota targets and the expectations of their members and voters. In the CDU/CSU the issue of women's representation appears to have made little impact on party organisation although it might have influenced the electoral choices of women.

Vallance and Davies have argued that regardless of party orientation, women MEPs have tended to support women's policies, notably EC initiatives to enhance equal opportunities and guarantee equal treatment of women in all spheres of society.[61] Since the women's movement has recently sensitised young generations to the continued limitations of equality and self-determination for women, those women who achieved elite positions may share interests and pursue partisan causes. But what of MEPs in general? Are they at the beck and call of their parties? Are they national ambassadors or standard-bearers of European integration? How did they rise to hold their present positions? What are their links with their parties, their electorates, the societies which elected them and which they should represent?

A survey of MEPs and non-elected candidates showed in 1979 that most had been members of their parties for at least ten years, were older than the average member of the *Bundestag* and between 70 per cent and 90 per cent had entered European politics after holding a top-level leadership position in their party at regional or national level.[62] To put it another way: for the larger parties with restricted organisational and personal mobility, at least, entry into European politics followed an extended career as a party functionary and such MEPs can be assumed to be seasoned and loyal party politicians. Ten years later, little seems to have changed. A 1989 study also showed that 81 per cent had held top positions in their party before being elected to the EP. Only one in three had parliamentary experience prior to Europe, and this had largely been at the local level.[63] Although a direct career path existed between *Bundestag* and the EP before 1979, since then dual mandates have been discouraged and the EP is creating its own brand of parliamentary politician. In the FRG, most of them have been party functionaries or elected members of assemblies at local government level. The EP has been the major arena to develop an approach to parliamentary politics and define the function of parliamentary representatives at European level. The role model of the member of the *Bundestag* or a *Landtag* does not appear to apply to Europe where MEPs have created their own parliamentary culture on the basis of extensive party service and first-time parliamentary experience. For small parties such as the Greens and now the Republicans, the conditioning through organisational work does not appear relevant since both are too new, too small and, in the case of the Greens, too committed to non-organisational recruitment of parliamentary representatives to fit the mould of the established parties.

MEPs relate, above all, to their party at the national and regional leadership level,[64] i.e. they retain the orientation of the party functionary; the question of renewed candidacies may also play its part. Contacts with party members, voters and even members of other parliaments are rare, although half the respondents stressed that they would welcome more frequent contacts.[65] Having made their way into European politics as long-serving party activists, the majority of West German MEPs see themselves as Europeans and regard their main purpose as representing the citizens of Europe.[66] In determining their approach to policymaking, MEPs are guided by two main considerations: loyalty to their party and loyalty to Europe, be it in the guise of hopes to advance European integration or as the positive experience of European party integration in their parliamentary experience. As a group, German MEPs do not see themselves as advocates, ambassadors or representatives of national interests or internal West German concerns. Given the new hesitancy about European integration and the topicality of national interests and national consciousness, the special breed of European who has emerged within the elected EP is oddly out of step with the sentiments that have arisen among the electorate. The Europeans in parliament appear to see themselves as torchbearers of a future without boundaries, national divisions, inter-governmental strife, social or economic discrepancies, let alone military conflict between member states; while West Germans, the former model children of Europeanism, have begun to lose their taste for supranational parliamentary democracy and prefer to find security in politics and values which they regard as 'made in Germany' and closer to their interests than the European perspectives.

NOTES AND REFERENCES

1. See T. Läufer, *Europäische Gemeinschaft, Europäisches Parlament, Europa-Wahl* (Bonn: Bundeszentrale für politische Bildung, 1989) and E. Jesse, *Wahlen. Die Bundesrepublik Deutschland im Vergleich* (Berlin: Colloquium, 1989).
2. H-J. Veen et al., *Trends in der öffentlichen Meinung im Vorfeld der Europawahl 1989* (Forschungsinstitut der Konrad Adenauer Stiftung, Interne Studien Nr. 12: Sankt Augustin, 1989), p. 26.
3. R. Stöss (ed.), *Parteien Handbuch* (Opladen: Westdeutscher Verlag, 1983), p. 19ff.
4. *Woche im Bundestag*, 28 June 1989, p. 12.
5. *Frankfurter Allgemeine Zeitung*, 20 June 1989, p. 3; see also Table 4.2.

6. See G. Smith, *Democracy in West Germany*, 3rd ed. (London: Heinemann, 1986).
7. S. Padgett and T. Burkett, *Political Parties and Elections in West Germany* (London: Hurst, 1986), p. 252ff.
8. See E. Kolinsky (ed.), *Opposition in Western Europe* (London: Croom Helm and PSI, 1987) and T. R. Rochon, *Mobilizing for Peace. The Antinuclear Movements in Western Europe* (Princeton: Princeton University Press, 1988).
9. See K. von Beyme, *Political Parties in Western Democracies* (Aldershot: Gower, 1985).
10. See E. Grabitz et al., *Direktwahl und Demokratierung. Eine Funktionenbilanz des Europäischen Parlaments nach der ersten Wahlperiode* (Bonn: Europa Union Verlag, 1988) and C. Schöndube, *Das Europäische Parlament vor der zweiten Direktwahl* (Bonn: Bundeszentrale für politische Bildung, 1983).
11. See J. Lodge, 'The European Parliament – from 'assembly' to co-legislature: changing the institutional dynamics', in J. Lodge (ed.), *The European Community and the Challenge of the Future* (London: Pinter, 1989), pp. 58–79.
12. *Das Parlament*, 6/16 June 1989, p. 20.
13. Veen et al., op. cit., p. 22.
14. See G. Almond and S. Verba, *The Civic Culture* (Boston: Little, Brown & Co., 1962) and L. J. Edinger, *Politics in West Germany* (Boston: Little, Brown & Co., 1968).
15. E. Kolinsky, 'Socio-Economic Change and Political Culture in West Germany', in J. Gaffney and E. Kolinsky (eds) *Political Culture in France and GermanY* (London: Routledge, 1989), pp. 34–67.
16. See A. J. Merritt and R. L. Merritt, *Public Opinion in Semisovereign Germany. The HICOG Surveys 1949–55* (Urbana: University of Illinois Press, 1980) and H-P. Schwarz, *Die Ära Adenauer 1949–1957. Gründerjahre der Republik* (Wiesbaden: Deutsche Verlaganstalt/Brockhaus, 1981), p. 336ff.
17. See L. J. Edinger, 'Patterns of German Elite Opinion'. in K. W. Deutsch et al., *France, Germany and the Western Alliance* (New York: Scribner's, 1967) and R. J. Shepherd, *Public Opinion and European Integration* (Farnborough: Saxon House, 1975) p. 106 and p. 139.
18. Veen et al., op. cit., p. 12.
19. See W. E. Paterson and G. Smith, *Developments in West German Politics* (London: Macmillan, 1989).
20. See M. Hättig, 'Nationalbewusstsein im geteilen Deutschland', in W. Weidenfeld (ed.), *Die Identität der Deutschen*, 2nd ed. (Munich: Hanser, 1983), pp. 274–293 and G. Schweigler, in *Europa Archiv*, 1989.
21. See P. Hassner, 'Zwei deutsche Staaten in Europa', in W. Weidenfeld, op. cit., pp. 294–323.
22. See M. Schmidt, 'Two Logics of Coalition Policy: the West German Case', in V. Bogdanor (ed.) *Coalition Government in Western Europe* (London: Heinemann, 1983), pp. 38–58.
23. *Independent*, 21 March, 5 and 14 April 1989.

24. The major sections of the electoral programmes of the CDU, CSU, SPD and the Greens have been published in *Das Parlament*, 9/16 June 1989, pp. 10–12; see also U. Lüke, *Die Dritte Direktwahl des Europäischen Parlaments* (Bonn: Internationes Sonderdienst SO 3, 1989), pp. 10–30.
25. Ibid., pp. 18–19.
26. Ibid., p. 20.
27. Ibid., p. 21.
28. See S. Henig (ed.), *Political Parties in the European Community* (London: Allen & Unwin and PSI, 1979) and O. Niedermeyer, *Europäische Parteien?* (Frankfurt: Campus, 1983).
29. H. Werner, 'Perspektiven und Probleme des Gemeinsamen Marktes 1993', in *Aus Politik und Zeitgeschichte*, B24–25, 1989, pp. 3–14.
30. H-J. Veen et al., *Die Europawahl in der Bundesrepublik Deutschland vom 18. Juni 1989. Eine erste Analyse.* (Forschungsinstitut der Konrad Adenauer Stiftung: Sankt Augustin, 1989), p. 38.
31. A. Volkens, 'Parteiprogramme und Einstellungen politischer Eliten: Konsens- und Konfliktstrukturen in Wahlprogrammen', in D. Herzog and B. Wessels (eds), *Konfliktpotentiale und Konsensstrategien* (Opladen: Westdeutscher Verlag, 1989), pp. 117–44.
32. *Deutschland in Europa*, 1988.
33. Liberales Aktionsprogramm für Europa, 1987.
34. Von Beyme, op. cit.
35. *Independent*, 27 April 1989.
36. Ibid., 29 April 1989.
37. *Der Spiegel*, no. 22, 1989.
38. *Die Zeit*, 2 June 1989.
39. *Der Spiegel*, no. 23, 1989.
40. H-J. Veen, 'The Greens as a Milieu Party', in E. Kolinsky (ed.), *The Greens in West Germany* (Oxford: Berg, 1989), pp. 31–60.
41. See R. Stöss, *Right Extremism in West Germany* (Oxford: Berg, 1989).
42. *Der Spiegel*, no. 22, 1989, p. 28ff and *Independent*, 24 June 1989.
43. Party Programme, 1988, p. 4.
44. Ibid., p. 3.
45. Ibid., p. 11.
46. See R. Stöss, 'Sozialer Wandel und politisches System in der Bundesrepublik Deutschland', Paper delivered on 14 March 1989 at Aston University.
47. Der Bundesminister des Inneren (ed.), *Betrifft: Verfassungsschutz* (Bonn: BMI, 1969ff. – annual published report).
48. Data compiled from *Statistisches Jahrbuch für die Bundesrepublik Deutschland* (Stuttgart and Mainz: Kohlhammer for the relevant years).
49. M. Frey, 'Ausländer in der Bundesrepublik Deutschland' in *Aus Politik und Zeitgeschichte*, B 25, 1982, pp. 3–16.
50. D. Just and P. C. Mühlens, 'Ausländerzunahme: objektive Probleme oder Einstellungsfrage?' in *Aus Politik und Zeitgeschichte*, B 25, 1982, pp. 28–40.
51. Veen et al., *Die Europawahl in der Bundesrepublik Deutschland vom 18. Juni 1989*, op cit., p. 52.

52. 'Aufbröselung' (V) in ibid.
53. See U. Backes and E. Jesse, *Politischer Extremismus in der Bundesrepublik Deutschland* (Cologne: Wissenschaft und Politik, 1989).
54. See R. Hrbek and U. Thaysen (eds), *Die Deutschen Länder und die Europäischen Gemeinschaften* (Baden–Baden: Nomos, 1986).
55. Forschungsgruppe Wahlen: *Die Wahl zum Europäischen Parlament vom 18 Juni 1989*. Vorbericht. Mimeo, Mannheim, 1989.
56. *Frankfurter Rundschau*, 20 June 1989.
57. See B. Hoecker, *Frauen in der Politik* (Opladen: Leske und Budrich, 1987) and E. Kolinsky, *Women in West Germany. Life, Work and Politics* (Oxford: Berg, 1989).
58. E. Vallance and D. Davies, *Women of Europe: Women MEPs and Equality Policy* (Cambridge: Cambridge University Press, 1986), pp. 159–60.
59. *Die Wahlbewerber*, 1989, pp. 9–10.
60. *Vorläufige Ergebnisse*, 1989, pp. 65–6.
61. Vallance and Davies, op. cit., p. 88ff.
62. K-H. Reif et al., 'Wer sind und was wollen die Deutschen im Europäischen Parlament?' in *Zeitschrift für Parlamentsfragen*, 3, 1979, pp. 332–54.
63. R. Hrbek and C. C. Schweitzer, 'Die deutschen Europa-Parlamentarier' in *Aus Politik und Zeitgeschichte*, B 3, 1989, pp. 1–18.
64. Ibid., p. 6.
65. Ibid., p. 7.
66. Ibid., p. 8 and Reif et al., op. cit., p. 351.

5 Greece

KEVIN FEATHERSTONE and SUSANNAH VERNEY

INTRODUCTION

The combination of the 1989 Euro-elections in Greece with a bitter contest for the national parliament threw into sharp relief the contrast between the growing consensus on EC matters and an intense polarisation in national politics. The 1989 Euro-elections thus suggested that EC membership was beginning to emerge as an integrative force in Greek society, at a time when domestic conflicts were having a centrifugal effect.[1]

Despite the long-term significance of the EC for Greek political life, the short-term impact of the EP election was minimal. Inevitably the combination of the national and the Euro-elections meant that the latter were greatly overshadowed by the former. The Euro-elections in Greece thus gave further confirmation to Reif's notion of such contests being of a 'second-order' to domestic parliamentary contests.[2]

RETROSPECTIVE

In recent years, the *Eurobarometer* polls coordinated by the EC Commission indicate that EC membership has become more popular with the Greek electorate. Asked about Greek membership of the EC, in March–April 1984, only 38 per cent thought that it was a 'good thing'. By October–November 1987, this proportion had increased to 58 per cent, though it slipped back to 51 per cent in spring 1988. Heightened awareness of EC affairs, due to increased media coverage during the Greek presidency of the Council of Ministers in the second half of the year, probably explains the significant increase to 66 per cent believing EC membership a good thing by October–November 1988. Most notably, asked whether Greece had benefited from EC membership, only 44 per cent agreed in March–April 1983, but 67 per cent did so by October–November 1988. Support for the EP has also increased a little. In March–April

1984 only 13 per cent of Greek voters had said that the EP was 'very important in the life of the EC'; by October–November 1988, this had doubled to 28 per cent. A majority of Greek voters would also like the
EP to become more important in the future (57 per cent in October–November 1988). Similarly, a majority said they had recently heard something about the EP (52 per cent in October–November 1988). In both cases, however, the proportion was actually higher just before the 1984 EP elections. This is probably due to the undivided attention able to be given to those elections, which unlike those of 1989 were held well clear of any national contest.

With voting compulsory in Greece, the biggest difference between previous national elections and those for the EP had been the greater fragmentation of electoral support for the parties in the Euro-elections.[3] In the first EP elections in Greece in October 1981, both PASOK (−7.9 per cent) and ND (−4.5 per cent) had done worse in the EP vote than that for the Athens Parliament. By contrast, the two communist parties both did better: KKE (+1.9 per cent) and the Euro-communist KKE-es (+3.9 per cent), as did the centrist social democratic KODISO (+3.5 per cent). Moreover, Greece's 24 MEPs belonged to six different national parties, whilst in the national parliament only three parties were represented. At the 1984 EP elections, there was no national contest to compare with, but PASOK again did worse than in its 1981 national contest. For both the 1981 and the 1984 EP votes, the Greek electorate clearly felt less constrained as there was no need to choose a government.

The 1984 elections had been a highly-charged confrontation between the PASOK Government coming to the end of its first term of office and ND desperate to establish its position in advance of the next national contest due within the following year. In the event, the ND challenge failed; PASOK could be well satisfied with its result when other EC governments were suffering setbacks. Within a few months, ND had changed its leader (Constantine Mitsotakis was elected). In the June 1985 national elections, after a temporary crisis over the election of a new president to replace Karamanlis, PASOK again managed to defeat ND and secure its second four-year term. In 1989, however, the EP elections were once more to coincide with a keenly-fought national contest, and after the tribulations of the Papandreou Government over the previous twelve months, the outcome seemed difficult to forecast.

During the 1984–89 period, various changes occurred within the Greek contingent of 24 MEPs. Two party leaders who had headed their respective lists resigned to pursue their domestic duties: Evangelos Averof (ND) relinquished his seat very quickly, followed by Leonidas Kyrkos (KKE-es) in January 1985. Moreover, Grigoris Farakos who had headed the KKE list resigned immediately, allowing Alexandros Alavanos to replace him, thus leaving the party's contingent of MEPs as before. Grigoris Varfis (PASOK) resigned at the end of 1984 prior to becoming a member of the Delors Commission. Another change was prompted by the death of Dimitris Evrigenis (ND), the main author of the EP's Report on Racism and Fascism. In addition, Manolis Glezos (of the leftist EDA elected on the PASOK list) resigned, to be replaced by Spyros Kolokotronis (EDA-PASOK), and Dimitris Adamov (KKE) resigned and was replaced by Dimitris Desyllas. A switch between groups occurred when Ioannis Boutos (ND) became an independent and joined the EDA (Gaullist EP Group).

The activity of Greek MEPs in the 1984–89 period reflected both national and party considerations. On issues of clear national interest – such as Cyprus, Turkey, the EC structural funds – strong unity was typically displayed in the EP by the Greek members, who were no doubt conscious of the domestic ramifications of a failure to do so. On other issues – for example, matters connected with the Social Charter and the Single European Market – Greek MEPs were more often differentiated according to their EP party group.

The conception of the role of the MEP varied. The Greek KKE MEPs, opposed to EC membership for much of this period, quickly learned to use EP procedures for their domestic advantage. They were very active, particularly in asking oral questions on controversial issues which they could have reported in the party newspaper, *Rizospastis*, back in Athens. The Communist Group remained one of the least cohesive in the EP, however. The ND MEPs probably achieved a higher EP profile and a higher reputation than did their PASOK counterparts. The ND MEPs were fully assimilated into the EPP group and their work was highly regarded.

On the whole, the EP and the work of the Greek MEPs received relatively high media coverage between 1984 and 1989. Greek State television gave rather more coverage to EP sessions, for example, than did many of their other EC counterparts.

The electoral system used for the 1989 contest was essentially the same as that used in 1981 and 1984. A party-list system was used in a single national constituency, which is different from the various systems adopted for recent national elections. However, as with national elections, voting in the Euro-elections was compulsory. Foreign EC nationals living in Greece were not allowed to participate in the domestic Euro-elections, but as in 1984 – as a result of Law 1427/84 – Greeks abroad were able to vote. As is traditional, the polling stations were open to coincide with the period between 'sunrise and sunset'. The position with respect to the dual mandate has changed: the 1981 electoral law made the EP mandate incompatible with being a member of the Greek Parliament, but Law 1443/84 introduced an exception (which is linked with clauses concerning the proportion of votes taken by each party) permitting the dual mandate for the first two candidates on each electoral list. The order in which candidates appear on a party's list is determined by the party itself, and unlike in the 1989 national parliamentary contest, the voter was not able to discriminate between EP candidates by the use of a 'preference cross'. A party forfeits a deposit if its national list obtains less than 3 per cent of the vote. Under the 1981 law, a retiring MEP is replaced by the highest-placed unsuccessful candidate on the party's original list.

By the end of the 1984–89 parliament, the Greek parties had become more assimilated into the EP's structures. Most notably, PASOK joined the CSP at a 1989 congress in Salerno, Italy, despite not being a member of the Socialist International, hitherto a prerequisite for affiliation. PASOK MEPs had been long-term members of the EP Socialist Group, however. ND continued to fully participate in the EPP, and the more broadly-based EDU. The Greek Communist MEPs remained in the loosely-organised EP Communist and Allies Group.

At the 1989 EP elections both PASOK and ND endorsed common EP group manifestos. For PASOK this was a significant innovation, and it paralleled its adhesion to the CSP. In the event, however, the party's endorsement was hesitant – it regarded the manifesto as merely constituting a suitable basis for discussion – and it did not distribute the Greek text very widely during the campaign. ND was a signatory to the EPP manifesto, with Mitsotakis attending the EPP Congress in Luxembourg in November 1988. Both ND MPs and MEPs participated in the negotiations over the manifesto, and the party considered its content to fully reflect its own domestic philosophy. The impact of the common manifesto on its own national programme was unclear, and again the EPP text was not used very prominently in the 1989 campaign. The EP Communist Group did not produce a common manifesto for the Synaspismos (left-wing coalitions) to use. The Group had earlier merely adopted a series of common statements on specific issues not directly related to the elections.

For the 1989 elections both the ND and the Synaspismos lists of candidates displayed a strong sense of continuity. Of the first ten ND candidates, seven had previously been MEPs. Heading the ND list was Ioannis Pesmazoglou, previously an MEP on the social demo-cratic KODISO list. His inclusion brought to the ND ticket clear European credentials, as he had been chiefly responsible for negoti-ating the 1961 Greek–EEC Association Agreement. Of the first four Synaspismos candidates, the three KKE MEPs had served in the previous EP and two of them were the only Greek MEPs to have served continuously since October 1981. The PASOK list displayed more change and proved more controversial. The first three candid-ates were ex-MEPs, followed by ex-National Economy Minister Panayotis Roumeliotis, who had been implicated in the Koskotas scandal. The fifth PASOK candidate was Dionysis Livanos who had switched from ND. More controversially, the list included Dimitrios Pagoropoulos who had chaired the much-criticised parliamentary investigation into the Koskotas affair; Sotiris Kostopoulos, the un-popular Government spokesman; and Ioannis Stamoulis, the lawyer for the disreputable tabloid newspaper *Avriani*. Thus, not only was the PASOK list a motley collection of political figures, several of them had been embroiled in domestic controversies and scandals. Moreover, in general their selection appeared to have had little to do with European criteria. The PASOK interpretation of the MEP's role thus seemed to differ from that of ND and the Synaspismos.

EURO-ELECTION 1989

The Greek European poll was a classic example of a second-order election. Probably under any circumstances the EP would have taken a back seat to the simultaneous national contest. But in 1989 the domestic political stakes were particularly high, given that the national election was expected to trigger a major restructuring of the party system.

Dramatic changes had occurred since the previous general elec-tion, when PASOK had shown every sign of dominating the Greek political scene for a long time to come. In 1985, after three-and-a-half years in power, the party's vote had suffered little attrition, falling only 2.25 per cent from its 1981 high of 48.07 per cent. In contrast, New Democracy's election defeat was followed in August 1985 by a damaging leadership contest after which the loser, Kostis Stephan-opoulos, left the party with nine MPs to set up Democratic Renewal (DI.ANA).[4] On the traditional Left the KKE, whose vote fell below 10 per cent in 1985, subsequently showed clear signs of decline, manifested particularly in student elections which were won by the Right for the first time since the fall of the dictatorship in 1974. Meanwhile, in 1986 the Fourth Congress of the KKE-es opted to dissolve itself and set up a new non-Communist party to rally the broad left. But the Greek Left (EAR), founded in 1987,[5] failed to attract support away from PASOK.

However, PASOK supporters' confident predictions of a third four-year term were confounded by revelations of wide-ranging scandals. The latter included alleged massive arms deal bribes[6] and the apparent diversion of public sector funds into PASOK coffers via George Koskotas' Bank of Crete,[7] with the common link being the abuse of the over-intimate relationship between the state and the governing party. The close identification between the latter and its leader, long noted by political commentators,[8] was never more obvious than during Prime Minister Andreas Papandreou's absence in England for heart surgery in autumn 1988. Subsequently the ageing Papandreou's very public relationship with a woman less than half his age, conducted with complete disregard for the strong Greek family tradition and for all political consequences, symbolised the political and moral decline of the PASOK state.

In spring 1989, facing the prospect of defeat, PASOK, like all its postwar predecessors,[9] opted to change the electoral law for the national elections. To deprive ND of a straight victory, it replaced the old reinforced proportional representation with a complicated new system under which an independent parliamentary majority required 46–47 per cent of the vote.[10] The KKE and EAR had already anticipated the imminent breakdown of the two party system. Their December 1988 Joint Statement,[11] implying the healing of the historic 1968 split in the traditional Left, was intended as the nucleus of a broader 'Coalition of the Forces of the Left and Progress' (henceforth Synaspismos after the Greek word for coalition) aiming to attract disaffected PASOK voters. With changes expected, not only in terms of which party governed but also of the whole process of government formation, it was unlikely that European issues could become the epicentre of attention.

In any case eight years after accession, the question of Europe, once the cause of bitter political controversy, had ceased to occupy centre-stage in Greece. In the 1960s the division on Greece's Association with the then-EEC had followed the anti-Left/Left political cleavage, at the time the fundamental axis of Greek political life.[12] While this had changed by the 1970s, due to Euro-communist support for accession, political party positions on EC membership had continued to symbolise very different perceptions of where Greece belonged in the world and the kind of political and economic system the country should have. However, in the late 1980s it seemed that Greece's EC orientation was finally becoming a matter of national consensus, which certainly had not been the case in 1984.

PASOK, whose anti-EC rhetoric in the 1970s had been one of the key elements in a strategy which turned the party into a major political force, in practice as the governing party since 1981 had opted for a tactical acceptance of EC membership.[13] In 1984 the party had evaded the whole issue of where it stood on Europe, by fighting the EP elections on a nationalist platform of 'Greece First'. But in autumn 1985, with Greece's serious economic problems forcing the government to contract an EC loan, Papandreou finally publicly admitted that Greece was in the EC to stay.[14] Subsequently, PASOK's attitude towards the EC has changed so much that one journalist has referred to 'a second accession'.[15] By December 1987 Papandreou was declaring the need for political and not simply economic union and calling on the EC partners to overcome the 'small problems' which divided them.[16] The symbolic shift from conflict to cooperation between the two EP elections can be illustrated by contrasting two of its election posters. In 1984, one of PASOK's main posters showed two muscular forearms engaged in an armwrestling contest, presumably demonstrating that PASOK meant strength in negotiations with the EC. Meanwhile a poster circulated two months before the 1989 election showed two arms reaching out for a handshake, with one of the arms being used as a bridge for a representative sample of the Greek people marching towards Europe with their heads held high.

Possibly even more striking have been recent KKE developments, indicating the end to thirty years of adamant opposition to any contractual relationship between Greece and the EC. Change in its EC stance has proved an essential element in the party's attempts to break out of the domestic ghetto to which its hardline policy had condemned it. After some tentative first steps in 1987,[17] the party effected a major shift in its March 1988 *Theses* on the unified European market[18] and the Joint Statement with EAR mentioned above. Adopting the Gorbachev vision of Europe as a 'Common Home' of its peoples, the KKE seems to have refocused its efforts on promoting closer relations between the EC and COMECON, a line which has allowed it to move from fighting the process of West European integration itself to a new strategy of encouraging the EC to move in a Leftward direction.

THE CAMPAIGN

The Euro-election in Greece was contested by twenty-one parties and coalitions. As in other member states these included both Greens (three different groupings had 'ecological' in their title) and the extreme Right, plus two protest parties led by former PASOK Ministers. However, none of the small parties made much impact on the campaign, probably due to the fact that the EP campaign was incorporated into the general national campaign. Hence as usual, the centre of attention was the duel between PASOK and ND, but this time with the addition of the Synaspismos as a third major player expected to mount a strong challenge. Although the campaign only officially started four weeks before the elections, in practice it had already been under way for several months, with major speeches by leading parties[19] and a generally tense political atmosphere.

Specifically European campaigning had been under way for even longer, with the lead being taken by the KKE. For about two years before the Euro-elections, a group from the party's European Parliament Department had been making regular trips to the provinces on an approximately monthly basis, both to carry out propaganda and to collect information about specific regional problems. In autumn 1988, New Democracy MEPs carried out an information campaign in the countryside, with financing from the EP.

In the immediate pre-electoral period, the three major parties tried to involve all their EP candidates in the campaign. On PASOK's tours of the countryside would-be MEPs accompanied other party speakers, giving a standard ten-minute introduction on European policy before the main speech. ND MEPs also toured the country-side, with major speeches being made notably by the first two candidates on the list, Ioannis Pesmazoglu and Marietta Giannakou. The extensive travels of the four leading Synaspismos candidates included a trip to Western Europe by Vassilis Ephremidis to speak to Greek migrant workers. However, in the highly charged pre-electoral atmosphere, it was difficult for EP candidates to focus solely on Europe and their speeches tended to cover the general political situation too.

In contrast to the flood of general election material, party publications on the EC were comparatively thin. It is striking that PASOK's 80-page manifesto, *The Programme for the Third Four-year Term*, did not include a section on EC policy. The party did, however, produce a 28-page glossy colour pamphlet on the main aspects of its EC policy in an easy-to-read format.[20] Instead of a manifesto, ND circulated a 24-page illustrated brochure explaining its main policy positions. The penultimate page, dealing with European policy, was also reprinted and circulated as a separate leaflet.[21] The Synaspismos devoted one-and-a-half pages of its 32-page programme to 'the European prospectus', which included East–West relations as well as EC policy. It also produced an eight-page pamphlet, *The Aims of the Coalition of the Left and Progress for the 1989 Euro-elections*. Both PASOK and the KKE published accounts of their service in the EP. In PASOK's case, this took the form of an expensively-produced 240-page book detailing the interventions of the party's MEPs under thematic headings[22] and a 40-minute videocassette shown in all PASOK electoral centres. Meanwhile the KKE's 32-page pamphlet, published two months before the elections, provided an impressionistic presentation with no real text.[23]

There were also non-party sources of information. Greek television (ERT) showed the advertising 'spots' produced by the EP's Audio-Visual Service encouraging people to vote. ERT cooperated with the EP office in Athens in producing a one-and-a-half hour documentary, broadcast in May, and also a videocassette.[24] Five thousand copies of the latter were sent to schools, political parties and various other organisations. Both the documentary and the cassette concentrated on providing information about EC institutions, which the EP office saw as its main role in the campaign. The latter also produced a glossy portfolio describing the EP's history, responsibilities and composition and discussing the 'democratic deficit'. Fifty thousand copies of the latter were distributed, some through political parties. As in 1984, the EP office's own information campaign ended at the end of April. However, the budget provided was understood to be only one-quarter of that of 1984.

Media coverage of the 1989 elections was exhaustive. At the end of

May the Deputy Minister for Press and Information proudly announced that a total of more than 50 hours' TV time had been set aside for the party campaigns,[25] and this was subsequently increased to give more time to smaller parties.[26] But in the midst of this saturation coverage, the EC was comparatively neglected. While small parties only fighting the EP elections got a 15-minute slot each, parties also contesting the national elections received no additional allocation.[27] Consequently, apart from the Synaspismos, which broadcast a 30-minute interview with EP candidate Michalis Papayannakis, the major parties paid little attention to European affairs. Not one of the five two-hour round-table debates was devoted to the EC, although admittedly there was some discussion of EC issues in the foreign policy session. In general, TV time was devoted to straight political party broadcasts on all issues or to coverage of the larger parties' main electoral rallies in Athens and Thessaloniki, with no debates between party leaders.[28] While TV coverage came under the control of an inter-party committee during the pre-electoral period, this did not prevent some opposition protests concerning the use of news bulletins for pro-government propaganda.[29]

A new element in the 1989 campaign was provided by the plethora of radio stations, both private and municipally-owned, which had sprung up following the end of the state radio monopoly in 1987. Despite earlier proposals to the contrary, radio was not brought under government control during the pre-electoral period and consequently played an important role, supplying a much wider range of information and comment than had been available in previous elections. Many radio stations broadcast interviews with EP candidates or referred to EC issues in discussion and phone-in programmes, although here again the general coverage of EC affairs amounted to no more than a fraction of the attention paid to the national campaign.

Newspapers also devoted comparatively little space to the Euro-election. Indeed, a section of the press was instrumental in setting the depressingly low tone of the 1989 election campaign, which was characterised by what became known as *Avrianismos* in honour of its leading exponent.[30] Salacious revelations concerning the private lives of Papandreou and Mitsotakis and the mud-slinging allegations that leading members of the Synaspismos owned luxurious yachts and villas,[31] became the major focus of public interest.

The election campaign was indicative of the state of crisis in the Greek political system. In the weeks immediately preceding the poll, urban terrorist groups, calling on the electors to spoil their ballot papers, carried out bomb attacks against a number of public buildings including the Ministries of Health and Justice[32] and an assassination attempt against a former Minister who was allegedly heavily involved in the Koskotas scandal.[33] While it is usual for Greek governments to tempt the voters with pre-electoral handouts, in 1989 this assumed unprecedented proportions. The most blatant example occurred on the eve of the elections when it was revealed that the public telephone company had promised hundreds of applicants that if PASOK won Sunday's elections, a job would be waiting for them the following Tuesday.[34] From the start the call for a clean-up had been the major theme of the election campaign, with each of the three major parties, including PASOK, claiming the greatest commitment to the cause. But by the time of the election, the demand for *katharsis* extended beyond the immediate need to prosecute those responsible for the scandals, to the necessity of ending the clientelist system by breaking the suffocatingly incestuous relationship of governing party and state.

With so much at stake domestically, none of the parties placed major emphasis on European affairs. In the immediate pre-election period, the reactions of the political parties to the massacre of students in China was certainly a more important issue than their stances on matters related to Greece's EC membership. To some extent this also reflected the fact that the EC had ceased to be the epicentre of controversy. The KKE's change of heart meant that all the major political forces were in agreement on certain basic points, such as the need to strengthen the EC's regional policy to the benefit of countries like Greece. In the past, the KKE had opposed EC funding on the grounds that it merely aggravated Greece's dependence on capitalism. Now as the leading member of the Synaspismos, the party joined its voice to the unanimous call for a more efficient use of the structural funds. Consensus marked other policy aims, such as the need for a more effective EC environmental policy. All the parties agreed on the need to strengthen the EP's powers. Again, this marked a remarkable shift for the KKE, which had always opposed the transfer of national powers to supranational institutions, a position which it had earlier shared with PASOK.

In the 1970s and early 1980s, European policy had been a favourite subject for point-scoring between the parties. But in 1989, the differences which certainly existed on EC matters in some sectors, such as defence policy, hardly featured at all in the parties' bitter attacks against each other. Indeed, from their Euro-election campaign literature, it would appear that the major difference between PASOK and ND now lay in their disagreement over which party deserved the credit for the benefits which both agreed EC membership had brought Greece. But neither made much of this issue, reserving their fire for matters of domestic policy.

From one point of view, the low profile of EC issues in the 1989 elections thus had its positive side. From another, it suggested a somewhat superficial approach to the problems involved. For example, references to the magic date of 1992 were incorporated into the campaign, but in a purely symbolic fashion. While ND's election material included a picture of a clock standing at five to twelve, with the figure 12 being replaced by 1992, some of PASOK's posters featured the legend '1989–1992: The Crucial Four-Year Term'. Both parties thus added to the general feeling of apprehension about the unified European market, without initiating any substantial debate on what was actually involved. The overheated domestic climate provided little opportunity for a sober assessment of the EC's future development and Greece's relationship to it. Consequently, in the 1989 Euro-election, there seemed little awareness that Greece was electing members to a European Parliament which would see rapid and fundamental changes in the Community.

THE RESULTS

The conduct of the 1989 elections in Greece became the subject of opposition protests[35] and seems to have reflected the general disorganisation of the state machine. In many cases, the supervisory committees required at each polling station simply did not turn up, while other polling stations remained closed until midday due to the absence of the statutory legal representative. A number of the smaller parties protested that their ballot papers had not been available at many polling stations.[36] More than a week after the poll, the EP election results remained incomplete with the Interior Ministry still missing the total from one polling station.

In the 1989 EP elections the distribution of party support was again more fragmented than in national elections. As in 1981, the elections coincided with voting for the national parliament. However, in 1989 there was much less difference between the electoral systems used in the two simultaneous elections. The system adopted nationally was

Table 5.1   Greek elections to the European Parliament, 1981, 1984 and 1989

| | 1981 | | 1984 | | 1989 | |
	% Vote	Seats	% Vote	Seats	% Vote	Seats
PASOK	40.2	10	41.6	10	36.0	9
New Democracy	31.4	8	38.1	9	40.4	10
KKE	12.8	3	11.6	3⎫	14.3	4
KKE-es	5.3	1	3.4	1⎭		
KODISO	4.2	1	0.8	0	–	–
DI.ANA	–		–		1.4	1
Extreme Right	2.0	1	2.3	1	1.2	0
(1981: Progressive Party; 1984–89: EPEN)						
Greens*	–		–		2.6	0

*Combined vote for 'OIK.ENAL: Ecologists-Alternatives'; 'OI.KI.P.AN: Ecological Movement-Political Renaissance' and 'EDOK: Greek Democratic Ecological Movement')

closer to the simple PR used in the Euro-elections than to the reinforced PR system of the 1981 national elections. The discrepancy between the national and the EP results in 1989 is thus all the more notable, affected not so much by the type of electoral system used as by the perceptions of the greater flexibility available to the voter in a 'second-order' election. With a greater prospect of being able to elect candidates from the smaller parties, the electorate limited this opportunity to Europe.

As in 1981, the two main parties fared worse in the EP elections than in the national contest, although the discrepancy was not quite so great. In 1981, PASOK's EP vote had been 7.9 per cent lower than its national parliamentary score; in 1989, it was only 3.2 per cent lower. Showing less change, the ND EP vote had been 4.5 per cent lower in 1981; in 1989, it was 3.9 per cent lower. This discrepancy was maintained for both parties across the country in the local electoral districts.[37] As in 1981, the Communist vote was higher in the EP than in the national elections: in 1981 it had been 1.9 per cent higher for the KKE and a very significant 3.9 per cent higher for KKE-es; in 1989, it was 1.2 per cent higher for the Synaspismos combined. Most of the other smaller parties fared better in the EP as opposed to the national elections. The extreme right EPEN, despite losing its single EP seat, received a significantly higher share of the vote in the Euro-elections, whilst the new centre-right DI.ANA did moderately better.

In both the national and EP elections of 1989, ND was the first-placed party in the EP contest – an achievement it had not matched since the 1977 national elections. EP representation for ND and PASOK became the mirror image of that in the old parliament: only one seat changed hands between them. The Synaspismos failed to gain any more seats than the KKE and EAR had held between them in the outgoing assembly, leaving the most notable change that of the loss of the EPEN seat and the gain of the DI.ANA member.[38]

A relative failure was the performance of Greece's self-proclaimed 'Green' parties. At the 1989 Euro-elections there were three such parties: the 'Ecologists: Alternatives', (OIK.ENAL); the 'Ecological Movement: Political Renaissance' (OI.KI.P.AN); and the Greek Democratic Ecological Movement (EDOK). None of them constituted an organised political party and their profile during the campaign remained low. The votes of the three parties (1.11, 0.42 and 0.04 per cent respectively), however, would, if combined, have been sufficient to elect Greece's first Green MEP.

Given the background to these elections, ND's failure to achieve a higher share of the vote was more notable than the drop in support for PASOK. Its relatively poor performance seemed to reflect its inability since 1981 to establish a favourable and distinctive image for itself on EC affairs. In PASOK's earlier years, ND seemed defensive and obliged to dispute the responsibility for the benefits gained from the EC with the Papandreou Government. More recently, it still seemed unable to defeat PASOK on the EC and it settled for a rather low profile, loose consensus on these matters. By contrast, the Papandreou Government had taken care to highlight its achievements within the EC. The superiority of ND over PASOK in 1989 was undoubtedly a reflection of their changing domestic fortunes, rather than of a change in opinions on the EC.

CONCLUSIONS

The results of the 1989 Euro-elections confirm the hypothesis of their 'second-order' nature. Not having to elect a government, the voters expressed a different set of political preferences. This may have been due to the perception that there was no 'lost vote' under the simple PR system used for the Euro-elections or that the latter offered a chance to opt for a second party choice. It is unlikely that it was a response to European issues.

It is striking that while the national election results produced major changes in the balance of power in the Greek Parliament, the outcome of the Euro-election indicated continuity in the distribution of seats between the parties. Indeed in the three EP elections held so far, the distribution of seats has hardly changed. In total, the balance between ND and PASOK has shifted by only two seats. In 1984 ND won the seat formerly held by the KODISO MEP, Ioannis Pesmazoglu. By 1989, when ND picked up another seat from PASOK, Pesmazoglu was heading the ND list.

More fundamental to long-term stability in the Greek approach to Europe, however, was the consensus over EC policy between the Greek parties which emerged in the run-up to the 1989 elections. Prior to Greek accession when there had been major policy divergences on Europe, no thoroughgoing debate as to the implications of membership had taken place.[39] The paradox is that now there is consensus, this debate is still not occurring. Greece has yet to confront the problems and issues that will arise from a Single European Market.

NOTES AND REFERENCES

1. On the connection between EC membership and democratic stability in Greece, see S. Verney, 'Political Parties and Democratic Consolidation in Greece: To be or not to be within the European Community', in G. Pridham (ed.), *Securing Democracy: Political Parties and Regime Consolidation in Southern Europe* (London: Routledge, forthcoming).

2. See K. Reif (ed.), *Ten European Elections 1979/81 and 1984: Campaigns and Results* (Aldershot: Gower, 1985).

3. On the previous Euroelections in Greece see the chapter by K. Featherstone in J. Lodge (ed.), *Direct Elections to the European Parliament 1984* (London: Macmillan, 1986).

4. See *Vima*, 1.9.85 and *The Times*, 14.9.85.

5. On the foundation of EAR, see Susannah Verney, 'The Spring of the Greek Left: Two Party Congresses', *Journal of Communist Studies*, 3:4, December 1987, 166–70.

6. For the most serious allegations, see the resignation letter of Deputy Defence Minister Stathis Yiotas, published in *Eleftherotypia*, 15.12.88.

7. The first 'instant book' (in Greek) on the Koskotas affair was Kostas Bakatselos, *The Ideology of Love: Who Corrupted Whom* (Athens: Roes, 1989). No doubt there will be others.

8. A notable recent example is Michalis Spourdalakis, *The Rise of the Greek Socialist Party* (London: Routledge, 1988).

9. See Richard Clogg, 'Greece' in V. Bogdanor and D. Butler, *Democracy and Elections: Electoral Systems and their Political Consequences* (Cambridge: Cambridge University Press, 1983).

10. The electoral law and an explanation of how it works can be found (in Greek) in Pontiki, *The Electoral Law* (Athens: Pontiki Publications, 1989).

11. Published in *Rizospastis/Avghi*, 8.12.88.

12. The outstanding work on Greek political attitudes towards the EEC during this period remains Michalis Pateras, 'From Association to Accession: Changing Attitudes of Greek Political Parties Towards Greek Relations with the European Communities, 1957–1975', unpublished PhD thesis for the London School of Economics, 1984.

13. On PASOK's EC policy, see Kevin Featherstone, 'Greece' in Juliet Lodge (ed.), *Direct Elections to the European Parliament 1984* (London: Macmillan, 1986).

14. In a German TV interview, also shown on the Greek state-controlled ERT. The transcript of the interview was published in *Ta Nea*, 4.10.85.

15. Nikos Nikolaou of *Kathimerini*.

16. At the press conference after the Copenhagen Summit. See *Eleftherotypia*, 7.12.87.

17. See articles by Euro-MP Alekos Alavanos in *Proti*, 29.1.87 and 22.9.87. See also *Avghi*, 25.2.87 on the KKE vote for the Seeler Report, the first time the whole of the Left in the European Parliament voted in favour of a report on East–West relations.

18. Published in *Rizospastis*, 24.3.88. For an analysis see Susannah Verney, 'The New Red Book of the KKE: The Renewal that Never Was', *Journal of Communist Studies*, 4:4 December 1988.

19. The market research company Nilsen-Hellas estimated that in the period from January to March 1989, New Democracy had spent 47.55 million drachmas renting hoardings for posters and 47.17 million drachmas placing advertisements in newspapers and magazines. The corresponding figures for PASOK were much lower: 9.1 million and 2.76 million drachmas respectively. See *Eleftherotypia*, 2.5.89.

20. 'PASOK is Here for a Europe with a Human Face'.

21. 'In United Europe with the Greeks United'.

22. '1984–1989: The Work of the PASOK Parliamentary Group in the European Parliament'.

23. 'The KKE in the European Parliament: A Creative Dynamic Presence for a Progressive Greece in a Context of Pan-European Co-operation'.

24. Entitled, 'Yesterday, Today, Tomorrow'.

25. *Eleftherotypia*, 24.5.89.

26. See for example *Eleftherotypia*, 25.5.89 and 7.6.89.

27. As the extreme Right-wing EPEN, in particular, bitterly complained.

28. For Papandreou's refusal to enter a TV dialogue with Mitsotakis, see *Eleftherotypia*, 9.5.89.

29. See, for example, *Eleftherotypia*, 22.5.89.

30. Yannis Gkinis, *The Avriani File: A Personal Testimony* (in Greek) (Athens: Basdekis Publications, 1982) provides some insight into the *Avriani* phenomenon, although the newspaper had acquired considerably more political influence in the years since the publication of this book.

31. For the Synaspismos' protest, see *Eleftherotypia*, 9.6.89.

32. See the press for 2.6.89 and 14.6.89.

33. See the press for 9.5.89.

34. See the afternoon papers for 17.6.89.

35. See the Greek press for 21.6.89.

36. For example see *Proti*, 19.6.89 for protests by the Greek Socialist Party and the Greek Radical Movement.

37. On the past geographical distribution of party support see chapter by K. Featherstone in K. Featherstone and D. K. Katsoudas (eds), *Political Change in Greece: Before and After the Colonels* (London: Croom Helm, 1987).

38. A former Greek member of the EP Socialist Group, Spyros Kolokotronis, had stood on the Synaspismos list in 1989, but he failed to be elected. The DI.ANA candidate elected was Dimitrios Nianias.

39. See S. Verney, 'Panacea or Plague: Greek Political Parties and Accession to the EC, 1974–79', forthcoming PhD thesis for King's College, University of London.

6 Spain and Portugal
RICHARD GILLESPIE[*]

The Iberian EP elections in 1989 were of particular significance. They were the first Euro-elections held in Portugal and Spain that were not combined with national elections and that coincided with elections in the rest of the Community; the countries involved were of course the EC's most recent members; and in the Spanish case added prominence was given to the poll by the country's holding the EC presidency. But, of course, the Iberian polls, like normal EP elections, were also expected to provide important pointers to future general election results. In Portugal the election was seen as an opportunity for a mid-term popular verdict on the government of Anibal Cavaco e Silva, while in Spain a general election was only a year away. In both countries government policies had recently met with widespread labour opposition and in Spain the ruling Socialists' continuing ascendancy had also been placed in question by recent cooperation between the parties to their right.

THE BACKGROUND

Upon joining the EC in January 1986 Spain had initially filled its 60 seats at Strasbourg by party nomination of existing national deputies and senators. Spain's 'provisional' MEPs sat until June 1987 when an EP election was combined with municipal and regional elections, while in Portugal a Euro-election was combined with the general election in July. Although opinion polls showed a clear majority of Spanish and Portuguese alike to be well satisfied with the first year of membership, these first EP elections were bound to be overshadowed by the national elections (although in the Spanish case opinion polls found greater interest in the European than in the regional elections).[1] Former prime minister Leopoldo Calvo-Sotelo later lamented that the Spanish poll had been 'just one more episode in the domestic political struggle; they were seen as a mock general election, a recount of the votes or a nationwide opinion poll'. One party had not even indicated which group its members would join at Strasbourg.[2] Iberia was not alone in 'nationalising' its Euro-elections, a tendency perhaps inevitable, given the parties' preoccupation with national office, the electorate's lack of understanding of the Community and the EP's lack of power. Nor did the electoral systems help: the visibility of the campaigns was restricted by decisions to use single nationwide constituencies; proportional representation by party-list system meant that the contests were managed by the same *clase política* that dominated the national elections, and celebrities such as Suárez were eventually dissuaded from standing in Spain when the possibility of dual mandates was suppressed. The decision to set the minimum voting age at 18, while following the EC norm, excluded the recently politicised youngsters who had mobilised against changes affecting university entrance in Spain.

The Spanish triple election took place against a background of social unrest, with secondary school students successfully resisting measures announced by Education Minister José Maravall and trade unionists resorting to industrial action in support of wage demands, efforts to achieve a new social contract having failed. The governing Socialist Party (PSOE) experienced some electoral slippage as a result, falling from 44.8 per cent in the June 1986 general election to 39.4 per cent. However, this still left it with enough support to feel fairly confident about retaining its absolute majority of the seats in the Spanish parliament, for which the threshold is about 40 per cent. The Socialists were heartened by the failure of the main opposition parties to advance appreciably since 1986: the right-wing Popular Alliance (AP), led by Antonio Hernández Mancha since the resignation of Manuel Fraga the previous December, lost ground, while there were only small improvements in the performances of Adolfo Suárez's Democratic and Social Centre (CDS) and the Communist-led United Left (IU). At regional level, the most striking feature was the performance of the pro-ETA People's Unity (HB) which, in spite of being anti-EC, managed to win a seat, in part through winning protest votes beyond the Basque Country, especially in Catalonia.

In Portugal, the following month, the most interesting feature of the EP poll was that, whereas most party results differed little from general election performances, there was one marked discrepancy. The Centre Social Democrats (CDS) lost half of their vote to the governing Social Democratic Party (PSD) in the general election, leaving them with only 4.34 per cent of the poll, yet in the EP election they gained four MEPs by winning 15.41 per cent of the votes. The explanation lay in tactical voting, with many CDS voters prepared to support the PSD against the Left in the general election, and some PSD voters returning the favour in the EP poll.[3]

Iberian MEPs have tended to regard Strasbourg unenthusiastically as a luxurious place of exile. However, right from the start Spanish MEPs made a bigger impact within the EC and not simply because they greatly outnumbered the Portuguese, 60 to 24. Spain's substantially greater economic strength is reflected in a far higher degree of national self-confidence at elite level. There are no nationwide parties in Spain opposed to EC membership, as the Portuguese Communist Party (PCP) and the more uncompetitive sectors of Portuguese industry initially were. Although it is true that the motivation behind Spain's entry was pre-eminently political,[4] Spanish ambitions extend to becoming an important economic partner, respected by the Germans and French. Following the easy optimism associated with the pre-entry phase, Spain's achievement of the fastest growth rates in the EC has since maintained this ambition.

Spain's first-division aspirations have also been reflected in the country's international alignment within the Community. While membership certainly has prompted the Iberian states to tackle some of the disputes that marred their relations in the past, there is no sentimental feeling of Iberian community among them; and the Spanish government has stated repeatedly that there are too many differences of interest for either an Iberian or a Mediterranean bloc to emerge. Spain's most cordial relations arguably have been with the Germans, building upon close PSOE–SPD contacts since the 1970s and the understandings that were reached during the process of Spanish EC entry. The closest, if at times stormy, relationship, however, has been with the French. France has the greatest economic involvement of any EC country in Spain, and geographical contiguity has forced France and Spain to reach agreements both to ensure improvements in communications (essential to Spain's modernisation plans) and to combat ETA, whose leadership has been based in France. Between 1984 and 1986, France gradually abandoned its traditional tolerance of ETA, influenced by the advent of Spain's EC membership and by the eruption of Basque violence at home, in the form of death-squad assassinations of ETA suspects by the Antiterrorist Liberation Groups (GAL).

As a result of Madrid's greater ambition, Spanish parties have taken the matter of EC representation more seriously than the Portuguese. The original Spanish 'provisional' MEPs were of high calibre and included five former ministers and one former prime minister (Calvo-Sotelo). Although the latter departed after the 1987 election, the number of ex-ministers grew. The former Socialist foreign minister Fernando Morán and the ex-Francoist minister Manuel Fraga became MEPs, as did the former Basque regional president Carlos Garaikoetxea. Moreover, the Spanish contingent has proved remarkably stable. While it is true that most of the 'provisionals' of 1986 had hoped for a speedy return to national politics, nine-tenths of them remained in post following the 1987 election and there were similarly few changes in 1989: just four MEPs dropped from the PSOE list and three (including Fraga) from the Popular Party (PP, former AP) list.[5]

In general Spanish MEPs have been energetic and have raised issues hitherto neglected, such as the problems of Latin America. MEPs from other countries have been reminded of the regional diversity of Spain, for example when Garaikoetxea addressed the EP in *Euskera* (after first taking the precaution of distributing his speech in Spanish). Clearly the PSOE contingent, given its numerical strength and the emphasis it places on fielding qualified people,[6] has had the biggest impact. With 36 MEPs in 1986–7, the Spanish Socialists became the largest body within the Socialist Group, the largest EP group. They were therefore able to propose former Spanish Transport, Tourism and Communications Minister Enrique Barón for the EP presidency in January 1987. Barón's narrow defeat at the hands of Sir Henry Plumb showed that ideological divisions are fundamental among the Spaniards at Strasbourg: the AP deputies preferred to vote with fellow European Conservatives than see a socialist compatriot obtain the presidency (Barón nonetheless became a vice-president). On the Right, Manuel Fraga also played an energetic EP role initially, but before long he began to devote more attention to his pursuit of the Galician regional presidency and to salvaging AP, which was refounded as the PP following the incorporation of Christian Democrats in January 1989. The man leading this moderate influx, Marcelino Oreja, had also contributed to Spain's European presence as general-secretary of the Council of Europe.

CAMPAIGNS AND ISSUES

The immediate political context of the EP elections was less exciting in Portugal than in Spain. Compared with 1987, there was a more general feeling that EC membership was bringing benefits. With Portugal receiving Ecu 700m in 1988 and Ecu 1bn in 1989 to promote agricultural and industrial modernisation, assist the backward regions and finance job-training, even the traditionally anti-EC PCP chose a pro-European, Carlos Carvalhas, to head the United Democratic Coalition (CDU) list, although of course the new line of the PCP also denoted the influence of Gorbachevism. However, as Carvalhas himself lamented, 'Most voters don't know where Strasbourg is, let alone what the European Parliament does'.[7] Under the circumstances, the main issue in the Portuguese election was not surprisingly the performance of Cavaco e Silva's government.

The governing PSD claimed credit for recent growth and productivity improvements, and for a successful EC integration accompanied by a massive influx of EC funds. Much more controversial was the government's privatisation programme and its weakening of job security, moves facilitated by the absolute majority won by the PSD in the 1987 general election, which enabled it subsequently, with Socialist Party (PS) support, to revise the Constitution of 1976. The widespread antagonism of labour caused by these measures was seen in the way in which the social democratic General Workers' Union (UGT), formed a decade earlier as a moderate rival to the Communist-led unions, had itself taken the initiative in calling a general strike early in 1988. More worrying for the PSD, however, were signs of erosion within its own middle-class social base, caused by an over-confident government having acted in a high-handed manner towards the financial community, management, civil servants, and the legal and medical professions, while introducing unpopular tax as well as labour reforms.

In Spain the immediate context was also of a modernising government, with a record of economic success, having alienated part of its social base through its policies and arrogance. Here, though, the labour challenge to the government had been more formidable, thanks to a united action agreement reached by the socialist and communist trade unions in February 1988. Given that Spain had achieved high rates of economic growth, recalling the 'miracle' of the 1960s, the unions were much more assertive here when demanding a 'social shift' in policy to rectify growing social inequalities, and opinion polls showed a majority of the country sympathising more with their case than with the government's response. Labour unrest reached a climax in the general strike on 14 December 1988, which even González admitted to be a political defeat for his government. Since then, the Socialists had regained some ground, chiefly by forming a united front with the PP when socio-economic policy was examined by parliament in the 'state of the nation' debate the following February. Nonetheless, the EP election was to provide the first real test of the electoral implications of the Socialist Party alienation of its organised labour base. For the first time ever, the Spanish General Workers' Union (UGT) did not urge its 800 000 members to vote for the PSOE.

Even more immediately, the Spanish election was influenced by Opposition manoeuvres designed to establish a more credible centre-right alternative to the PSOE. As noted already, the AP had tried to overcome its unappealing authoritarian right-wing image by bringing in more moderate Christian Democrats and 'refounding' the party as the PP in January 1989, although the former Francoist Manuel Fraga simultaneously returned as president in an attempt to stem the decline that had occurred under Hernández Mancha. However, even with Oreja selected to lead the PP into the Euro-election, and the party's decision to join the Christian Democratic rather than the Conservative Group in the EP, it was clear that Fraga's party still lagged a long way behind the PSOE.

Thus most strategic thinking about ways to upset the PSOE's putative 'predominance' in the party system centred upon the possibility of forming a broad right alliance incorporating Fraga's forces and Suárez's CDS. This was not exactly a 'natural' alliance. Fraga had been disappointed when Suárez had been chosen as prime minister in 1976 and many former Francoists had felt betrayed by Suárez's subsequent legalisation of the Communist Party (PCE) and eventual concession of autonomy to the Basque Country. They had also seen Suárez during the first Socialist government (1982–6) attempt to attract votes both to the left and to the right of the PSOE. While seeking to project a progressive image, the CDS had no interest in becoming associated with Manuel Fraga. Nor did Fraga's eventual seduction of the Christian Democrats exactly help, for Suárez had always blamed these people for the destruction of his former party, the Union of the Democratic Centre (UCD). However, pragmatism, and the fear that the CDS might before long outgrow an intransigent conservative party, eventually led Fraga seriously to pursue a conciliatory course.

Suárez's party had most to lose from an alliance, for it would be the weaker partner in terms of seats, organisation and finance, and by committing itself to a centre-right alignment it would preclude the possibility of an agreement with the PSOE, were it to hold the balance of power after the next general election. The explanation behind Suárez's shift to the right may well reside in personal ambition. It is much easier to conceive of him returning to the Moncloa Palace at the head of a centre-right coalition, given the PP's lack of an 'electable' leader, than it is to see him as premier leading a coalition with the *felipista* PSOE.

The CDS decision to join the Liberal International, announced in September 1988, signalled a move to the right which was confirmed less than two months before the EP election when it signed a pact with the PP. With a view to acquiring greater credibility as an alternative of government, the two parties agreed to use their combined forces to censure and bring down Socialist administrations in a number of municipalities and regions, commencing in Madrid. In self-defence the PSOE attempted to secure defections from the enemy camp, with some success at the Madrid regional level.

By this time, the Socialists' public image had become quite tarnished as a result of exposés of corruption and high-living among some of the PSOE's representatives; undoubtedly this had already proved damaging to the party, contributing to public solidarity with the general strike. Now, however, the Socialists were showing signs of unscrupulousness; they seemed prepared to hang on to power at any cost. However, the same characteristic was seen among the centre-right forces too, as they made their bid for power. Admittedly the PSOE had earlier resorted to 'unholy alliances' itself – for example, to win regional power in Galicia – but now a far more extensive and just as unprincipled move was being made by the CDS and PP, and the former party in particular seemed to have shifted too far, too fast, to retain much credibility. By the time of the election the PP was also being accused of corruption, after an IU deputy claimed to have been offered a huge bribe to support a censure motion against the Socialist regional president of Madrid.

Hardly any of the main Spanish parties had a 'clean' image by now. Even the PCE, while not accused of corruption, had disappointed some of the hopes raised by the election of Julio Anguita to its leadership in February 1988, by subsequently reaching an accommodation with a more Stalinist party led by Ignacio Gallego. Moreover, one of the deputies elected on the IU ticket at the 1986 general election, the economist Ramón Tamames, had since joined the CDS without resigning his seat.

Although in principle the parties had decided to call a halt to inter-party transfers that involved politicians disposing of their seats as if they were their own private property, the public image of political parties collectively was now worse than at any time since the mid-1970s. To differing degrees, the three leading parties, at least, were seen as unscrupulous, remote and susceptible to corruption. Together with labour's disaffection from the government, these sentiments gave rise to expectations of a significant protest vote and high level of abstention in the EP election. One newspaper cartoon captured the mood when it depicted two old ladies inspecting the election posters, and one saying to the other: 'I'm going to vote for the lot of them, so that they get out of Spain and leave us in peace'![8]

During the election campaigns, the governing parties of both Portugal and Spain were accused of taking unfair advantage of their position. In Portugal, Cavaco was accused of manipulating the electorate by feeding it an unusual amount of 'good news' (the slowing-down of inflation, the concession of teachers' demands, an extraordinary increase in the minimum wage). The Spanish Opposition meanwhile protested that the 'institutional' campaign undertaken by the government chiefly favoured the PSOE, since as in Portugal the emphasis was upon the importance of voting, and clearly the governing party was the one most vulnerable to high abstention. However, while Portuguese TV viewers were urged, 'Be a 12-star citizen! Vote in the European election', it was not only the PSD government that tried to motivate the electorate: President Soares, the former PS leader, also made an eve-of-poll appeal to the 'civic duty' of the voters to participate in order to give 'credibility' to Portugal's MEPs.[9] More controversial were the unmistakable similarities between the Spanish state's and the PSOE's propaganda in Spain. The European 12-star emblem featured in state and party posters alike and whereas the institutional slogan was 'Vote with Europe', the PSOE slogan was 'Vote PSOE' followed by 'In Europe with Strength'.[10]

However, these issues did not overshadow the campaigns. In Portugal, the government's record was the main focus of controversy, although among its achievements the PSD was emphasising successful EC integration and the amount of EC funding received. This enabled the Socialists, while acknowledging that the funds had financed infrastructural improvements and had helped businesses and farms to modernise, to claim that the PSD's recent electoral success had relied upon such funding. The Opposition highlighted the government's lack of influence in EC decision-making and its inefficient supervision of job training grants, which had allowed money to be siphoned-off through phantom enterprises. Communist municipal government was pointed to by the CDU as a counter-example of the efficient use of EC structural funds to improve services.[11] Thanks to the presence within it of a small Green party (alongside the PCP and a fellow-travelling wing of the Popular Democratic Movement), the CDU hoped to capitalise upon a growing ecological awareness in Portugal.

All the Portuguese parties spent a good deal of time attacking their rivals, but one individual exception was the charismatic former CDS president and EP list leader Lucas Pires who, unlike party leader Diogo Freitas do Amaral, avoided right-wing attacks on Cavaco and tried to focus the party campaign on European issues. Meanwhile the sights of the leading opposition party, the PS, were upon reducing the lead of the PSD prior to challenging for office in 1991. Internally there was a degree of disunity, with critics of general-secretary Jorge Sampaio claiming that the PS alliance with the originally pro-Eanes Democratic Renewal Party (PRD) was a strategic error.

The Spanish campaign was somewhat livelier as a result of the recent PP–CDS pact, the expectation of an earlier general election, and Spain's presidency of the EC. On the face of it, the PSOE mounted a genuine Euro-campaign. Not only were the Socialists the only Spanish party to campaign on a joint programme shared by its European allies: they had also had a major input into the Socialist Group's manifesto, it having been drafted originally in Spanish by a committee headed by Barón.[12] The PSOE reminded the electorate that it was the most European of Spanish parties by holding a conference of 'Socialism and Europeanism' in May, attended by Jacques Delors, Oskar Lafontaine and the Spanish Socialist EC Commissioner Manuel Marín, who had led the negotiations on Spain's entry. The party presented the alternatives as being Thatcher's Europe or a Citizens' Europe. However, the main purpose of this dichotomy was to support a strategy of polarising the electoral contest within Spain. By making out that the PP–CDS agreement was an all-purpose pact, and by repeatedly claiming that the CDS had become a PP 'satellite', the Socialists were suggesting that the only real alternative to themselves were the Spanish Thatcherites. The motive here was clearly to try to hold on to working-class votes, threatened by the dispute with the unions. This was also the idea behind deputy prime minister Alfonso Guerra's campaign claim that the PSOE was still the party of the 'shirtless ones' – a claim belied by the embarrassing publication during the campaign of the Economic and Social Committee's report on Spain, which echoed trade union concerns about the emergence of a dual society.

The three main parties' campaigns had more to do with the situation in Madrid than debates in Strasbourg. There was no serious assessment of Spain's presidency of the EC, party opinions on this being all too predictable. So much hinged anyway on what would be the outcome of the Madrid summit that would be held only after the election. The predominant public attitude seemed to be that, while the Spanish presidency had been efficient enough, it had not seen any giant strides towards objectives valued by ordinary people. Through their inexperience in the EC, the Socialists had encouraged inflated views of what the presiding member could achieve, and there was now some sense of disappointment, although offset by a readiness to await the outcome of the Madrid summit. Socialist attempts to generate enthusiasm for the draft Social Charter were doomed by the disappointment surrounding the PSOE's domestic social policies and by the general European trade union verdict that the proposed Charter would be ineffective.

Among the other party campaigns, that of the PP was hampered by the lack of panache of its leading candidate. Oreja's presence gave the PP campaign respectability but there was nothing exciting about him, and informed voters were aware that if his list did well, then he would most likely resign before long to head the PP list for the general election. On the other hand, while the party was seeking to project a more modern image, Fraga's presence in the party presidency suggested to some that the diehard right-wingers could make a comeback at any time.

The published programme of the PP focused exclusively on the kind of Europe that the party favoured,[13] but its more visible media campaign, like that of the CDS, emphasised the defects of the González government (which, besides being negative, implicitly conceded that the PSOE was unbeatable). The CDS produced a detailed, genuinely European programme,[14] but its advertisements advocating better communications (especially motorways), health, education and pensions, would have been more suitable for a national election. The IU programme, meanwhile, called for a social Europe, full civil and political rights, a stronger EP, a non-nuclear, non-Atlanticist Europe, and 'economic growth compatible with the environment'.[15] Headed by PCE leader Julio Anguita and list-leader Fernando Pérez Royo, a Sevillian with a passion for bull-fighting, the IU campaign was unusual in that it was based on a full explanation of the programme. IU hoped to attract fresh votes from the UGT, which had decided that this option – together with the People's Left

(IP) led by Juan María Bandrés and the Spanish Workers' Party (PTE) of Santiago Carrillo – was one of the most sympathetic to the union's views on social policy. However, the attractiveness of the IU list was limited by the predominance of PCE candidates: the former PSOE deputy mayor of Madrid, Alonso Puerta, was the only socialist placed high enough to win a seat.[16]

Among the smaller Spanish parties, a novel feature of the campaign was the presence of the Greens who, by running a national campaign for the first time, seemed likely to win their first seat. Their prospects were enhanced by Spain's appalling record of environmental neglect, but were jeopardised by internal divisions. Since 1987 the 'Greens' and the 'Confederation of the Greens' had united to present the 'Green List', affiliated to the European Greens, but the electorate was confronted with three other ecological lists; and one of these, the 'Ecological Greens', linked to the right-wing *La Comunidad* sect, seems to have competed only to split the Green vote. Responsibility for the confusion, however, also lay with the Socialist authorities who had allowed several 'Green' groups with similar names to register as political parties, whereas in the late 1970s the PSOE had resisted the registration of socialist parties with similar names.[17] Complicating the ecological option still further, IP, based primarily on the social democratic Basque Left (EE) party, also received support from the Rainbow Group.

Spanish interest lay also in the performance of the peripheral nationalist parties or alliances based upon them. Although Basque Nationalist Party (PNV) leader Xabier Arzalluz favoured unity among the Basque nationalist forces within Europe, for Bandrés the ideological divisions were more salient than the bonds of nationalism. IP and the PNV-based Nationalist Coalition (CN) each brought together ideologically likeminded forces from various parts of Spain, as did the People's Europe (EP) ticket headed by former Basque president Carlos Garaikoetxea. Meanwhile HB was without allies, and had even considered withdrawal. Madrid increased its isolation by refusing main-channel television time to its MEP, Txema Montero, the justification being the Basque alliance's rejection of institutional participation. The government clearly hoped that HB would lose votes as a result of the failure of the recent ETA–government peace talks, ETA's drift towards indiscriminate terrorism (such as the bombing of a Catalan supermarket) and HB's declared ambition to establish an anti-EC bloc in Strasbourg.

Also standing alone were the much more moderate Catalan

nationalists of Convergence and Unity (CiU). The possibility of CiU–
PNV cooperation had evaporated when the Basques rejected the idea
of representational rotation in the EP: the PNV wanted a permanent
Basque presence in Strasbourg to sell Euskadi in Europe and
promote the development of the Atlantic flank of Spain.

The other regionally-based contender was the *Partido Andalucista*
(PA), headed by the popular mayor of Jérez de la Frontera, Pedro
Pacheco. In Andalucía, where 25 per cent of the Spanish electorate is
based, the populist PA seemed set to do well by taking advantage of
accusations of corruption levelled against the Socialist regional
authorities and the internal divisions afflicting the regional federation
of the PSOE. Andalucía was also the home of the entrepreneur José
María Ruiz-Mateos, who presented himself as a defender of entre-
preneurs against politicians and technocrats. He blamed Socialist
ministers personally for the expropriation in 1983 of his huge but
tottering holding company, Rumasa. By June 1989 he was wanted by
the authorities on charges of fraud, misappropriation, illegal currency
operations, falsification, insulting the head of state, and assault on
the minister who ordered Rumasa's nationalisation; none the less,
disguised in wig and dark glasses, he was able to attend a press
conference given by Economy Minister Carlos Solchaga, and even
obtained his autograph! Ruiz-Mateos thus injected an element of
buffoonery into the Spanish election campaign.

THE RESULTS

Spanish opinion polls proved a fairly accurate guide to the actual
results, their most notable error being in relation to the PSOE vote.
A poll published on 9 June suggested that the Socialists would win
only 35.3 per cent of the votes, a drop of 4 points since 1987, and
would lose 3–5 seats.[18] Even an exit poll published 10 days later put
the PSOE result at 35.4 per cent, meaning a loss of 2–4 seats.[19] This
discrepancy with the actual results probably indicates a reluctance to
vote for the PSOE on the part of Socialists who eventually decided
that it was the lesser evil. Although banned, opinion poll results were
also published by the Portuguese press on the eve of polling: these
tended to give the governing PSD more votes and the opposition
parties less than they eventually received.[20] It is difficult to assess
whether foreknowledge of other European results from elections
held on 15 June had a real impact in Portugal on 18 June, but

Table 6.1   Spanish EP election results, 1989 and 1987

Party/ Alliance	1989		1987	
	Seats	% Votes	Seats	% Votes
PSOE	27	39.56	28	39.44
PP	15	21.42	17	24.89
CDS	5	7.14	7	10.36
IU	4	6.06	3	5.30
CiU	2	4.19	3	4.47
Ruiz-Mateos	2	3.65	–	– —
PA	1	1.88	0	0.97
CN	1	1.87	–	– —
IP	1	1.83	0	1.37
HB	1	1.71	1	1.89
EP	1	1.51	1	1.71
Others	0	9.18	0	9.60
TOTAL	60		60	

Participation: 1987 68.93%
1989 54.82%

Source: *El País*, 20 June 1989

certainly the information supplied by exit polls led the PSD to hope for a 'Spanish' result (notwithstanding the formal political differences between the PSOE and PSD), while the PS was encouraged by the British result.

The Spanish results provided the PSOE with considerable relief. The Socialists increased their lead over their immediate rivals, the PP and CDS, while the leftward swing favouring IU was moderate and translated into just one extra seat. The PSOE lost only one seat while the PP and CDS each lost two, compared with the 1987 results.[21] However, the PSOE lost no fewer than 1.3m votes, mainly through abstention. For the most part, their discontented supporters preferred to stay away rather than transfer their votes, or they decided at the last minute to vote Socialist. The size of the protest vote was limited by the recent PP–CDS operation in Madrid, which had made the 'threat' from the right seem much more real, and by the proximity of the next general election, which encouraged socialists to behave 'responsibly'.

For the centre-right forces, the results were deeply disappointing. A question mark was immediately placed against the future of PP–CDS cooperation (though the takeover of Madrid's town hall went ahead) and the whole question of the PP's leadership was thrown into the air. The combined vote of the two parties represented a loss of 2.2m: approximately one-third of their combined total in 1987. For the smaller party of the two, the CDS, the outcome was a real disaster and it may be tempted to revert to its former, less ambitious, general election strategy based on the hypothesis of a hung parliament.

It would seem that the centre-right had misread the signs concerning popular reactions to PP–CDS antics in Madrid. A poll carried out in early June had found 49 per cent of those questioned believing that the inter-party agreement would make the centre-right a real alternative to the governing PSOE; however only 29 per cent had thought it would enable the centre-right to win the next general election.[22] The Madrid results of the EP election contain the clearest verdict on the shenanigans of the major parties. The PSOE, whose desperate efforts to secure opposition defections there had been condemned as 'vote-buying' by many critics, lost over 100 000 votes, as did both the PP and CDS (compared with the 1987 EP results). The PP fell less drastically (30.6 to 28.0 per cent) than the PSOE (40.8 to 35.4 per cent) and CDS (14.2 to 9.3 per cent) in the Madrid region, where abstention at 41.5 per cent was well below the national 45.18 per cent. IU benefited from the swing to the left there: its vote rose from 125 000 to 179 000, and its proportion of the vote went from 5.2 to 8.5 per cent. IP led by Bandrés also saw its support grow in Madrid, from 21 000 to 33 000 votes.[23]

Of the four main Spanish contenders, IU was the only one that could claim to have progressed, both in terms of seats and proportionally. However, its total national vote of 959 000 was below its 1987 achievement of 1 012 000 votes and still further below earlier PCE electoral performances. By staying out of the party imbroglio in Madrid, IU avoided the electorate's punishment of the politicians and it picked up some UGT votes, though far fewer than it had hoped for. The Communist-dominated alliance had hoped to win several additional EP seats but had to be content with consolidating its electoral position and challenging the CDS for third place nationally.

The other contender benefiting from protest votes was Ruiz-Mateos whose 609 000 votes carried not only the fugitive but also his son-in-law, Carlos Perreau de Pinninck Domenech, to Strasbourg. This unexpected result can partly be explained in terms of the situation in Madrid, where the ticket achieved its best mainland result: 129 000 votes, 6.1 per cent of the total. However, more generally Ruiz-Mateos picked up votes from former Fraga supporters who disapproved of the pact with Suárez or who saw Oreja as too weak a PP candidate.[24] Although some ultra-right activists took part in his campaign, Ruiz-Mateos's success does not portend a right-wing revival, for the ultra-right itself attracted only a derisory vote. His supporters include people who lost out as a result of the Rumasa expropriation and above all those who feel that the politicians are corrupt, remote and self-serving.

If the sixth position of Ruiz-Mateos embarrassed the political elite and worried the centre-right, the parties at least derived a degree of common satisfaction from the decline of HB. The pro-ETA alliance saw its national vote drop from 361 000 votes in 1987 to 270 000. It suffered quite a minor reversal in the Basque Country and Navarra, but lost heavily elsewhere (falling from 40 000 to 15 000 votes in Catalonia). In the Basque Country, only the People's Europe ticket headed by Garaikoetxea did worse, losing 24 per cent of its 1987 votes while HB lost 12 per cent. The most successful Basque party was the most moderate: the PNV. Its Nationalist Coalition (CN) ticket outperformed the PSOE in the Basque Country, while the moderate Catalan nationalists of the CiU were beaten regionally by the PSOE and lost an MEP. The Catalan result confirms the dominance of the PSOE in supra-regional elections in Catalonia and the weakness of the CiU when its list is not headed by the charismatic regional president, Jordi Pujol. Finally, in Andalucía the PSOE managed to increase its share of the vote (from 48.6 to 50.2 per cent) in spite of high abstention in the region. It lost over 200 000 votes there, but the PP lost more and support for the CDS and IU also declined. The minor beneficiary of these setbacks was Ruiz-Mateos, the major one the PA, which went from 5.3 to 10.5 per cent of the regional vote and thus took Pedro Pacheco to Strasbourg.

Overall, the results provided an illustration of how high abstention in Spain helps minor parties to gain representation, especially in EP elections when (unlike Spanish general elections) there are no sub-national constituencies. No fewer than 11 Spanish tickets won representation, compared with seven in 1987 when the turnout was 68.9 per cent. The 14-point drop in participation in the more recent election was more than the PSOE had predicted but less than they had feared. Although the Socialists will try to win back some of their former supporters in time for the next general election, chiefly by improving public services, they will feel reassured by the evidence that the centre-right remains as unattractive to the electorate as in the past.

The Spanish result also underlined the importance of party alliances under the D'Hondt system. The ecological movement paid heavily for its disunity, the Catalan nationalists lost a seat because of their lack of allies in other parts of Spain, and HB's growing isolation within Spain proved less than fatal only because of the relative stability of its support in the Basque Country.

Unlike the Spanish results, those in Portugal showed the gap between government and opposition parties narrowing significantly. There a governing party with a far lower profile in Europe saw its vote drop almost five points since the last EP election. It lost a seat while the Socialist list gained two and the Communist-led CDU gained one. The left was able to celebrate the first defeat of Cavaco e Silva and also cheered the loss of a seat by the right-wing CDS. Pointing to the reduction from 15 to 4 points in the distance separating the PSD from the PS, Socialist leader Jorge Sampaio declared 'Portugal is changing'.[25] His view was that the result left the PS as the only rival to the PSD, and thus poised to win power in 1991. However, the Socialists' progress was more apparent than real. The closing of the gap owed more to PSD abstentions than to genuine PS growth, for the increased Socialist share of the vote can be largely explained in terms of the incorporation of PRD candidates who in 1987 had featured in a separate list. The votes of the two parties then had totalled 27.2 per cent, against 28.5 per cent now. It has been calculated that at least 40 per cent of the abstentions came from the governing party.[26]

The Socialists had been hoping for CDU and CDS failures to move

Table 6.2   Portuguese EP election results, 1989 and 1987

| Party/ | 1989 | | 1987 | |
Alliance	Seats	% Votes	Seats	% Votes
PSD	9	32.7	10	37.4
PS			6	22.5
PRD	8	28.5	1	4.4
CDU	4	14.4	3	11.5
CDS	3	14.2	4	15.4
Others	0	10.2	0	8.8
TOTAL	24		24	

Participation: 1987 76.6%
                    1989 51.4%

Source: *Expreso* (Lisbon), 23 June 1989

Portugal in the direction of 'bipolarisation'. Instead, while the CDS suffered only minor losses, the CDU did remarkably well. Although the Communist Party has experienced a sharp decline in the 1980s, it was favoured on this occasion by various factors: the new, more positive, image presented by CDU list leader Carlos Carvalhas; the presence of Green deputy Maria Santos in fourth place on the CDU list; the availability of PRD votes as a result of the Renewal Party's effective breakup; and the commitment of Communist militants which helped 'deliver' the CDU vote amid a generally low turnout.

While far from a disastrous election for the PSD, the Portuguese outcome will be keener competition in future between a less confident government and more optimistic Socialist opposition. The Portuguese results do not, however, indicate a shift to 'bipolarisation': instead the four-party system that emerged during the mid-1970s appears to have reasserted itself through the effective disappearance of the PRD, which rose and fell in quick succession in the mid-1980s. None of the eight smaller parties (six of the radical left and two of the extreme right) managed to win seats.[27]

CONCLUSION

The Iberian EP elections had several common features – party campaigns dominated by national issues, similar electoral systems, a marked fall in electoral participation, and a substantial erosion of support for ruling parties – yet they also produced several major contrasts. While in Portugal fewer party lists gained representation in Strasbourg than had done so in 1987, the opposite tendency was present in Spain, largely because of the solid base that the peripheral parties enjoy in nationalist communities and the ability of most of them to unite with similar regional parties elsewhere in Spain. Moreover, in contrast to Portugal, the Spanish result indicates the continuing lack of a convincing opposition alternative to the government. This relates to the divisions that still exist between the 'authoritarian' and 'modern' elements within the Spanish right and the way in which conservative unity is thwarted by major centre–periphery cleavages. Lastly, although this may be a short-term trend, exacerbated by the situation in Madrid, the Spanish election gave rise to an anti-party protest vote that has no effective counterpart in Portugal. However, the new Iberian protest votes were in no way anti-EC protests; and while the hostile HB found itself reduced to its

Basque heartlands, the previously anti-EC Portuguese Communists advanced, in part by adopting a more positive attitude towards Europe.

NOTES AND REFERENCES

* Research for this chapter was undertaken with assistance from the Estimates and Grants Committee, University of Warwick. The author also wishes to thank Tom Gallagher for providing information about the Portuguese election.

1. *El País* (Madrid), weekly edn, 8 June 1987.
2. Calvo-Sotelo, 'Las Euroelecciones de Junio de 1987', *Anuario El País 1989* (Madrid: PRISA, 1989), p. 64.
3. Tom Gallagher, 'Goodbye to Revolution: The Portuguese Election of July 1987', *West European Politics*, 11:1 (1988).
4. Benny Pollack and Graham Hunter, *The Paradox of Spanish Foreign Policy* (London: Pinter, 1987), Ch. 6.
5. *El País*, 1 June 1989.
6. Of the PSOE's 60 candidates in 1989, 85 per cent had higher education qualifications. There were 18 university lecturers plus 5 professors, 13 civil servants, 5 lawyers, 3 journalists, 3 party officials, 2 administrators, 2 public officials, 2 students and only 1 of any other occupational group. The average age was 44 and there were 20 women. *El Socialista* (Madrid), 15 May 1989.
7. *Financial Times*, 6 June 1989.
8. *El Independiente* (Madrid), 9 June 1989.
9. *El País*, 19 June 1989.
10. The institutional campaign cost the taxpayer £6m. The PSOE invested £5.6m in its party campaign, less than the legal maximum of £7.2m. *El Independiente*, 9 June 1989; *El Socialista*, 31 May 1989.
11. *Financial Times*, 6 June 1989.
12. *El Socialista*, 31 May 1989; *Por una Europa unida, próspera y solidaria. Manifiesto de la Unión de los Partidos Socialistas de la Comunidad Europea* (Brussels, 10 February 1989). It is worth noting that the document (pp. 6, 22) was supportive of the idea of *concertación social*, which the González government had by now abandoned.
13. Partido Popular, *Europa unida, democrática, solidaria, popular* (Madrid, May 1989).
14. Centro Democrático y Social, *Paso al centro* (Madrid, June 1989).
15. Izquierda Unida, *Es Tiempo de alternativas* (Madrid, May 1989); *Mundo Obrero* (Madrid), 17 May 1989.
16. *Boletín Oficial del Estado* (Madrid), no. 115 (15 May 1989), p. 14.
17. *El Independiente*, 2 June 1989.
18. *El País*, 9 June 1989.
19. Ibid., 16 June 1989.

20. Ibid., 19 June 1989.
21. In fact, since 1987 the PSOE had acquired an additional MEP through the defection from the CDS of Carmen Díez de Rivera.
22. *Cambio 16* (Madrid), 16 June 1989. In the same poll, 66 per cent of the respondents said they intended to vote for the same party in the EP and general elections; 13 per cent said they would vote for different parties.
23. *El País*, 20 June 1989; and for the 1987 EP results, *Anuario El País 1988*, pp. 114–23.
24. Pilar Díez, 'La galaxia electoral que eligió a Ruiz-Mateos', *Cambio 16*, 3 July 1989.
25. *El País*, 20 June 1989.
26. See Tom Gallagher, 'Portugal', *Electoral Studies*, forthcoming.
27. *El País*, 19 June 1989.

7 France

PAUL HAINSWORTH

INTRODUCTION

The third EP elections took place amidst a climate of growing electoral apathy. Since the French presidential contest of April–May 1988 (and an 80 per cent voting turnout) a succession of diverse elections – legislative, cantonal, municipal and so on – had produced low levels of participation. In turn, opinion polls suggested that the turnout for the EP elections would register new degrees of apathy with possibly one in two voters abstaining. After all, the June 1989 election constituted the tenth visit to the polls in fourteen months for some electors and a certain poll-weariness seemed likely. The (French) President of the European Commission, Jacques Delors, exhorted political parties to mobilise the electorate but ex-President of France, Valéry Giscard d'Estaing, was doubtlessly correct in his diagnosis that while Europe interested the French people the EP elections did not.

BACKGROUND

Eurobarometer polls revealed consistently high levels of French support for European integration, France's membership of the EC and the onset of 1993 (i.e. '1992'). Despite understandable anxieties over the Single European Market and *some* adverse polls, opinion remained basically optimistic about competing in the Europe of the 1990s. Certainly, the main political forces supported the Single European Act. Socialist President, François Mitterrand had signed the document, made European integration an important part of his successful presidential re-election platform[1] and, clearly, viewed progress in the European arena as a priority of his political agenda. In his May 1989 press conference, Mitterrand set out the priorities for the forthcoming French presidency of the Council of Ministers: economic and monetary union, the social dimension, cultural matters, the environment and a citizens' Europe. Similarly, the two foremost movements on the French right – the neo-Gaullist *Rassemblement pour la République* (RPR) and the Giscardian-created *Union pour la*

Démocratie française (UDF) – shared the pro-European sentiments of the *Parti socialiste* (PS), albeit with different emphases. With the broad consensus on Europe across these three main organisations, it was left to the smaller movements – the *Front National* (FN), the *Parti communiste français* (PCF) and the *Verts* (Greens) – to mark their differences and propose alternative, more critical, European visions.

The nature of the electoral system for the EP elections in France made it likely that all the above parties would be represented at Strasbourg. Indeed, as Reif has pointed out,[2] there is a considerable difference between the two ballot majority systems (*scrutin d'arrondissement*) used for national elections since 1958 and the single ballot system of proportional representation adopted by President Giscard d'Estaing for the 1979 EP elections and retained thereafter. Essentially, the latter system treats France as a single Euro-constituency with its allotted quota of 81 seats. Each competing list or party submits the names of 81 candidates and electors are not allowed to change the order of the list, which receives seats proportional to votes obtained. However, no list achieving under five per cent of actual voters is allowed representation or the return of their 100 000 francs deposit – a regulation which penalised minor parties (especially Trotskyists and Ecologists) in previous EP elections.

In the 1984 EP election[3] the RPR and UDF submitted a joint list under the leadership of Simone Veil. The election was seen as a mid-term verdict on the French Socialist Party, elected to high office in 1981, but increasingly unpopular by 1984. Consequently, the UDF–RPR list triumphed with approximately 43 per cent (41 MEPs) against the PS's 20.7 per cent (20 MEPs). The 1984 election was significant particularly for the emergence and success of the National Front (FN) – 11 per cent, 10 MEPs – and the decimation of the PCF – 11 per cent, 10 MEPs – which lost half its 1979 voters and MEPs. To some extent, the 1984 election was a watershed in French politics as the FN became established with further electoral successes, and the PCF continued to decline. At the same time, Laurent Fabius replaced Pierre Mauroy as premier, thereby confirming the Socialists' drift towards the centre, whilst the right pursued union as a means of winning elections.

The entry of the extreme right-wing FN to the European Parliament resulted in the creation of a Euro-right transnational party group centred on a Franco-Italian (MSI) axis with the FN's Jean-Marie Le Pen as President. Opponents of the extreme right reacted vigorously by rejecting all Euro-right proposals, ostracising the movement and drawing up an anti-racist report. Obviously, the PS, inside the CSP and the EP's Socialist Group, and the PCF, attached to the Communist and Allies Group, took part in these processes. The group attachments of the traditional French right (RPR, UDF) were characterised by division as their joint Euro-list split into three separate groups: the RPR Gaullists (20 MEPs) combined with the Irish Fianna Fail in the European Alliance for Renewal and Democracy, the Christian Democratic wing of the UDF (10 MEPs) joined the European People's Party and the remaining UDF 11 MEPs sat with the European Liberal, Democratic and Reform group. A significant feature of the French contingent inside the EP, therefore, was the clear fragmentation and Balkanisation of the 81 MEPs. In terms of voting on and conceptualising European integration, the picture was further complicated as some UDF representatives had more in common with the PS than their right-wing colleagues. Similarly, the PCF and RPR MEPs shared a common, longstanding mistrust of supranationalism and perceived threats to national sovereignty. Two other noteworthy features of the French pattern were, first, the low estimation of an MEP's status compared to membership of the French National Assembly or even lesser elective offices and, second, bad attendance. As regards the latter, FN MEPs were the best attenders in the years 1984–89, with an overall participation level of 70 per cent and the PCF MEPs worst, with an overall participation rate of 51 per cent.[4] However, at 94 per cent, a single PCF MEP (Robert Chambeiron) held the best attendance record. A notorious relapse occurred recently when, by a narrow majority and with decisive French absentees, the EP voted to approve the construction of an EP building in Brussels. In theory, the Socialist government's reform of the *cumul* (that is, the simultaneous accumulation of various elected offices) should mitigate against bad attendance after June 1989. Unsurprisingly, attendance at the EP emerged as an issue in the campaign, to which we now turn.

CAMPAIGN

The immediate political context of the 1989 EP election campaign was of the left in office. Apart from 1986–88, when the right won a parliamentary but, significantly, not a presidential, majority, the PS and allies had monopolised the major levers of political office since

May 1981, following Mitterrand's ousting of Giscard as President of the Republic. Subsequently, the 1988 presidential and parliamentary elections had left Mitterrand with an impressive presidential majority and a Socialist minority government. Astutely, Mitterrand appointed ex-rival Michel Rocard (PS) as premier and the EP elections followed, therefore, a year of 'moderate' socialist rule, incorporating various ministerial recruits from the centre-*cum*-right, converts to the PS's policy of *ouverture*. Primarily, both Mitterrand and Rocard practised consensus-orientated politics and reaped the rewards with high personal opinion poll ratings, well above all political rivals and parties. As the celebrations for the bicentenary of the French Revolution proceeded, observers even commented on the monarchical status of President Mitterrand, reminiscent of de Gaulle. Rocard's success rested on a mixture of factors: improved economic indicators, sensitive management of the New Caledonian problem, willingness to dialogue and compromise to contain social unrest, practice of political *ouverture*, favourable municipal election results and so on. Certainly, the personal standings of Mitterrand and Rocard should not be interpreted as an absence of problems or a consensus within the PS. This would be erroneous. Nevertheless, the Socialists enjoyed the luxury of a very divided opposition, much in evidence in the years 1988–89.

Right-wing divisions spilled over into the EP election campaign. In brief, the right was divided on questions of leadership, strategy, structures and tactics. In fact, throughout the 1982–89 period, the right had continually failed, except in 1986, to turn an apparent electoral majority on the first ballot of elections into a winning formula on the decisive second ballot. Fratricide, the FN's presence and skilful manoeuvring by Mitterrand all contributed to this situation. In 1989 accumulated right-wing failures released a well-publicised multi-dimensional movement of self-criticism, embracing demands for renovation and reform of the right.

Initially, this development threatened to swamp the right's EP campaign. An articulate, media-conscious, cross-party nucleus of younger politicians increasingly set the agenda following the municipal elections (March 1989). Galvanised by defeats and the unwelcome prospect of another decade in opposition, they wanted *inter alia* new structures and leaders, political decentralisation and greater freedom of expression within their respective parties. At first, it seemed likely that these so-called *rénovateurs* would present their own list in the EP elections – unless one of them headed a united right-wing list. In the event, the French right's *two* lists were championed by familiar faces, Giscard and Veil. The *rénovateurs* declined places on these lists, took up respective, dutiful positions within the support committees for the two right-wing candidates and, in part, postponed their crusade until after the election. However, to retain their momentum, the *rénovateurs* tabled a pre-election motion of censure in the National Assembly against the Socialists' European policy. Mitterrand, Rocard and Co. were charged with insufficient preparation for 1993 in spheres such as competitiveness, training and fiscal harmonisation. In practice, the censure motion did not trouble seriously the government but revealed the divisions on the right, as many RPR parliamentarians refused to support the motion in protest against the demands and impatience of the *rénovateurs*.

Turbulence on the right spilled over into the EP election campaign. The latter represented both a stage and parenthesis in right-wing soul-searching. The right's campaign was characterised by division, personified by the two lists. The RPR and most of the UDF favoured a single electoral list headed by Giscard with the RPR's general-secretary, Alain Juppé, second on the list. According to Giscard, a united list was capable of achieving about 40 per cent of the poll, as in 1984, and inflicting a crushing defeat on the PS. RPR leader and ex-premier Jacques Chirac supported this logic and acted as president of the list's national support committee. In contrast, the Christian Democratic wing of the UDF, the *Centre des démocrates sociaux* (CDS), favoured separate lists on the basis that the strategy would maximise the right-wing vote, equilibriate the French right towards centre-rightism and respect the identity of different components of the right. Supporters of this viewpoint claimed that elections would be won or lost in the centre ground of French politics, as Mitterrand had demonstrated. Hence, Simone Veil's list was presented as a complement, not as a threat, to the UDF–RPR list. Moreover, it was argued, the electoral system encouraged separate lists and worked against the traditional advice to 'vote usefully'. Unsurprisingly, this interpretation was not shared by the UDF–RPR camp, which portrayed Veil and her supporters as divisive and prone to future seduction by the Socialist Party.

Giscard and Co. tried to point out that there were no basic differences on the right over the EC. Allegedly, the RPR had abandoned its reservations about European integration – evident in the 1979 campaign[5] when Veil and Giscard opposed Chirac – and an identity of views prevailed. This was underlined via the Madelin

(UDF) – de la Malène (RPR) report which pioneered the common UDF–RPR platform, *Pour Une Europe Unie*. However, Giscard's promise to campaign 'in the centre' was not appreciated by the arch-Gaullist wing of the RPR. For instance, Michel Debré – who in 1979 had led (with Chirac) the RPR list – now counselled ballot-spoilation. Also, ex-Interior Minister (1986–88) and RPR leader in the Senate chamber, Charles Pasqua, publicly accepted the list 'without enthusiasm', feeling the RPR had sacrificed identity, voters and seats in an unhealthy compromise. For Pasqua, the RPR needed to affirm its Gaullist roots more emphatically and circumvent the defection of working-class 'popular' voters to the FN. In short, 'union at any price' or 'fusion in confusion' was rejected. For Chirac, union was not an end in itself but 'a decisive stage in the task of reconstruction and renovation' of the right.[6] Yet, according to some critics, the RPR had been outmanoeuvred tactically on the right, leaving the UDF with two access routes (via Giscard or Veil) to the EP and, more seriously, providing Giscard with a pedestal to resurrect his political credibility – and possibly once again lead the French right. Clearly, therefore, there were domestic considerations at stake in the formation of right-wing lists with the leadership and nature of the French right on the agenda.

In an attempt to defuse reservations about his leadership, Giscard played down any intentions of using the EP election for domestic advantage. He promised not to be a candidate for the French presidency – except in 'exceptional circumstances'![7] Instead, other worthy positions would be retained or coveted – the presidencies of the National Assembly's Foreign Affairs Committee, the European Liberal Democratic and Reform (ELDR) group and, possibly, the EP or even the EC – if European integration moves in this direction. In many respects, Giscard was an ideal leader for the UDF–RPR list. As ex-president of France, his international status was assured. As president, he had played a major role in such initiatives as the European Council, the European Monetary System and the first direct elections to the EP. Since defeat in 1981, Giscard had assumed the role of right-wing federator and architect of union – notwithstanding his preference for *two* Euro-lists on the right in 1984! Further, despite his image as 'a politician of the past' he partook of many of the *rénovateurs*' hopes for reconstructing the French right in the parameters of a single confederation or movement. Indeed, his writings of the 1970s[8] called for the modernisation of French politics and, for Giscard, an obvious route was evolution towards a *de facto* two-party system.

Against Veil's list, Giscard enjoyed the lion's share of right-wing support including 90 per cent of the RPR's national council, over three quarters of the UDF's national council, eighteen (out of nineteen) presidents of France's twenty-two regional councils, the right-wing majority in the Senate (including CDS senators) plus the backing of various minor right-wing parties and socio-professional interests throughout the country. To appease the mounting cacophony for reform, Giscard was careful to present a young Euro-list with dynamic forty-year-olds in 'electable' positions – Juppé (2), François Léotard (3), Michèle Barzach (4) and so on. As regards list formation, order of placement is crucial since only the higher-placed individuals are assured of election. Lower positions, therefore, are useful for enlisting declarations of support, encouraging future leaders or recognising the merits of various individuals or causes. Two notable names on the UDF–RPR list were Alain Pompidou (20) and Charles de Gaulle (39), son and grandson respectively of former right-wing presidents. The UDF–RPR list placed candidates in rotation – one UDF followed by one RPR – with a few places reserved for 'outsiders' to testify to the openness of the list, and reassure diverse lobbies. However, compared to some other lists, the UDF–RPR camp demonstrated few *ouvertures* and, consequently, was attacked by Veil as a list of *apparatchiks*, 'a cold and monolithic right'.

Veil's supporters also criticised the UDF–RPR list as a temporary, opportunist marriage of convenience, combining European federalists with diehard nationalists. Allegedly, it would disintegrate once the 1995 presidential election intervened – a distant but omnipresent preoccupation. Veil's camp persisted with the accusation that the RPR and UDF cherished different conceptions of Europe. For Veil, the RPR had 'neither the same programme, nor the same enthusiasm or ambition' for Europe as the UDF. From this perspective, Giscard had abandoned the UDF leadership and diluted policies for the cause of an 'unnatural alliance'. In the light of Veil's leadership of a joint UDF–RPR list in 1984, this argument involved some contortions. Veil contended that the circumstances of all-out opposition to the PS–PCF coalition in 1984 provided a different context to 1989. Now, she tried to pinpoint the policy difference between her centre list and Giscard's UDF–RPR coalition. Consequently, Veil criticised the UDF–RPR's over-cautious time-scale for European integration and economic and monetary union, singling out the social dimension, a citizens' Europe and votes for all Europeans in local elections as distinguishing policies. Another key theme was morality in politics: none on her list had compromised with the FN.

Veil's list exhibited more openness than Giscard's with 40 per cent of places reserved for non-CDS individuals such as the film director, Claude Lelouch (thirteenth). According to Veil, her list was not centrist (that is, CDS) but a centre-orientated list drawing in civil society – and even boasting a sole RPR rebel (Jean-Louis Borlanges, in an electable seventh position). Certainly, there were some reservations inside the CDS about adopting a non-CDS individual as their candidate.[9] Also, as President Giscard's Minister of Health, her pioneering of abortion liberalisation had offended Catholic sentiments.

However, Veil's popularity would appeal to a wider audience than the CDS's electorate. Like Giscard, she was a political 'heavyweight' with good European credentials, notably as the first president of the directly-elected EP and party group leader therein. Moreover, she had headed a list in three consecutive EP elections. In 1979, as Giscard's standard-bearer, she had outdistanced easily the RPR, PS and PCF lists. In 1984, too, her joint UDF–RPR list topped the poll comfortably. In 1989, she now opted for a separate list to provide the potential right-wing voter with more choice. Additionally, Veil represented a French centre-*cum*-centre-right liberated from the dominant *Parti républicain* (PR) inside the UDF. The Christian Democratic and centrist CDS rested uncomfortably within the UDF alongside the free-market liberals of the PR – Léotard, Madelin and Gerard Lonquet, principally. The EP elections, then, consummated a gradual growing-apart of these elements – a process accelerated in June 1988 with the creation of a *Union de Centre* (UDC) separate group within the National Assembly and under Pierre Méhaignerie's CDS leadership. Veil's number two on the Euro-list, Jean-Louis Borloo, located the list as equidistant from the PS and UDF–RPR lists but, in fact, Veil expressed closer proximity to Giscard whilst marking the differences between lists. Inevitably, posing as the centre *and* the right simultaneously raised identity problems – not least since Giscard and Veil would sit in the same ELDR group at the EP.

In terms of policies, Veil's manifesto for European unity was predictably pro-European: support for a new European treaty to achieve political union before the Year 2000, a citizens' and people's Europe, a European bank, stronger European institutions – including the EP, economic and monetary union, European defence policy, an effective European environmental agency and so on. Targeting the

UDF–RPR list in particular, Veil promised full attendance and participation at the EP. Of course, she needed to exaggerate the differences between the two lists to justify her candidature. In fact, Giscard also incorporated a heavy dosage of 'Europeanism' in his programme – stronger EC institutions, a new treaty, economic and monetary union, European defence and so on. In short, the two platforms were very similar. Opinion polls confirmed this. In one poll, 52 per cent (against 20 per cent) perceived little or no difference between the two right-wing lists. Furthermore, 42 per cent (against 29 per cent) saw little or no difference between Veil and the PS on European policies.[10]

Giscard and Veil agreed with the main objectives of Mitterrand's European policy whilst contesting the details. Nevertheless, in the EP campaign, the two sides attacked each other for different conceptions of Europe. According to Giscard, there was an 'enormous difference' between 'a liberal and social Europe' and 'a bureaucratic and socialist Europe'[11] Both Giscard and Veil (and the PCF especially) were unwilling to let the Socialists monopolise the social dimension of 1993. In turn, the PS proposed a Europe of social progress against the right's *laissez-faire* view of 1993. The social dimension constituted the main plank of the Socialists' programme, echoing the broad manifesto of the CSP. For the leader of the PS's list, Laurent Fabius, it was a stark choice between 'the Europe of Thatcher' or 'the Europe of Mitterrand'. Certain pan-European left-wing issues were given priority in Fabius' campaign: job creation, a European charter of fundamental social rights, solidarity with the Third World, social justice (coupled with economic efficiency), reversal of the EC's 'democratic deficit' and, hence, stronger powers for national and European parliaments. Like his rivals, Fabius adapted his discourse to his audience. In Quimper (Brittany), therefore, where the Greens were strong and ecology a regional concern, Fabius referred to the environment as 'our principal worry'. Elsewhere, unemployment, a 'Europe for the regions' or reassurances for French overseas areas predominated as themes. Moreover, various proposals were common to the PS and the French right, such as economic and monetary union, a European bank and environmental agency. In fact, *République moderne*, the left-wing *courant* inside the party under Jean-Pierre Chevenement's inspiration, criticised the 'soft' consensus on Europe and demanded (unsuccessfully) a more radical critique of European integration, incorporating reservations about economic liberalism, loss of sovereignty and Atlanticism. Fabius was challenged by Giscard to a televised debate about Europe but, tactically (and possibly recalling a bruising experience with Chirac on television), Fabius refused to face Giscard without Veil.

Fabius was seen as Mitterrand's choice for leading the Socialists' European list. Since 1984, Fabius had emerged as the preferred *dauphin* of the president. In 1984 (–86), Fabius became Mitterrand's young premier, replacing Pierre Mauroy (1981–84) and rapidly acquiring a reputation for managerial socialism, centre-leftism and consensus politics. In 1988, though, Fabius was unable to recapture the premiership – as Mitterrand opted for the more popular Michel Rocard – or the leadership of the Socialist Party, which went to Mauroy. In compensation, Fabius acquired the presidency of the French National Assembly and used this base to establish his candidature in 1989. In truth, few colleagues wished to lead the EP campaign since EP elections were not seen as good occasions for mobilising support. In 1979, Mitterrand's list had polled 22.3 per cent, with Lionel Jospin's list falling to 20.7 per cent in 1984. The only serious contenders to Fabius, hinted at, were Jacques Delors, currently Commission President and the recently-elected mayor of Strasbourg, Catherine Trautmann, a 'Rocardian'.

To Fabius, the EP election had potentially useful domestic connotations. First, electioneering would provide an opportunity to raise his profile and refine a somewhat austere public image. Second, success would help to re-establish his credibility as a contender for the highest political offices after Mitterrand's departure. Fabius hitched his campaign to Mitterrand's European policy, a step not fully appreciated by some Socialists – fearful of a bad result lowering the president's high popularity ratings. Campaign literature or posters showed Mitterrand with Helmut Kohl, and Fabius in the company of dignitaries such as Mitterrand, Mikhail Gorbachev and George Bush. Fabius depended naturally upon fellow-socialists to mobilise support, with campaign material targeting locally and regionally elected figures as well as seven million selected voters. In practice, Mitterrand (as president) played no conspicuously active role in the campaign and Rocard and Mauroy provided loyal but hardly enthusiastic backing. Fabius promised a 'short, powerful and Europedagogic' campaign, which was personalised and Kennedyesque. Ostensibly, it appealed to an audience wider than the PS but, ultimately, failed to mobilise the party sufficiently. Jospin and Mauroy enjoyed a better rapport than Fabius with party militants, some of whom were unimpressed by the spectacle of Fabius' campaign, premier Rocard's dilution of socialism and the government's and Euro-list's openings to external personalities. Collectively, these factors limited the party rank and file's input in June 1989. Probably anticipating the difficulty of mobilising militants throughout a consensual period, Mitterrand did at least encourage Interior Minister Pierre Joxe to reform Pasqua's legislation to restrict the conditions of entry and residence of foreigners. This reform, introduced during the election campaign, served to pacify rank-and-file Socialists and the immigration lobby, besides throwing a usefully divisive semi-dormant issue to the French right.

As with opponents, list formation was a delicate operation for the Socialists. Internal party tendencies or *courants* were already flexing their political muscles in preparation for the 1990 conference which would discuss the nature of contemporary French socialism. Fabius needed to ensure representation on the Euro-list for the main *courants*. Also, roughly every fifth position was reserved for outsiders to enhance the practice of *ouverture* and reflect the 'presidential majority', which included a quota of non-socialist ministers in Rocard's administration. Second on Fabius' list was Catherine Trautmann – young, dynamic, Strasbourgeois *and* female. Elsewhere, there were electable places for allies on the left and right – the (MRG) Radicals and the *Association des Démocrates*, respectively. The promotion of Alain Bompard, the PS's 'green' Euro-specialist, was an indication of the concern with ecological issues *and* rivals (the Greens). In 1979, Bompard occupied the thirty-third rung, and in 1984 the ninth position; in 1989 he ranked fourth. Amongst the places of *ouverture* were André Sainjon (fifteenth) and a former PCF/ CGT trade union leader, Nora Zäidi (twentieth) from *SOS Racisme* and two prominent individuals from the world of medicine, in fifth and eleventh positions. The composition and focus were reflected in the official title of the list, *Majorité de progrès pour l'Europe*.

An interesting campaign initiative was the meeting between Mauroy and Achilles Occhetto, the Italian Communist Party (PCI) leader. This was interpreted as an attempt to revive the 'Euro-left' idea, undercut the PCF and further drive a wedge between the pro-European PCI and more negative PCF. In 1989, the PCF's European list was led not by party-leader George Marchais, as in 1979 and 1984, but by Philippe Herzog, a party intellectual. Although a member of PCF's Central Committee and co-author of a recent book on 1993[12] Herzog was not well-known throughout France so image-building was expedient.

L'Humanité, the PCF's daily press, called for a real debate on Europe to replace the prevalent 'consensual fog'. Herzog's manifesto emphasised especially the themes of justice, peace, sovereignty and wider European cooperation. In particular, the PCF campaigned against the SEM and pointed to the discrepancy between the PS's 'demagogic' rhetoric and actual practice, as regards the social dimension. For the PCF, European integration was synonymous with social regression, national demise, overarmament and multinational capitalism. Opinion polls tended to portray the PCF as the least European party in France, but Herzog rejected the charge of anti-Europeanism, opting instead for a Europe built via 'popular' social struggles as opposed to 'a Europe of capitalists and speculators', a Europe for 'a golden elite'.

To boost the PCF's campaign, ex-government minister Jacques Ralite (number ten on Herzog's list) organised a declaration of support from various national and international figures from the world of culture – such as artists, musicians and film directors. Also, trade-union backing was evident at the forty-third *Confédération générale des travailleurs* (CGT) conference just before the election. Henri Krasucki, the CGT's general-secretary, adhered to the PCF whilst ex-CGT leader, Georges Séguy was on Herzog's list. The latter was primarily a party list with only token practice of political *ouverture*. The PCF was confronted by a rival list of mainly ex-PCF militants and *rénovateurs* – besides growing internal dissent from so-called *reconstructeurs*. The 1980s had witnessed the decline of the hitherto powerful party, with the 1984 EP election registering significant losses (see above). In 1989, like the PS, the PCF feared the demobilisation of its (already declining) electorate – via abstentions – as well as potential losses to the Socialists, the Greens and the FN.

As usual, there were distinctly Gaullist nuances to the PCF campaign, with the party posing as the sole defender of national sovereignty. In fact, this attribute was shared by the National Front. Ironically, in view of the FN's bitter condemnation of de Gaulle over Algerian independence, the extreme right-wing now campaigned as the best exponents of 'a Europe of *patries* and nations'. Giscard's inclination to campaign in the centre and the RPR's apparent conversion to further European integration left FN leader, Jean-Marie Le Pen, as the unlikely usurper of Gaullist values. Of course, the UDF–RPR leadership was conscious of the threat posed by the FN. Giscard was careful to include nationalist references and immigration control in his speeches. RPR voices, too, were more inclined to stress the nation-state dimension. Giscard's preference was for 'a union of European states' rather than a United States of Europe or a Europe of *patries*. Within this context, the conversion of Yvan Blot (number five on Le Pen's list), ex-RPR parliamentarian, was a useful coup. Blot initiated the nascent French committee for a Europe of *patries* – inspired by Margaret Thatcher's Bruges speech (1988) and de Gaulle's anti-supranationalism – and urged Gaullists to vote for Le Pen.

According to Le Pen, the construction of Europe was 'useful and necessary' – particularly in the defence sphere, where the FN wanted further integration – but the choice was essentially between 'a geographically, politically and culturally defined Europe' or 'a cosmopolitan and multiracial Europe', a 'resolutely patriotic' Europe or 'a socialist *mondialiste*, utopian, adventure'.[13] Much of the FN's campaign was anchored around the theme of French identity ('a French France in a European Europe') with strong reservations about the opening of frontiers (to immigrants? or terrorists?) via the Single European Act. In particular, the movement opposed the right to vote in any European local Elections, construing this as leading to the right of immigrants to vote.

As to the list formation, Le Pen picked his team virtually single-handed after soundings from colleagues. Priority was given to efficiency and specialisms to contend with the technical nature of much European business. Consequently, less-favoured was the more populist and extremist 'old guard', in part associated with the late Jean-Pierre Stirbois. The pro-Vichy film-maker, Claude Autant-Lara, enjoyed a position of opening but, apart from Blot, the list was not marked by electable *ouvertures*. Again, the title of the list, *Europe et patrie*, summed up the emphasis.

If the FN constituted the Achilles heel of the French right, the Greens threatened the left in a similar manner. Antoine Waechter, leader of the Greens and French presidential candidate in 1988, managed to commit his movement to a depoliticised 'neither left nor right stance'. Yet, voting analyses and opinion polls tended to locate ecologist voters primarily to the left of the political spectrum.[14] Ex-presidential candidate (1981) Brice Lalonde perceived ecologist voters as 'leaning to the left without toppling over'. However, the Greens were unhappy with left-wing critiques of ecological politics and, in turn, critical of government policy. In 1989, the Greens resisted attempts – notably by the New Left elements such as Pierre Juquin (ex-PCF and 1988 presidential candidate) – to penetrate the movement with a view to promoting an 'ecosocialism'. Similarly, Waechter opposed the influence of the West German Grünen allies, interpreting the latter's active support for communist *rénovateurs* (the MRC) as 'very unfriendly' and 'regrettable'.[15] Waechter aspired to consolidate *and* equilibriate the Greens' presence in the EP, redirecting the movement away from the dominance of the left-orientated radicalism of the Grünen and the eclectic disorganisation of the Rainbow Group.

The Greens' manifesto stressed the themes of regionalism and solidarity, with the list entitled *Les Verts – Europe – Ecologie: Pour une Europe des régions et des peuples solidaires*. Besides the obvious themes of environmental protection, energy resources, the quality of life and anti-nuclearism, the manifesto urged solidarity with the Third World, the regions, the unemployed, the young and the old. The Greens expressed strong reservations about the SEM, fearing that free-market profiteering would outweigh the social and ecological dimensions. Consequently, the Greens were criticised by the Environment Minister (Brice Lalonde) for anti-Europeanism. Ecologist concerns were illustrated by the high degree of *ouverture* on Waechter's list, openings which might easily deflate Waechter's aim for greater coordination at Strasbourg. For example, 20 of the 81 places were reserved for outsiders, albeit only three in electable positions. Amongst the causes espoused, thereby, were second-generation immigration, regionalism (with Corsican Max Simeoni in third place), the Third World and the unemployment lobby. Prominent on the list were veterans of political ecology who had led the challenge in previous diverse elections – Réné Dumont, Solange Fernex, Didier Anger and Yves Cochet.

The five per cent quota threshold had prevented ecologists taking up seats in 1979 and 1984. In 1989, however, good municipal election, by-election and opinion polls suggested that Waechter would double his 1988 presidential share of the poll (approximately 4 per cent). Of course, the 1980s had witnessed a growth in green politics across Europe, with the French Greens increasingly amongst the vanguard. The 1988 presidential campaign had realised an influx of new members. The holding of the fifth conference of European greens in Paris, before the European elections, was a useful tribute to the growth of the movement – as, indeed, was Waechter's invitation to the prestigious *L'Heure de Vérité* television programme.

As well as the main parties, the electorate was faced with a myriad of smaller lists – including Trotskyists, dissident communists, animal-lovers and hunters. These are too many to discuss here; suffice to say that, in 1979, eleven lists contested the election, in 1984 fourteen, and in 1989 fifteen. When the campaign closed, voters were left with the impression of an election of limited passion, debate or interest compared to other occasions. Presentation and perfection of electoral communication techniques were in evidence virtually as much as policy. Nevertheless, certain themes (European and national) predominated, such as the place and identity of France in the emerging Europe of the 1990s; the near-widespread mandatory condemnation of 'Eurocracy', 'technocracy' or other vote-conscious labels; the willingness to practise or preach *ouverture*; and the social-*cum*-environmental dimensions. Besides the European agenda, French political forces were preoccupied with discussion about domestic and intra-party concerns. Generally, the PS managed to restrict debate (about French socialism) until after the election but, for the right, this proved less easy – not least since the existence of three rival lists (Giscard, Veil, Le Pen) illustrated graphically the problem of division facing the right. The results of the election would, of course, contribute to these questions.

RESULTS

With some exceptions, the polls predicted a victory of sorts for the UDF–RPR list. Unable to achieve a single right-wing list, Giscard's modest target was to surpass Fabius. Veil aspired to about 15 per cent although real expectations were slightly lower. Optimistically, Le Pen hoped to double his number of MEPs (to twenty) or, at least, recapture his 1988 presidential share of the poll (14.4 per cent). Fabius, again modestly, aimed to improve on Jospin's 1984 poll (20.7 per cent), the PCF to likewise emulate 1984 returns, whilst the Greens aspired to about ten per cent of voters and between five and ten MEPs. Much depended on turnout.

As anticipated, abstentions were high and, at 48.8 per cent, turnout was down on 1984 (66.7 per cent) and 1979 (60.7 per cent). Various reasons were offered for the low poll: electoral weariness, apathy, lack of interest in the election, distraction of world events (China, Iran, USSR), the demobilising consensus on Europe, and so on. Three of the principal lists (Waechter, Le Pen and Giscard) had some cause for satisfaction but the others (Fabius, Veil and Herzog) suffered major disappointments. Amongst the smaller lists, the

Table 7.1   The 1989 European Election in France

	Votes	%	Seats
Union UDF–RPR (Giscard)	5 241 354	28.80	26
Centre (Veil)	1 528 931	8.42	7
Socialist Party (Fabius)	4 284 734	23.61	22
National Front (Le Pen)	2 128 589	11.73	10
Greens (Waechter)	1 922 353	10.59	9
Communist Party (Herzog)	1 399 939	7.71	7
Others	1 639 688	9.06	–

Source: European Parliament EP News

'hunters' (*Chasse, pêche et tradition*) scored a creditable 4.13 per cent against Brussels' 'interference' in traditional leisure pursuits. All the smaller lists lost their deposits. Overall, political commentators interpreted the election as a blow to established political parties since, due to abstentions and the proliferation of lists, the two main lists aggregated only one in four voters.[16]

At almost 29 per cent, Giscard signalled his return to the forefront of French politics and achieved the twenty-six seats roughly targeted. Fabius's 23.61 per cent (twenty-two seats) surpassed Jospin's 1984 percentage and won two extra seats but trailed decisively behind Giscard, and well behind 1988 PS returns in the presidential and parliamentary elections. Abstentions and the rise of the Greens clearly hit the PS but, outside Rocard and Mitterrand, it is arguable whether another individual could have improved upon Fabius's result. In short, EP elections are not the PS's forte. Certainly, there were some misgivings on Fabius's part about the failure of the PS to mobilise support. Equally, within the party, there were criticisms about his campaign style. Fabius's result is not a very positive base to relaunch his leadership intentions although, collectively, the right had lost eight seats and about six percentage points since 1984. At 8.42 per cent (seven seats) Veil's poll was a failure for French centrism as an autonomous political force and a disincentive to reconstruct a movement outside the main parties. Veil regretted the failure of local elites ('betrayal by *notables*') to mobilise support but, clearly, the strategy of two lists backfired.

Outside the PS–UDF–RPR galaxies, Le Pen's performance (not for the first time) limited right-wing success. At 11.73 per cent (ten seats), Le Pen polled the highest FN share of the poll apart from the 1988 presidential election. The movement had now maintained its position in French politics over a number of years and diverse elections since 1983, indicating stabilisation of the extreme right's electorate. In the Provence–Alpes–Côte d'Azur region (21.18 per cent) especially, the movement maintained its high profile, leaving the UDF and RPR with the familiar problem of facing up to the FN's influence. Predictably, Le Pen used his results to reiterate the fact that without the FN the right lacked a majority.

For the PCF, decline continued as Herzog recorded only a marginally better share of the poll (7.7 per cent, seven seats) than André Lajoinie (6.8 per cent), the PCF's 1988 presidential candidate – but, on a lower poll, many less actual voters. Reporting to the Central Committee,[17] Marchais claimed the vote did not reflect real party support, blaming the absence of debate and events in China for the PCF's losses. Herzog interpreted the results as a blow against the actual form of European integration.

Internal and external critics, however, blamed Marchais' leadership and the lack of genuine *perestroika* for the results. Without doubt, the most striking feature of the EP election was the good performance of the Greens (10.59 per cent, nine seats), a breakthrough reflected across Europe. In Waechter's Alsace (18.30 per cent) and Simeoni's Corsica (15.49 per cent) the Greens polled well. Waechter viewed the Greens' success as a victory for the ecologists' independent strategy and a vote for new environmental perspectives within *la classe politique*.

AFTERMATH

Following the election, attention reverted to the domestic debates on the reform of the right and the nature of French socialism. For example, Mauroy sent a letter to all militants affirming the need for the PS to identify itself in a period of consensual politics. Giscard translated his European vote as a referendum for union, even fusion, but rivals resisted his attempt to force through an immediate reconstruction of the right. The RPR – despite Juppé's and Chirac's roles – found it impossible to deprive Giscard of *his* Euro victory but, still, opted for a piecemeal process of reform. Younger political leaders, notably Léotard, looked with impatient frustration at the prospect of Giscard's rehabilitation via Europe. Indeed, Giscard now emerged as the most popular figure on the right with vastly improved opinion-poll ratings and good support for his policy of right-wing union. To enhance unity, Giscard hoped all the French right-wing MEPs would sit together, but a familiar pattern of disintegration recurred. The neo-Gaullist MEPs renewed the alliance with Fianna Fail whilst the UDF divided along usual lines (see above). Divisions were evident elsewhere involving France's MEPs as the PCI moved away from alliance with the PCF, the Italian MSI parted company with the FN and the Greens marked their distance from the Rainbow Group. The consequence of all these developments was to leave French MEPs more fragmented than ever with *six* European lists feeding into *nine* European groupings.

Nevertheless, in mid-1989, the French influence – particularly the PS's – across Europe was very pronounced. Mitterrand (European Council), Delors (European Commission) and Catherine Lalumière (Council of Europe), all headed important institutions. Also, no less than five French politicians were elected presidents of the eleven Euro-groups in the new European Parliament: Giscard (Liberal, Democratic and Reformist Group), Jean-Pierre Cot (Socialist Group), Christian de la Malène (European Democratic Alliance), Jean-Marie Le Pen (European Right) and Réné-Emile Piquet (Left Unity). In addition, Antoine Waechter became chairperson of the Regional Policy and Planning Committee. Abstentionism and apathy at home did not dilute the important ongoing French political elite contribution to the construction of Europe.

NOTES AND REFERENCES

1. See F. Mitterrand, *Lettre à tous les français*, electoral manifesto, (Paris, 1988). P. Hainsworth, 'The Re-election of François Mitterrand: The French Presidential Election of 1988', *Parliamentary Affairs*, Vol. 41, no. 4, October (1988) 536–47.
2. K. Reif, 'France' in K. Reif (ed.), *Ten European Elections*, (Aldershot: Saxon House, 1984) p. 87.
3. J. and M. Charlot, 'France', in *Electoral Studies*, 3:3 (1984) 274–7.
4. *Libération*, 17/18 June 1989.
5. J. C. Hollick, 'The European Election of 1979 in France: A Masked Ball for 1981', *Parliamentary Affairs*, XXXII No. 4 (1979), 459–69.
6. *Le Figaro*, 20 April 1989.
7. *Le Monde*, 31 May 1989.
8. V. Giscard d'Estaing, *La Démocratie française* (Paris: Fayard, 1976).
9. Veil belongs to the *adhérents directs* component of the UDF.
10. *L'Express*, 16 June 1989.

11. *Le Monde*, 23 May 1989.
12. P. Herzog and Y. Dimicoli, *Europe 92: Construire autrement et autre chose* (Paris: Messidor/Editions Sociales, 1989).
13. Jean-Marie Le Pen, *L'Espoir* (Paris: Albatros, 1989).
14. See *Le Nouvel Observateur*, 22–8 June 1989.
15. *Le Monde*, 16 June 1989.
16. For a comprehensive area-by-area analysis of the elections see 'Résultats des Elections Européennes (Juin 1988). L'embellie des Verts', *Le Monde, Dossiers et Documents*, July 1989.
17. *L'Humanité*, 23 June 1989.

8 Ireland
MICHAEL GALLAGHER

INTRODUCTION

The EP elections, held in Ireland on 15 June, fell two years and four months after the previous general election. The February 1987 election had produced a Fianna Fail minority government which had embarked on a programme of austerity, stabilising the foreign debt by cuts across the board, including the health services. Despite being in a minority (it won just 81 seats out of 166), the government seemed in a secure parliamentary position, as the second and third largest parties, Fine Gael and the Progressive Democrats, broadly supported its economic policies, with only the small number of left-wing TDs providing wholehearted opposition. The centre-right consensus on the economy meant that Fianna Fail's policies had actually increased its popularity since the election, and the party was registering more than 50 per cent support in the opinion polls. The EP elections, it seemed, would provide a kind of mid-term test of whether the electorate really was as happy with the spending cuts as the polls suggested.

These expectations were rudely shattered on 25 May, when prime minister Charles Haughey dissolved the Dail (the lower house of parliament) and announced that a general election would be held on the same day as the EP elections. From this point on, the EP elections were virtually lost from sight amid the domestic battle.

The elections (both EP and domestic) were contested by seven different parties plus a number of independents. Ireland's largest party, Fianna Fail, joined the French RPR (Gaullists) in the 1984–89 EP in the European Democratic Alliance. A centre-right party with a populist touch, it attaches more importance to the achievement of an all-Ireland republic than do the other main parties, and tends to be conservative on issues touching on church–state relations. The second main party, Fine Gael, is part of the Christian Democrat/EPP group; it too can be seen as centre-right, with a more middle-class support base than Fianna Fail. It attaches a greater priority to the achievement of consensus within Northern Ireland than to the attainment of an all-Ireland republic, and since the late 1970s has been relatively liberal on church–state issues such as divorce.

The third strongest party at the 1987 election was a newcomer on the scene, the Progressive Democrats (PDs). The PDs were formed in December 1985 by some former Fianna Fail TDs (Dail deputies) who had become disaffected with that party and especially with its leader, Charles Haughey. The PDs adopted a broadly Thatcherite approach to the economy, while espousing policies on Northern Ireland and church–state issues similar to those of Fine Gael. Indeed, once the general election was announced, the two parties concluded a 'pact' and announced that their aim was to form a coalition government if they won enough seats.

On the left, the Irish Labour Party is an orthodox member of the Socialist group. The smaller and more left-wing Workers' Party had not joined any European grouping by the time of the elections, and did not say with whom its MEPs, if any were elected, would sit.

Sinn Fein, the political wing of the IRA, has little support in the Republic of Ireland, but decided to contest the EP elections in any case. Ireland's seventh party, the Greens, had always been completely insignificant in electoral terms prior to the 1989 elections.

The electoral system used for both contests was the single transferable vote (STV), which is employed for all public elections in Ireland. STV is a particular variant of proportional representation which enables the voter to rank all candidates, regardless of party, in order of preference. Candidates are certain of election if their vote total reaches the Droop quota, which is defined as the next integer above the figure obtained by dividing the number of votes by the number one greater than the number of seats. In other words, in a three-seat constituency, the quota is one more than a quarter of the votes, in a four-seat constituency one more than a fifth, and so on. If insufficient candidates reach the quota on first preferences, the counting process proceeds by eliminating the lowest-placed candidate and transferring his or her votes according to the second preferences marked, or by distributing the 'surplus' of candidates whose vote totals exceed the quota. Consequently, even if a candidate's number of first preferences does not reach the Droop quota, he or she can still hope to be elected by attracting second and lower preferences from other candidates who are either eliminated from the count through having low support or are elected with a surplus of votes over and above the quota.[1]

The qualifications for voter-eligibility in Ireland are being aged 18 years or over, ordinarily resident in the constituency of registration, and a citizen of Ireland or any other EC state. Irish people based overseas, a large number given the rate of emigration, are not entitled to be on the register. As regards candidacy, anyone not eligible to stand at Dail elections may not do so at an EP election. This excludes non-Irish citizens, those under 21, and the usual list of disqualified persons (the insane, judges and so on). As well as the other categories excluded under EC law, such as government ministers and certain EC officials, Irish law also excludes the Attorney-General. Candidates holding certain other offices, such as the speaker or deputy speaker of the Dail or the Seanad (the upper house of parliament), or that of junior minister, will be deemed to have resigned from that position upon taking up membership of the EP, but are not debarred from standing.

Ireland's 15 MEPs were returned from four multi-member constituencies: Munster returned five MEPs, Dublin four, Leinster and Connacht–Ulster three each. This allocation has remained unaltered since the first EP elections in 1979, but is now anomalous, as the Dublin electorate exceeds that of Munster. The fairest allocation within the existing boundaries would have given three MEPs to Connacht–Ulster and four to each of the other constituencies.

There is no entirely satisfactory way of filling casual vacancies under STV. The method adopted between 1979 and 1984, allowing the party of the vacating member to nominate the successor, attracted considerable criticism when eleven different people occupied Labour's four seats. In 1984 a new approach was adopted; the parties picked in advance, and made available to the voters, an ordered list of 'substitutes' who would fill any vacancies arising. This procedure bore at least a superficial resemblance to the idea of having a party list whose lower names could fill seats vacated by those elected by virtue of having a higher list position, and thus seemed to satisfy the EP. Over the following five years, only two MEPs resigned their seats (Ryan to become an EC Auditor and MacSharry to become Minister for Finance), and the system of substitutes was used again in 1989.

The previous two EP elections had produced contrasting results (see Table 8.1). In 1979, the two major parties had fared poorly; Fianna Fail and Fine Gael each won only about a third of the votes, and between them they captured just 9 of the 15 seats. Labour, with only 14 per cent of the votes, won 4 seats. In addition, two independents were elected: Neil Blaney, a hardline traditional nationalist who had been expelled from Fianna Fail in 1972 took a seat in Connacht–Ulster, and T. J. Maher, a former leader of a major farmers' interest group, was elected in Munster.

Table 8.1   Ireland: results of previous EP elections and 1987 Dail election

	EP election 1979 % Votes	Seats	EP election 1984 % Votes	Seats	General election 1987 % votes
Fianna Fail	34.7	5	39.2	8	44.1
Fine Gael	33.1	4	32.2	6	27.1
PDs	–	–	–	–	11.8
Labour	14.5	4	8.4	0	6.4
Workers' Party	3.3	0	4.3	0	3.8
Others	14.4	2	15.9	1	6.7
TOTAL	100.0	15	100.0	15	100.0
Turnout	61.2		46.4		72.7

In 1984, the major parties struck back.[2] Although their combined vote rose little, they picked up five extra seats. Labour lost all of its MEPs, leaving Ireland as the only EC member state with no representative in any of the left-of-centre groups in the new EP. Fianna Fail took Blaney's seat, and only Maher, who by now had joined the Liberal group in the EP while remaining an independent at home, prevented Fianna Fail and Fine Gael between them making a clean sweep of the seats.

The common theme in 1979 and 1984 had been a swing against the government. The 1979 election came at a low point in the fortunes of the Fianna Fail administration, and the party's poor performance may have speeded up the retirement plans of the then prime minister Jack Lynch. In 1984 a Fine Gael–Labour coalition was in office, and suffered a mid-term rebuff. Labour's loss of all its EP seats strengthened the conviction of anti-coalitionists within the party that coalition with Fine Gael was an unwise tactic, though without fundamentally altering the intra-party balance of forces.

THE CAMPAIGN

It would be fair to say that no Euro-election campaign *per se* ever emerged. Nevertheless, the parties did make efforts, especially before the general election was finally announced, to set out a European agenda.

Manifestos

All parties issued manifestos relating to the EP elections specifically. In many cases these were shortened versions of the manifestos issued by the respective EP grouping, and sometimes omitted any reference at all to areas of controversy.[3] Thus Fianna Fail's manifesto did not commit itself on the question of whether the EP should have additional powers, and the Fine Gael manifesto also did not mention the subject, though the EPP manifesto favoured enlargement of the EP's role.

The PDs' manifesto was rather fuller, urging that the EP 'should be given the power to veto any major Community act that is not supported by a majority of MEPs'. The PDs also wanted Ireland's MEPs to be allowed to attend the Dail (though without having the right to vote there), to contribute to Dail debates, and to ask parliamentary questions on European affairs. The Irish Labour Party also favoured increased power for the EP, like the Socialist group generally, and secured a reference in the Socialist manifesto to Ireland's neutrality. In any case, the almost complete lack of interest shown in the EP manifestos by voters and commentators alike meant that any possible contradictions or oversights contained therein went entirely unremarked.

The candidates

A total of 53 candidates (only seven of them women) stood. A few were chosen late in 1988, but most of the candidate selection conferences took place between January and March 1989. Selection practices vary slightly from party to party, but in essence are the same. Each party held a selection conference in each constituency, attended by delegates (a total of several hundred in the case of Fianna Fail and Fine Gael) from each part of the constituency organisation.

In some cases the head offices of the parties were active in the period before the selection conference, seeking to line up big names from outside the party ranks. Two such candidates eventually emerged, both in the Munster constituency. Fianna Fail persuaded Paddy Lane, a former leader of the Irish Farmers' Association, to take his chance at the party's selection conference, while Fine Gael were able to attract John Cushnahan, former general-secretary of Northern Ireland's cross-community Alliance Party. Both were selected to run in the election. The low salience of EP party group labels in Ireland meant that Cushnahan's decision to stand for Fine Gael rather than the PDs (with whom Alliance were linked through both parties' membership of the Liberals group) caused little comment in itself.

There were no major surprises at the selection conferences. Four MEPs retired (Barrett and Flanagan of Fianna Fail, Clinton and O'Donnell of Fine Gael), and the other 11 were all reselected. In addition, a number of TDs went before the selection conferences, keeping the vexed question of the dual mandate alive. All the Irish parties oppose the dual mandate in principle, but in practice find it hard to resist the temptation to use proven vote-winners as their EP candidates, for want of alternatives. The formula usually adopted by the parties is that any TD elected to the EP will have to decide at the next general election whether to retire from the Dail or resign his or her EP seat. While this had generally been adhered to, each fresh EP election has thrown up a new crop of dual mandate holders, and the cycle has begun again. Going into the 1989 EP election, none of the Irish MEPs also sat in the Dail, but 11 TDs were selected to run in the election. When the general election was called, two of these decided against running for the Dail again, but the other nine, as well as ten other candidates, stood in both elections.

Under the STV electoral system, parties have to decide how many candidates to run in each constituency. Obviously, every party will run at least as many candidates as it hopes to win seats. Running more than this number has its advantages and disadvantages. It probably means that the party will win more first-preference votes, as with a wider geographical spread of candidates in the constituency the ticket will attract more votes. On the other hand, an argument for running the minimum number is that every time one of a party's candidates is eliminated from the count, some of his or her votes will 'leak' away to other parties, perhaps to candidates from the same part of the constituency, even though most will transfer to the eliminated candidate's running mates. Generally speaking, the main parties adopted the latter line of thought, and nominated fewer rather than more candidates. Fianna Fail and Fine Gael each ran nine candidates, the Workers' Party had six, Labour five and the PDs only four. Sinn Fein, which said it was standing in order to raise the profile of some of its Dail candidates rather than because it expected to win any seats, had seven candidates, and the Green Party ran two.

In addition, there were 11 independents, undeterred by the IR£1000 deposit demanded of candidates (returned only to those whose total of votes exceeds a third of the Droop quota at some stage of the count). Two of these were heavyweights, outgoing MEP T. J. Maher in Munster and former MEP Neil Blaney in Connacht–Ulster. Blaney (who had belonged to the Technical Coordination Group in the 1979–84 EP) announced that he would join the EP Rainbow group if elected. Two other independents were of particular interest. Father (though his clerical status was itself a matter of dispute) Patrick Ryan, who had narrowly avoided being extradited from Belgium to Britain where the police wanted to question him about alleged IRA activities, stood in Munster, claiming that a vote for him was a vote against Margaret Thatcher. Sinn Fein stood aside in the constituency in his favour. In Dublin, Raymond Crotty, whose successful challenge to the constitutionality of the Single European Act in 1987 had necessitated a referendum on the issue, ran in the hope of picking up support from the 34 per cent of Dublin voters who had voted against the SEA. The other independents were of varying degrees of seriousness, the least likely MEP being one William Abbey of the Holy Cross Fitzsimons, who ran in Munster and also, for good measure, in seven Dail constituencies (he duly lost all eight of his deposits).

The issues and campaigning techniques

Any hopes, slim in any case based on the experience of 1979 and 1984, that a genuinely 'European' election campaign might develop, disappeared once the general election was called. Most candidates put the focus on domestic politics, while trying to work-in a European angle.

The main theme of Fianna Fail's election literature was the party's record in government over the previous two years, and the 'great progress' it had made 'along the road to national recovery'. In European terms, it claimed that the Fianna Fail MEPs in the 1984–89 EP 'have been active and effective in protecting our vital agricultural interests, pressing for European initiatives to tackle unemployment, raising environmental, consumers' and women's issues, promoting the rule of law and defending our neutrality'. Fine Gael and the PDs tended to lay more stress on the merits of their individual candidates. For example, outgoing Dublin MEP Mary Banotti was described as being 'recognised as a leading member' of the EP and as having been 'a prominent and forceful champion' of Dublin in the EP, while the PDs urged voters to 'send Ireland's very best' (i.e. *their* candidates) to represent Ireland in the EP.

Labour and the Workers' Party, in contrast, appealed for votes almost entirely on the basis of their opposition to the government's programme of cuts in public expenditure. There were few references to a European dimension in their literature, and these tended to be very general in nature. For example, Workers' Party leader Proinsias de Rossa's campaign leaflet promised that 'in the European Parliament he will stand up for the people of Dublin and make sure we get our fair share from the new Europe'. The Green Party's literature stressed environmental issues (the ozone layer, greenhouse effect, and so on), though without any indication of how it would use the EP if it won a seat there. Perhaps surprisingly, it was Sinn Fein, of all the parties, whose campaign literature gave most attention to European issues. The party adopted an anti-EC position, arguing that EC membership had brought about higher unemployment, prices and emigration. Sinn Fein MEPs, it said, would 'demand international support for British withdrawal' from Northern Ireland, and would act as 'watchdogs' on behalf of the Irish people, a rationale for participation in the election which other anti-EC candidates also adopted.

Individual candidates tended to say even less about Europe than their parties' literature did. They were prone to speak of the low standard of Irish infrastructure such as the transport network, and announce their intention to try to ensure, if elected, that the country (and especially their constituency) received a higher share of the Regional and Social Funds. Candidates with a background in farming referred to the need to maintain spending on the CAP, while Dublin candidates criticised the food price-rises they said it had produced. Generally, though, they soon concluded that the public was not very responsive to a European dimension. In the words of Munster PD candidate Pat Cox, 'Nobody is asking us about Europe. They're all complaining about the health services and the inability to get into hospitals.'[4]

In the Munster constituency, Northern Ireland emerged as an issue because of the candidacies of Patrick Ryan and John Cushnahan. Whereas most of the other candidates studiously ignored Ryan, Cushnahan criticised his refusal to condemn the violence used by the IRA. Cushnahan himself was the target of what seemed to be an orchestrated campaign by Irish-Americans of a republican hue, who wrote letters to the provincial papers, often couched in very similar terms, denouncing him particularly for his past efforts in the USA to prevent the adoption of the MacBride principles (which had the effect of discouraging American investment in Northern Ireland). Munster readers were informed by letter-writers from Colorado, Illinois and Massachusetts that they 'must reject the candidacy' of 'John Cushnahan of Belfast', or else Ireland would 'face a crisis',

Margaret Thatcher would derive satisfaction, and Cushnahan's presence at Strasbourg would 'set Western European standards back a hundred years or more'.[5] This tactic, with its obvious overtones of external interference in the election, was almost certainly counter-productive in its effects.

The mass media, obvious scapegoats for those who believe that European issues should have been brought more strongly to the public's notice, in fact did their best to highlight specifically European perspectives when these arose. RTE, the national broadcasting authority, staged admittedly uninspiring debates between candidates in each of the four constituencies. The national newspapers reserved a certain amount of their election coverage for the EP contest, with snippets of candidates' statements and assessments of the likely outcome in each constituency. Many provincial papers, too, gave reasonable coverage of the EP election, often focusing on candidates from their own area of the constituency.

The candidates (other than the independents) campaigned within the framework of a strategy devised by their party within their constituency. In most cases, the parties attempted the technique of 'vote management' which sometimes pays off under STV. Suppose a party runs two candidates and wins 120 000 first-preference votes in a constituency where the Droop quota (which secures election) is 80 000. If one of its candidates wins 80 000 votes and the other 40 000, the trailing candidate will probably not be elected. But if each candidate receives 60 000 first preferences, there is a much better chance that the party will win two seats, as both will remain in the count longer and can hope to float up towards the quota on a tide of votes transferred from eliminated candidates. The aim of managing the votes, then, is to ensure that the party's two leading candidates (if the party is aiming at two seats) win approximately the same number of first preferences. This is achieved by dividing the constituency into two equal parts, on the basis of the estimated party vote in each portion of it, and asking voters to give their first preference accordingly. For example, in the Connacht–Ulster constituency, the Fianna Fail organisation 'awarded' one candidate, Sean Doherty, the northern part of the constituency (which contains his own home base), and asked voters there to give him their first preference; the same was done for the other candidate, Mark Killilea, in the southern part.

Once the division had been sorted out, candidates in the three rural constituencies roamed around their allotted territory in garish campaign buses, 'marking' it like big cats with posters on what seemed to be every available telegraph pole. Each candidate kept a wary eye on the other, watching for any attempts to poach personal votes outside the agreed area. The general technique was to attempt to show the candidate's face in as many parts of 'his' (or 'her') territory as possible. A report in a provincial paper[6] on the campaign of outgoing MEP Mark Killilea conveys the flavour:

> Where every vote in the general election is gathered through personal contact, the Euro vote is sought through the less sophisticated psychology of noise and notice. It's only scratching the surface, Mark admits, but there is no other way the message can be got across in a constituency as big as Connacht–Ulster. You home in on every possible town and village with a cacophony of taped talk and music. You attract attention. Like predators, the workers pour from the coach; distribute literature to a few central houses; ask for support. And after ten minutes they're back, speeding towards the next destination.

When soliciting support, candidates are expected to ask voters to give their second preference to a party colleague. Sometimes, though, the literature issued was extremely personalised, making little or no mention of the candidate's running mates or even party. In Dublin, especially, attempts at vote management and dividing up the constituency seemed to break down in some cases, and candidates treated it as an open city, seeking first preferences wherever they could get them. In reality, candidates often regarded their so-called 'running mates' as their deadliest rivals rather than as partners.

THE RESULTS

Most of the general election results were known by midnight on Friday 16 June, and given that Fianna Fail's failure to obtain an overall majority had triggered off intense debate as to how the next government would be formed, the EP election results had the role of a light dessert after the main course. The counting of the votes began at 9 on the morning of Sunday 18 June, but no results were revealed, or probably even reached, until polling had ended in all other EC countries. The final results were not known until Monday evening.

Turnout, boosted by the general election, was up 19 per cent over 1984 (see Table 8.2). It was also up on the 1979 figure, which had itself been raised by local elections having been held on the same day.

Table 8.2   Ireland: results of 1989 EP and Dail elections

	EP election % Votes	EP election Seats	Dail election % Votes
Fianna Fail	31.5	6	44.1
Fine Gael	21.6	4	29.3
PDs	11.9	1	5.5
Labour	9.5	1	9.5
Workers' Party	7.5	1	5.0
Greens	3.7	0	1.5
Sinn Fein	2.3	0	1.2
Others	11.9	2	3.9
TOTAL	100.0	15	100.0
Turnout	66.6		68.4

There had been fears on this occasion that turnout might fall to not much above 40 per cent. The calling of the general election, though it had swamped the EP election as such, at least ensured that many more people bothered to vote.

In terms of past EP election results, both Fianna Fail and Fine Gael fell back to a level below even their 1979 performances (compare Tables 8.1 and 8.2). Between them, the two parties won just 53.1 per cent of the votes, the lowest they have ever won at a nationwide electoral contest. Each party lost a seat in Dublin, and Fianna Fail also dropped one in Connacht–Ulster, while Fine Gael lost one in Munster. Both major parties were disappointed with the results, having hoped to improve on or at least maintain their 1984 standing.

The left was slightly more satisfied with the election outcome. Labour's vote went up only slightly on its 1984 figure, and its one seat (which came in Dublin) was well below its 1979 achievement. Its Leinster candidate fell just 10 votes (in a poll of nearly 400 000) short of unseating one of the sitting Fianna Fail MEPs, and the party subsequently initiated legal action, still pending at the time of writing, seeking the overturning of certain decisions of the returning officer concerning the validity of some ballot papers. The Workers' Party won its first-ever EP seat; this was gained in Dublin, where its candidate outpolled Labour. However, its success brought it some dilemmas. The first concerned the question of which EP group to join. In many ways the Communist group seemed the most logical choice, but some party members feared that open identification with communism at European level might cost electoral support at home.

In the end the party put its doubts aside, and joined the more hardline of the two Communist groupings in the new EP, along with the French, Greek and Portuguese parties, rather than the 'Euro-communist' group dominated by the PCI. The second dilemma was that its successful candidate, Proinsias de Rossa, is also party-leader and a TD, so he will have either to dissipate his energies in tackling three jobs simultaneously or to risk opprobrium by soon handing over his EP seat to a relative unknown.

The PDs performed very creditably, winning a seat through Pat Cox (the party's general secretary) in Munster at the expense of Fine Gael. Given the party's major setback at the general election (see below), Cox's election at the head of the poll gave a much-needed boost to his party's morale. The Greens, who had amazed even themselves by winning a seat at the general election, were further encouraged; they took 8.3 per cent of the votes in Dublin, where they outpolled the PDs, and 6.3 per cent in Leinster. Sinn Fein performed dismally, all of its candidates losing their deposits. Among the independents, two (Blaney and Maher) were elected. Patrick Ryan won over 30 000 votes (6.3 per cent) in Munster, nowhere near enough to give him a chance of election, while in Dublin Ray Crotty lost his deposit with 25 000 first preferences.

In some constituencies the battle within parties was as intriguing as that between them. In Dublin, both major parties had two outgoing MEPs fighting for one eventual seat. Within Fianna Fail, Niall Andrews defeated Eileen Lemass, but on the Fine Gael side of the fence Mary Banotti outpolled Chris O'Malley, to return to Strasbourg as Ireland's only female MEP. In Munster, Fine Gael's controversial nominee John Cushnahan ousted outgoing MEP Tom Raftery, the final margin between them being less than a thousand votes. Despite some misleading reports to the contrary, Cushnahan received very few (just 4.7 per cent) of the votes transferred from Ryan when the latter was eliminated, though Raftery received even fewer.

There was general surprise in Connacht–Ulster when Fianna Fail's one seat went to Mark Killilea (who had become an MEP in 1987 by stepping into the place of the retiring MacSharry) rather than the better-known Sean Doherty, who had suffered an even more un-expected loss of his Dail seat a couple of days earlier. It was widely speculated that Doherty's attempt to win two seats, which had produced charges of 'double-jobbing', had counted against him in both contests. As a result of the election, only two of Ireland's MEPs (Blaney and de Rossa) now hold a dual mandate.

Bearing in mind the extent to which the EP election campaign was obscured by the general election, it might be expected that the voting pattern at the two elections would be almost identical. This was far from the case (see Table 8.2). Using Pedersen's well-known volatility index,[7] which is calculated simply by adding the differences between the performances of each party at the two elections and dividing the result by two, we obtain a figure of 20.3 per cent. This means that at least a fifth of voters cast their votes differently at the two elections. In Munster the figure rises to 29.8 per cent, indicating that at least this proportion of voters split their votes.

Fianna Fail and Fine Gael fared considerably worse at the EP election; Labour and the Workers' Party did about the same at each; and the PDs, the Greens and others did rather better. Part of the explanation is that the latter parties did not run candidates in every Dail constituency, so they could win votes at the EP election where this was not possible at the general election. For example, the Greens ran a candidate in only one of the 8 Dail constituencies in Leinster, but at the EP election their candidate could attract votes from all over Leinster. In addition, the PDs in particular ran high-profile candidates at the EP election, who may have appealed to more voters than their Dail nominees. Moreover, the more successful independents, such as Blaney, Crotty, Maher and Ryan were virtually absent from the Dail electoral scene (the exception was Blaney, who stood and was re-elected in Donegal North-East). Nonetheless, it seems likely that some voters did approach the two elections in a different frame of mind, voting at the Dail election with government formation uppermost in their thoughts while using the EP election as an opportunity to express some kind of protest against the two main parties.

The main significance of the election for Ireland is probably the greater number of EP groups in which the country will now be represented. Between 1984 and 1989 there were Irish MEPs only in the EDA and EPP groups (plus the independent Maher in the Liberal group), but there will now also be a Labour MEP in the Socialist group, a PD MEP sitting perhaps uneasily alongside Maher with the Liberals, a Workers' Party MEP in one of the Communist groups and Blaney in the Rainbow group. Given that the EP operates through the parliamentary groups rather than through national blocs of MEPs, the 1989 elections in Ireland have had the outcome of increasing the country's voice in the EP.

NOTES AND REFERENCES

1. For explanations of the operation and impact of STV in Ireland, see G. Hand, 'Ireland', in G. Hand, J. Georgel and C. Sasse (eds), *European Electoral Systems Handbook* (London: Butterworth, 1979); M. Gallagher, 'The Political Consequences of the Electoral System in the Republic of Ireland', *Electoral Studies*, V (1986), 253–75.
2. For the 1984 campaign, see N. Collins, 'Ireland', in J. Lodge (ed.), *Direct Elections to the European Parliament 1984* (London: Macmillan, 1986).
3. See review of the manifestos by Joe Carroll in *Irish Times*, 30 May 1989.
4. *Irish Times*, 29 May 1989.
5. The quotes are taken from examples of such letters in the *Limerick Leader*, 3 and 10 June 1989.
6. Sean Rice, in *Connacht Tribune*, 9 June 1989.
7. M. N. Pedersen, 'The Dynamics of European Party Systems: Changing Patterns of Electoral Volatility', *European Journal of Political Research*, VII (1979), 1–26.

9 Italy
PHILIP DANIELS[*]

The third election to the EP was held in Italy on 18 June 1989 against the background of a government crisis caused by the resignation of prime minister Ciriaco De Mita some four weeks before polling day. The turbulent domestic context, with a caretaker government in office, ensured that the 1989 EP election campaign focused primarily on national issues and concerns, thus repeating the pattern of the 1979 and 1984 elections.

PARTIES AND PUBLIC OPINION ON EUROPEAN INTEGRATION

EC membership arouses genuine enthusiasm among both Italian political elites and the public. Once the left's initial hostility to European integration had subsided, a consensus emerged across the party system in favour of the EC. A pro-European consensus has also developed among the Italian public, so much so that since the mid-1970s mass support for European integration has for much of the time been higher in Italy than any other member state. Surveys consistently show that the public perceive tangible benefits deriving from EC membership, strongly favour moves to unify Western Europe and support the further development of common policies.[1]

However, this strong and consistent support for European integration has not always been matched by a capacity or willingness to fully implement European policies. As a result, Italy's idealistic commitment to integration is often dismissed by critics, at home and abroad, as 'verbal' or 'liturgical' Europeanism.[2] Italy's poor record of compliance with EC laws and decisions is in large part due to the shortcomings of national institutions and bureaucratic–administrative structures. Governmental instability, the lack of effective political authority at the apex of government and cumbersome parliamentary procedures hinder the implementation of EC policy.[3] In an attempt to alleviate this problem, new parliamentary procedures have been introduced to accelerate the passage of EC directives into national law, a reform viewed as essential to keep pace with the large amount of legislation required to complete the internal market.

Throughout the 1980s Italy has played a prominent role in the efforts to reform the EC's institutions. Italy has consistently adopted a 'maximalist' stance in the reform debate, pressing for a significant increase in the EP's powers, an enhanced role for the Commission and the extension of EC competence into new spheres of policy. The Single European Act was received with disappointment in Italian circles. In accordance with resolutions passed by the two houses of parliament in early 1986, Italy's eventual assent to the SEA was accompanied by a government statement which expressed 'deep dissatisfaction' with the results achieved in Luxembourg. The Government undertook to work for the full implementation of the limited reforms and to continue to press for further changes to the EC's institutional balance. In some circles, the 'minimalist' reforms provoked calls for a 'two-speed Europe', with the most *communautaire* member-states forging ahead towards European Union 'even at the cost of losing some travelling companions'.[4]

DIRECT ELECTIONS TO THE EP

While turnout in EP elections has been lower than in national elections, voting in the EP elections in 1979 (85.5 per cent) and 1984 (83.9 per cent) was high compared with most member states. For EP elections Italy is divided into five large constituencies with the 81 seats allocated between them according to population size (the North-West returns 22 MEPs, the North-East 15, the Centre 16, the South 19 and the Islands 9). The parties present lists of candidates for each constituency and seats are assigned to the parties on the basis of proportional representation. Voters may also indicate preferences for candidates on a party list.

The most notable feature of the 1984 EP election was the significant advance of the PCI which, with an increase in its vote of 3.4 per cent compared to the 1983 national parliamentary elections, became the largest party for the first time. While the DC temporarily lost its position as the leading national party, its percentage share of the vote increased slightly compared to the 1983 national elections (up from 32.9 per cent to 33 per cent). For the PSI the 1984 result was a disappointment. Hoping to accrue electoral dividends from the high-profile premiership of its leader Craxi, the party in the event lost support compared with 1983 (down from 11.4 per cent to 11.2 per cent). The joint list presented by the PRI and PLI won 6.1 per cent of the vote, down from the total of 8 per cent achieved by the two parties standing independently in 1983.[5]

The 1984 elections produced a rather high turnover in the Italian contingent of MEPs: of the 81 MEPs who sat in the 1979–84 EP, only 35 returned to the newly-elected parliament. Recent research has shown that Italian MEPs are among the most *communautaire* in their conception of their role in the EP; almost 80 per cent of respondents saw Europe as their principal concern rather than national or local commitments, although they acknowledged that this was likely to be at odds with their voters' expectations.[6] Italian MEPs do not escape the general lack of esteem which characterises public perceptions of the political class in Italy. Italian MEPs' rather poor attendance in the EP is frequently criticised with some justification. This poor attendance record is in part explained by the MEPs' need to keep in close touch with the constituency power-bases at home. In addition, some MEPs hold a dual mandate in the national and European parliaments and many prominent politicians (including party secretaries) with EP seats rarely attend (e.g. Claudio Martelli, a leading Socialist, did not attend at all in the 1988 session).[7]

THE NATIONAL POLITICAL CONTEXT

The run-up to the 1989 EP elections was dominated by a domestic political crisis. The Christian Democrat prime minister Ciriaco De Mita, leading a *pentapartito* (five-party) coalition of the DC, PSI, PRI, PSDI and PLI, resigned on 19 May 1989 after a turbulent thirteen months in office. De Mita's position as prime minister had looked vulnerable since February 1989 when he had lost the post of DC party secretary to Arnaldo Forlani. The government's main preoccupation was the burgeoning budget deficit and in spring 1989 measures were announced to cut public expenditure and to increase public service charges (including medical costs). The issue, which divided the coalition, was badly mishandled and provoked a general strike. The simmering political crisis came to a head in the spring season of party congresses with a series of attacks on the government's performance from coalition partners. De Mita announced his resignation after a barrage of criticisms by Socialist ministers at the PSI congress and a scathing denunciation of the government's leadership in Craxi's closing address. The motives and timing behind the Socialists' decision to bring down the government were seen as largely electoral, with the party hoping to distance itself from a lacklustre government. While the DC and PSI have been coalition partners throughout the 1980s, relations between the two parties have been highly conflictual and competitive as each has sought to secure electoral advantage from participation in government. With no other coalition formula available while Communist participation in government is ruled out, the DC and PSI have been condemned to work together but with little policy cohesiveness or willingness to cooperate.

Following the government collapse the parties were provided with an early test of their popular standing in partial local elections, mainly in southern Italy, at the end of May. All five parties which had served in De Mita's government achieved some success. The most notable feature of the results was the PSI's success in overtaking the PCI. This setback for the PCI, the latest in a steady electoral decline spanning most of the decade, was widely interpreted as an indication that the PSI would close the gap on the Communists or even overtake their rivals on the left in the EP elections. More cautious analyses pointed to the specific local factors in communal elections, the voters' greater knowledge of candidates and the variations in voting behaviour between local and nationwide contests. The Communists, alluding to their reputation as 'the party with clean hands', reacted to their defeat by claiming that their vote had fallen in those areas where clientelistic politics and organised crime were most rife.

THE 1989 EP ELECTION

The candidates

The selection of the candidates for the 14 party lists was largely settled by early May: 994 candidates were selected, 220 more than in 1984. As in 1979 and 1984, the respective lists contained prominent national politicians (for example, Andreotti, Goria, Martinazzoli and Colombo for the DC, Occhetto and Napolitano for the PCI, Craxi for the PSI, and La Malfa, Altissimo, Visentini and Pannella for the PRI–PLI–Federalists); leading party figures in local government (e.g. Renzo Imbeni, PCI mayor of Bologna); and the presence of academics (e.g. Margherita Hack, the astrophysicist for the PCI), journalists and broadcasters (e.g. Giuliano Ferrara for the PSI) and well-known figures from the cultural world. The selection of prestige candidates, fittingly described in the Italian idiom as 'flowers in the buttonhole', is a common feature of both national and European elections and is designed to enhance the parties' electoral appeal. The most novel element of the lists for the 1989 EP elections was the inclusion of nationals of other EC states as candidates for the first time. A law passed in January 1989 made provision for this and it survived a challenge in the Constitutional Court at the end of May. The most notable non-Italian selections were Maurice Duverger (a French political scientist) for the PCI, David Steel (a British SLD MP) for the PRI–PLI–Federalists, and Leonid Pljusc (a Russian exile and human rights' activist) for the PSDI.

The presence of fourteen separate party lists was symptomatic of the state of flux in the party system and only served to complicate the choices available to the electors. The PRI and PLI, which had presented a joint list in 1984, this time joined with the Radical Party in the so-called *alleanza laica* (lay alliance) of federalists. However, the role of the Radicals in this electoral alliance was rather ambiguous, since Radical candidates were also on the lists of the Rainbow Greens, the PSDI and the Anti-Prohibitionists, and the party actively encouraged their voters to support particular candidates on other lists. Just as confusing was the presentation of two 'green' lists, one for the official Greens (with the smiling sun symbol) which had entered the national parliament in 1987 with almost one million votes, and the other for the Rainbow Greens (with the daisy symbol) which brought together candidates from mainly left-wing political backgrounds, including members of the PR and DP. Plans to present a joint list had foundered on the issue of political alignment (with the Rainbow Greens supporting a left alternative in Italy) and the unwillingness of local Greens' organisations to give prominent figures from other parties an elevated position on Green lists. The PSI lists included three candidates (Romita, Amadei and Moroni) from the Democratic Socialist Union (UDS) which had broken away from the PSDI when the party had rejected a merger with Craxi's Socialists. The presentation of lists by local and regional parties, of which there has been a recent proliferation, further complicated the electoral scene; these included the Lombard League, the SVP, the Pensioners, and the Federalism list made up principally of parties from the Val d'Aosta and Sardinia. The lists included a new formation, the Anti-Prohibitionists, whose single issue appeal was against the criminalisation of drug use.

Party strategies

The EP election strategies of the leading national parties reflected a
blend of national and European themes. The PCI, as in 1984,
emphasised its 'European left' strategy which has evolved over the
last decade and seeks to develop close links with socialist and social
democratic parties in Europe.[8] The PCI's ideological renewal in
recent years, which was given new momentum at the party's eighteenth congress in March 1989, has brought it closer to socialist parties
in Europe. With regard to European issues like workers' rights, environmental protection and East–West relations there is considerable
convergence between the PCI and the socialist left in the EC. The
PCI's 'European left' strategy is in part an attempt to compensate for
the domestic political exclusion which the party has had to endure
throughout the 1980s as the DC and PSI have joined forces in
government. The declared strategy of Craxi's PSI, to isolate the PCI
and to supplant it as the leading party of the Italian left, has provoked
acrimonious relations between the two parties. This fierce domestic
competion has inevitably spilled over into the European arena. In
March 1989 the Socialists cancelled a proposed meeting with the PCI
in Brussels after the Communist leader Occhetto had allegedly told a
journalist that Craxi was the obstacle to a better PCI–PSI rapport.
The Socialist decision to cancel the meeting, at a time when relations
between the two parties were showing signs of improvement, was
widely seen as a ploy to perpetuate the PCI's isolated image and to
undermine its contacts with parties of the European left in the run-up
to the EP elections. Much to the annoyance of the Socialists, the PCI
made great play of its links with other European left parties
throughout the 1989 campaign.[9] Duverger played a prominent role in
the election campaign, stressing the PCI's progressive Europeanism,
its affinities with the French Socialists, and missing no opportunity to
attack Craxi. In early June the PCI and the French PS organised a
joint press conference in Paris to promote their common policy for a
'cultural Europe'. The presence of Laurent Fabius and Jack Lang was
regarded as something of an electoral bonus for the PCI. The PCI's
keenness to emphasise its links with the European left was reflected
in the party's slogans during the 1989 campaign (e.g. 'In Europe. To
the Left with the New PCI'). In electoral terms, the PCI's best hope
appeared to be to limit its likely decline and to hold off the challenge
of the PSI. The pessimism within the PCI was clearly illustrated a few
days before the EP elections when Occhetto admitted that he would

be satisfied with 23 per cent of the vote, 11 per cent less than the PCI had polled in 1984.

The DC's election strategy concentrated on traditional and well-tried themes. As in 1984, the party stressed its long pro-European tradition (exemplified by the slogan 'First in Europe') and contrasted it with the later conversion of the PCI to the idea of European integration. The DC made clear the link between the vote for the EP and the domestic political situation: 'Some think that the European elections concern a remote event, a problem which does not interest us much; in short, that it concerns elections of little importance. This is a serious error. Not only because Europe will increasingly affect us in our day-to-day life, but also because the stability of the Italian political situation depends on the result of the 18 June elections'. The DC thus stressed the national dimension to the EP vote, claiming that the party had an indispensable role in ensuring the governability of the country and warning against a dispersion of votes which would exacerbate political instability and undermine Italy's role in Europe. The DC party secretary, Arnaldo Forlani, made it clear that the PCI was regarded as the main electoral adversary but, with the distribution of ministerial posts in the next government looming, it went without saying that the DC wanted a good showing against their erstwhile coalition allies.

The PSI's strategy concentrated on the projection of its image as a modern, reformist party with close links with the socialist left in Europe. In electoral terms, the PSI aimed to narrow the gap between itself and the PCI. The PSI had advanced significantly in the 1987 national elections (up from 11.4 per cent to 14.3 per cent) and, with the fall in the PCI vote, many commentators had suggested that Craxi might emulate Mitterrand's Socialist Party and supplant the Communists as the leading party of the left. Indeed, the PSI and sections of the press had made much of the so-called 'French syndrome', depicting the PCI as an anachronistic party in terminal decline. The Socialists' ambitious expectations were pared down as election day approached and polls indicated rather modest gains: a few days before the election Craxi indicated that a one per cent increase on the PSI's 1987 showing would be regarded as a success.

A similar blend of domestic and European themes was evident in the strategies of some of the other parties. The PLI and PRI launched a common programme in April 1989 calling for a modernisation of national institutions, public services and the economy to enable Italy to participate fully in Europe. It invited federalists, environmentalists,

Radicals and others to join their lists for the EP elections. This so-called *polo laico* (lay pole) of centre parties was in part motivated by a desire to strengthen their electoral position and to counter the PSI's attempts to attract support from the small centre parties.

The campaign

The domestic political turmoil induced by the government crisis detracted from the EP election campaign, as national political issues overshadowed European themes. The fierce political competition among the erstwhile allies in government was intensified as the rival parties sought a good showing in the EP elections to strengthen their hands in the imminent coalition bargaining. The intense rivalry was evident in the barrage of attacks on President Cossiga after he had asked Giovanni Spadolini to explore the various alternatives for a new governing coalition. The DC and PSI claimed that the appointment of the Republican Spadolini, the president of the Senate and a former prime minister, would give his party and its 'lay' centre allies a high public profile and a significant advantage in the EP elections. President Cossiga was also criticised by the PSI when he asked De Mita to try to form a new government a few days before the elections. The PSI and the DC had made it clear that a resolution of the crisis would have to wait until after the EP elections. In the event, it proved impossible to refashion the five-party coalition in the context of an acrimonious election campaign.

European themes and the EP campaign were inevitably relegated to the inside pages of the newspapers as the tragic events which unfolded in China captured the headlines. The massacre in Tiananmen Square had an immediate impact on the European campaign, however, as other parties, in particular the DC and PSI, exploited it in an attack on the PCI reminiscent of the anti-communist campaigns of the Cold War period. In this atmosphere European themes were given little chance to become the focus of the campaign. Indeed, the PCI leader Occhetto complained that he had to spend much of his campaigning time responding to polemical attacks on his party.

European themes were of course prominent in the formal campaign literature of the major parties. Each party produced an extensive election programme which addressed European issues in great detail. The DC adopted the common programme of its transnational party federation, the EPP, and supplemented this with its own campaign literature which emphasised the DC's longstanding commitment to the idea of a united Europe and detailed the party's position on a whole range of European issues including peace, common security and the internal market. The campaign material also contained detailed proposals for EC policies for the family, youth and women. The PSI adopted the manifesto of the CSP (as did the PSDI) and in its own campaign literature called for more extensive powers for the EP and policies for a 'social Europe', environmental protection, high-technology research and employment. In his introduction to the transnational manifesto, Craxi paid particular attention to the new climate of East–West *détente* and the possibility of a new relationship for the two halves of Europe. With no equivalent communist transnational organisation, the PCI produced its own programme for the elections which dealt with European policies and EC issues in great detail. It stressed among other things the need for a social dimension to the EC to complement the single market, the new opportunities for Europe as a result of improved East–West relations, and the EC's essential role in promoting disarmament, employment, women's rights, protection of the environment and Third World development. The PRI–PLI–Federalists used the common programme of the ELD which, among other things, proposed an enhanced role for the EP in a European Union, a commitment to a genuine internal market, greater social justice and a more prominent EC role in world affairs.

While the formal election programmes addressed European issues in great detail, the parties' campaign slogans tended to be a mixture of national and European themes: 'To Give Stability to Our Country, to take Italy to the Centre of Europe' (DC); 'More Strength to the MSI–DN and Italy Wins'; 'A New Italy For The New Europe' (PCI); 'PSI. Italy Towards Europe'; 'The Alternative For Italy and For Europe' (PCI). This combination of European and national themes was also evident in election addresses and party publications. The PCI, for example, cleverly linked its call for an alternative government in Italy to its proposals for an alternative strategy for European integration. It contrasted two conflicting and opposed views of integration; on the one hand, the Europe of deregulation, single market unification and the liberalisation of capital movements, and on the other, the Europe of controlled competition, with a 'social space' and effective coordination of macroeconomic policy. Italy, so the PCI argued, was faced with a similar set of choices and a vote for the Communists in the EP elections would encourage an alternative national government and align the country with the progressives in

Europe ('In Europe One Chooses. Either With the Conservatives or the Progressives'). The national–European link was also apparent in the PCI's proposals for reform of Italy's political institutions and greater fiscal efficiency to enable Italy to play a full part in the EC. The DC likewise combined national and European themes as, for example, in its references to its governing role which it claimed provides the political continuity vital to safeguard Italy's interests in the EC. Similarly, the DC stressed the national economic success of the 1980s which had prepared Italy to take full advantage of the Single European Market. Of course the clear distinction between national and European concerns has blurred somewhat as the EC has increasingly assumed a role in policy spheres formerly the sole responsibility of national governments. Thus, parties could focus on themes which straddled the national and European dimensions; Occhetto, for example, campaigning in southern Italy, called for the region's economic development and a more effective EC regional policy to assist it.

While European themes were not entirely absent from the 1989 campaign, there was little real inter-party debate about the merits or demerits of the EC or its policies. This is not simply because membership of the EC is a 'valence' issue which no longer divides the parties. The pro-integrationist consensus is not matched by cross-party agreement on EC policies or Europe's future. Indeed, party differences have become more pronounced and more meaningful as integration has gathered a new momentum in recent years and the EC's future direction is being widely debated. The lack of real debate on European issues in the 1989 campaign had more to do with the parties' vote-maximising strategies. The parties tend to concentrate on those issues which are most likely to mobilise their voters or to secure electoral advantages over their rivals and in 1989 the most salient issues were national ones. In Italy, as elsewhere, voters on the whole were not well-informed on the details of EC policies and EC issues do not rank as the voters' most pressing concerns.

The lack of attention in the campaign to purely European themes was most clearly illustrated with regard to the national referendum held on the same day as the EP elections. The referendum asked voters if they were in favour of conferring constituent powers on the EP. They were asked to vote 'yes' or 'no' to the following question: 'Do you think that the European Communities should be transformed into an effective Union, with a government responsible to the Parliament, entrusting to the same European Parliament a mandate to draw up a draft European constitution for ratification directly by the competent organs of the member states of the Community?' While all the major parties supported European Union and an extension of EP powers in their election programmes, the referendum was virtually ignored throughout the campaign. The referendum had been proposed by senators and deputies in the European Federalist Movement and was a direct response to the EP's call for constituent powers. Provision for the consultative referendum had required a new constitutional law which completed its complex parliamentary passage by early April 1989. The strong party backing for the referendum again demonstrated Italy's 'maximalist' stance on the question of institutional reform. The sponsors of the referendum saw it as providing a lead to other member states and giving Italian MEPs the moral authority to push for European Union.

The party campaigns contained the usual mixture of television spots, press advertisements, party rallies, debates and free pop concerts. On the whole media coverage of specifically EC themes was scant. Foreign news stories, in particular the events in China and the death of Khomeini, dominated the media's headlines at the height of the campaign in early June. As in 1984, media coverage focused on the domestic orientation of the campaign. The press, not surprisingly, devoted attention to the more newsworthy domestic items to do with the government crisis, and detailed coverage of European issues was virtually absent until the last few days before the election. What little attention was paid to Europe in the press was often of a critical nature, focusing, for example, on the poor attendance record of Italian MEPs.[10]

Television coverage of the EP elections included news items on the campaign, party political broadcasts and question and answer programmes with journalists and party leaders. The use of television for party commercials has become a common feature of elections in Italy and the EP campaign was no exception.[11] All the major parties bought commercial spots on the private television channels which are not required to maintain a fair partisan balance. The PCI, for example, paid for eight 15-second commercials on the private networks featuring a blond baby and covering such themes as racial integration, peace and disarmament, the environment, a fairer taxation system and the role of women. The DC spent an estimated 75 per cent of its campaign budget on television spots using various images (e.g. a hammer smashing a piggy bank and a deflating ball) to convey the general message that the DC is the guarantor of security and progress. The PSI's commercials tended to focus on their leader Craxi and included one featuring other European socialist leaders.

The role of both public and private television channels in the campaign caused considerable controversy. The public channels, required to maintain balance and neutrality but under the control of political parties, came in for severe criticism. The Radical Party produced a report, supported by the PRI, PLI and PSDI, showing that the DC, PSI and PCI were receiving disproportionate coverage in news programmes.[12] The PCI was also highly critical of television's role in the campaign. PCI was particularly incensed by a programme broadcast on 14 June by the Socialist-controlled Rai-2 which examined the relationship between Stalin and the former PCI leader Togliatti. The PCI complained that the programme was biased against the Italian Communists and broadcast for electoral reasons.[13] The PCI also made a more general criticism, echoed by other parties, of the lack of neutral coverage and unequal opportunities for the parties on both the public and private networks. Particular concern was expressed about the complete absence of public controls or regulation of the burgeoning private networks, many under the control of broadcasting magnate Silvio Berlusconi and his Fininvest company. The parliamentary committee of control, responsible for the public broadcasting networks, had written to the private channels asking them to respect impartiality during the campaign but the PCI complained that this attempted voluntary control had failed. The Rai journalists' union (Usigrai) also criticised the unbalanced coverage and asked the President to intervene to guarantee a fair campaign.[14] The EP campaign also prompted renewed calls for regulations to control party commercials on the private channels after the DC and PSI had far outspent the other parties.

RESULTS

The 81.5 per cent turnout in the 1989 EP elections was once again high by European standards (only surpassed by Belgium and Luxembourg) but the trend of rising rates of abstention in national and Euroelections continued. Indeed, adding the 7.1 per cent spoiled or blank ballots to the abstainers gave a total of 25.6 per cent for Italy's so-called 'third party'. The rise in abstention was attributed to the bewildering proliferation of party lists, the domestic orientation of the campaign and voting on a single day rather than two as in national elections.

Table 9.1   Italy: the 1989 and 1984 European Election results and 1987
General Election results (Chamber of Deputies)

Parties	European Election 1989		European Election 1984		General election 1987
	% Votes	Seats	% Votes	Seats	% Votes Cast
DC (Christian					34.3
Democrats)	32.9	26	33.0	26	
PCI (Communists)	27.6	22	33.3	27	26.6
PSI (Socialists)	14.8	12	11.2	9	14.3
PRI (Republicans)[1]	} 4.4	} 4	} 6.1	} 5	3.7
PLI (Liberals)					2.1
PR (Radicals)	–	–	3.4	3	2.6
MSI–DN (Italian Social Movement–National Right)	5.5	4	6.5	5	5.9
PSDI (Social Democrats)	2.7	2	3.5	3	2.9
Verdi (Green List)	3.8	3	–	–	2.5
Verdi Arcobaleno (Rainbow Greens)	2.4	2	–	–	–
Lega Lombardo-Alleanza Nord (Lombard League–North Alliance)[2]	1.8	2	–	–	0.5
DP (Proletarian Democrats)	1.3	1	1.4	1	1.7
SVP (South Tyrol People's Party)	0.5	1	0.6	1	0.5
Federalismo (Union Valdôtaine–Partito Sardo d'Azione) (Val d'Aosta Union and Sardinian Action Party)[3]	0.6	1	0.5	1	0.5
Lega Antiproibizionista (Anti-Prohibitionist League)	1.2	1	–	–	–
Pensionati (Pensioners)	0.5	–	–	–	–
Others	–	–	0.5	–	1.9

Notes
1. In 1989 list of Liberals, Republicans and Federalists (including candidates from Radical Party).
2. In 1989 various local parties from the Veneto, Lombardy, Piedmont, Tuscany and Emilia Romagna grouped in this list. In 1984 the Veneto League won 0.5 per cent of the vote and 0.8 per cent in 1987.
3. In 1989 the Federalism list included other small regional formations (e.g. the Southern Movement). The 1987 result is the combined total of lists presented separately.

Thirteen of the fourteen lists presented in the 1989 EP elections won seats. The most significant features of the results were: the rise in the PCI's share of the vote; the DC equalling its lowest-ever vote in a nationwide contest; the PSI's failure to advance significantly; the success of the two 'green' lists; and the setback for the lay alliance of PLI–PRI–Federalists. The most unexpected result was the PCI's increased percentage share of the vote compared with the 1987 national elections (up from 26.6 per cent to 27.6 per cent of the vote). The PCI did well in the large urban centres where it had been losing support since 1985: it recovered its position as the largest party in Milan and Naples (where it had come second to the DC in 1987), and it consolidated its primacy in Turin, Genoa, Florence and Bologna. A number of factors contributed to the PCI's relative success: its effective organisational machine enabled it to mobilise its vote more successfully than the other parties;[15] the party's leading role in the opposition to unpopular government policies such as the increases in health charges; a rejection by voters of attempts by other parties to delegitimise the PCI following the massacre in Tienanmen Square; and approval for the moderate 'new course' undertaken by the Occhetto leadership and approved at the PCI's eighteenth congress in March 1989.

For the Socialists, the 1989 results were a setback for the party's so-called 'long-wave' strategy of supplanting the PCI as the leading party of the left. While the PSI was the only party in De Mita's government to increase its vote compared to 1987 (up from 14.3 per cent to 14.8 per cent), this was less than the party's pre-election expectations and the electoral distance from the PCI rose from 12.3 to 12.8 per cent. The PSI attributed its disappointing result to the lacklustre performance of the De Mita government and indicated that it would insist on clear programmatic agreements before joining another *pentapartito* coalition. Some commentators suggested that the PSI had reached an electoral ceiling. The PSI's rightward drift under Craxi and the meagre reform record of the *pentapartito* coalitions make it difficult to attract support from voters on the left, particularly from the PCI with its strong subcultural vote that makes rapid electoral erosion unlikely. In addition, the PSI's attempts to absorb the votes of the 'third pole' of centre-left parties suffered a setback in 1989. The large losses of the PLI–PRI–Federalists' alliance did not accrue to the Socialists, the PSDI largely held its 1987 vote, and the success of the 'green' lists (with a combined vote of 6.2 per cent) indicated that the PSI had an important new challenger for votes.

The DC vote equalled its historic low with 32.9 per cent (down from 34.3 per cent in 1987) and confirmed the party's decline from the 1960s and 1970s when it consistently polled 38–39 per cent. The DC performed badly in the large urban centres, losing votes in Rome, Naples, Milan, Turin, Genoa, Bologna, Florence and Palermo. In all, the party lost 1.8 million votes compared to 1987. It attributed the setback to the higher levels of abstention, which it claimed had a disproportionate effect on its vote,[16] and to the voters' negative reaction to the collapse of the De Mita government. More critical voices within the DC claimed that the party's campaign, with its focus on political continuity, had been too negative and that the new, more conservative line which had emerged from the party congress in February 1989 had alienated some support. The party leadership claimed that the vote signified no change in the domestic political context and took some comfort in its claim that the success of the PCI had been exaggerated since the PCI had lost around 700 000 votes since the 1987 national election and 5.7 per cent since the 1984 EP elections.

The new electoral alliance of the PLI, PRI and PR fared badly. Support for the PLI and PRI had totalled 5.8 per cent in 1987 (when they ran independently) but fell to 4.4 per cent in the 1989 election. The performance of the 'lay alliance', which had aimed to establish itself as the new 'fourth pole' in the party system, was even more disappointing if the 2.6 per cent the Radicals polled in 1987 is taken into account. Some leading Liberals and Republicans had opposed the alliance with the Radicals on the grounds that it represented an incoherent grouping of government parties (the PLI and PRI) with an opposition party. There were disagreements among the parties over the lists of candidates and during the campaign Pannella, a maverick Radical and a candidate on the list, had invited electors to vote for other parties.

The two 'green' lists – the Rainbow Greens and the Greens – achieved a notable success with 2.4 per cent and 3.8 per cent respectively. The acrimonious split in early May appeared not to have damaged the parties. The combined vote of 6.2 per cent (up from the 2.5 per cent the single Green List obtained in 1987) confirmed a new force in national politics. There was much post-election discussion of a possible merger between the two lists but disagreements over political alignment, organisational structure and strategy remained. These difficulties were compounded by the presence of prominent ecologists in the lists of other parties and the resistance of non-political organisations like the Italian WWF and *Italia Nostra* (Our Italy) to a formal political party.

The far-right MSI–DN lost one of its MEPs as its vote fell to 5.5 per cent (from 6.5 per cent in 1984). The PSDI vote declined slightly but the party viewed this as a success after having suffered the loss of a breakaway group to the PSI. Of the other results, two in particular are worth noting: (1) the election of two MEPs for the Lombard League, a regionalist grouping with a populist appeal against the government in Rome and migrant workers from the South. The League won 8.1 per cent of the vote in Lombardy to emerge as the fourth largest party in the region. (2) The election of an MEP for the Anti-prohibitionists League which had formed shortly before the elections to oppose new anti-drug legislation.

There was a considerable turnover in the Italian representation in the EP with around 80 per cent of the MEPs elected for the first time. It was some days before the final list of MEPs was confirmed as candidates elected in more than one constituency decided which one to represent. In addition, some successful candidates with positions in the caretaker government had to choose between an EP seat or their ministerial office since the two are incompatible according to electoral law. The DC decided shortly after the election to introduce their own rule that membership of the EP would be incompatible with elected positions in the national parliament or regional councils. Craxi recorded the highest number of preference votes with over 650 000 in the South constituency and a total of 1.47 million in the three constituencies he contested. Of the foreign candidates, only Maurice Duverger (PCI list) was elected.

The referendum held on the same day as the Euro-elections saw a massive vote (88.1 per cent of the valid votes) in favour of the EP acquiring constituent powers to transform the EC into a political and economic Union. The result was in line with the strong pro-European sentiments expressed in opinion surveys and the all-party backing for the proposal. However, the seven million spoiled or blank ballots were perhaps indicative of a lack of interest or knowledge about the issue.

Most post-election comment concentrated on the domestic impact of the EP election results rather than on their EC-level significance. The outcome of the elections offered no clear indications for a speedy resolution of the government crisis with the relative strengths of the major parties largely unaltered. The combined vote of the parties in the *pentapartito* coalition fell by 2.5 per cent (from 57.3 per cent in

1987 to 54.8 per cent in 1989) but with no viable alternative coalition available and the DC and PSI unwilling to risk early elections, there was little doubt that the five-party government would be stitched back together. However, there appeared to be little promise of a stable period of government given the intense rivalries among the coalition partners and the lack of policy cohesion.

Beyond its immediate impact on government formation, the EP election indicated the possibility of some longer-term changes to the shape of the party system and individual party strategies. The 1989 results confirmed a trend in the evolution of the party system which has seen the combined votes of the DC and PCI (60.5 per cent in 1989) fall steadily in national and EP elections since 1976 (with the sole exception of the 1984 EP election). The declining bipolarism has not resulted, however, in the emergence of a cohesive 'third pole' of lay centre and socialist parties which is at the heart of the PSI's strategy.[17] As the 1989 campaign showed, there is intense competition among these parties and strong resistance to Socialist designs for dominance. The election of candidates from thirteen party lists in 1989 was consistent with a growing fragmentation of the vote which has seen the electoral advance of single-issue groups and local and regional lists. The proliferation of these new political groupings, already evident in the 1987 national election, reflects in part the inability of the established parties to aggregate particularistic interests. The fragmentation of the vote was also emblematic of the growing volatility of the Italian electorate.[18]

With regard to individual party strategies, the 1989 EP elections prompted much speculation about the long-term prospects for a new alternative coalition excluding the DC. In numerical terms a 'reformist alternative', embracing the PCI, PR, PSI, PRI, PLI, PSDI, DP and Greens, is a potential majority but the political differences between these proposed partners rule out any such governing formula in the foreseeable future. The PSI remains the pivotal party in any coalition formula and much post-election comment focused on the party's strategic alternatives following its failure to advance on the Communists.[19] Sections of the press argued that the PSI could not expect to oust the Communists as the leading party of the left in the short term, and therefore to 'unblock' the system it would have to cooperate with the PCI. A few days after the EP elections the two parties met at the Stockholm Socialist International gathering where the PCI was present as an 'observer' for the first time. However, little indication emerged that Craxi would change his combative approach to the Communists. Soon after the Euro-election the PCI indicated that it might leave the Communist group in the EP, with which it shares little in common on European questions, and seek a closer relationship with the Socialist group.[20] When the newly-elected EP held its first session in late July the PCI formed a new group, the European United Left. A meeting between its leader Luigi Colajanni and Jean-Pierre Cot, head of the Socialist group, indicated that the two alignments might reach common policy positions in the EP. This continuation of the PCI's 'European left' strategy, if successful, is likely to have significant repercussions in the domestic political arena and, in particular, on Communist–Socialist relations.

CONCLUSIONS

The 1989 EP election in Italy was contested by the parties on primarily domestic political issues. This domestic orientation, also a feature of the 1979 and 1984 contests, was inevitable given the potential impact of the Euro-election on the national balance of power. The parties regard EP elections as an extension of national political competition and focus on those issues which mobilise their support and maximise their electoral prospects. This 'internal-isation'[21] of the EP elections was even more pronounced in 1989 with the intense domestic political competition produced by the collapse of the De Mita government. Nevertheless, European issues were not entirely forgotten and a clearer picture emerged of growing party differences with regard to the future course of European integration. The parties also addressed issues with a European and domestic dimension (for example, regional development) and scope for this is likely to increase as the national and EC contexts of policymaking become more intertwined.

NOTES AND REFERENCES

*   The author would like to thank the Nuffield Foundation for the grant it gave to finance a research visit to Italy.
1.   See R. Inglehart, J-R. Rabier and K. Reif, 'The Evolution of Public Attitudes Toward European Integration: 1970–1986', *Journal of European Integration*, X (1987) pp. 135–55. A Doxa survey before the EP

elections found 83 per cent of Italians in favour of EC membership, 90 per cent in favour of efforts to unify Europe, 78 per cent in favour of the single European market, and 74 per cent in favour of the idea of a European government responsible to the EP (reported in *La Stampa*, 27 May 1989, p. 7). For similar findings see the results of a survey conducted for the Federalist Intergroup for European Union summarised in *La Repubblica*, 18 June 1988, p. 16 and the 'European Omnibus Survey' (October–November 1988) reported in *Dieci Anni Che Hanno Cambiato L'Europa 1979/89*, European Parliament, Luxembourg, February 1989, p. 85.

2. See, for example, the comments by Mauro Ferri (who served as President of the EP's Committee for Institutional Affairs and later on the Dooge Committee) reported in R. A. Cangelosi, *Dal Progetto di Trattato Spinelli All'Atto Unico Europeo* (Milan: Franco Angeli, 1987) p. 10; A. Giolitti, 'Italy and the Community After Thirty Years of Experience', *The International Spectator*, XIX (1984) 75–82; and *Il Mondo Economico*, 22 October 1988, p. 23.

3. On this see G. Pridham, 'Italy', in C. and K. Twitchett (eds), *Building Europe: Britain's Partners in the EEC* (London: Europa, 1981).

4. Cangelosi, op. cit., p. 31. There is evidence of public support for the notion of a 'two-speed Europe': the Doxa survey (op. cit.) found that 72 per cent of Italian respondents were in favour of proceeding towards European Union even at the cost of leaving out reluctant member states.

5. For details of the 1984 results see G. Pridham, 'Italy', in J. Lodge (ed.), *Direct Elections to the European Parliament 1984* (London: Macmillan, 1986); G. Mazzoleni, 'Italy', *Electoral Studies*, 3 (1984) 294–8; and G. D'Agostino (ed.), *Un Voto Per L'Europa Tra Desiderio E Delusione* (Naples: Guida Editori, 1987).

6. See the valuable comparative study of MEPs by L. Bardi, *Il Parlamento Della Comunità Europea* (Bologna: Il Mulino, 1989) p. 92 and p. 118. Also see F. Attinà, *Il Parlamento Europeo E Gli Interessi Comunitari* (Milan: Franco Angeli, 1986).

7. Reported in *L'Espresso*, 18 June 1989, pp. 18–19. Also see *Il Giornale*, 26 May 1989, p. 1 and *Il Sole – 24 Ore*, 29 May 1989, pp. 1–2.

8. See, for example, G. Napolitano, *Oltre I Vecchi Confini. Il futuro della sinistra e l'Europa* (Milan: Mondadori, 1989); Napolitano is a leading exponent of the PCI's 'European left' strategy. Also see E. Peggio, *1992 – La Sinistra, L'Europa, L'Italia* (Milan: Sperling and Kupfer, 1989).

9. For example, the PCI made much of the positive assessment of its role in the EP by Jean-Pierre Cot (French Socialist MEP): see *L'Unità*, 1 June 1989.

10. See the reports cited in note 7.

11. See E. Cheli, P. Mancini, G. Mazzoleni, G. Tinacci Mannelli, *Elezioni in TV: dalle tribune alle pubblicità* (Milan: Franco Angeli, 1989).

12. See *Il Sole – 24 Ore*, 15 June 1989, p. 2.

13. See *L'Unità*, 16 June 1989, p. 2 and 21 June 1989, p. 2.

14. See *La Repubblica*, 11/12 June 1989, p. 2.

15. On the same effect in 1984 see A. Agosta, 'Consistenza reale e linee di tendenza del voto comunista (Italia centrale ed Emilia Romagna)', in G. D'Agostino (ed.) op. cit.
16. See G. Sani in *Il Sole – 24 Ore*, 22 June 1989, p. 4.
17. See. M. Rhodes, 'Craxi and the lay-socialist area: third force or three forces?', in R. Leonardi and P. Corbetta (eds), *Italian Politics: A Review*, Volume 3 (London: Pinter, 1989).
18. On changing Italian electoral behaviour, see R. Mannheimer and G. Sani, *Il Mercato Elettorale*, (Bologna: Il Mulino, 1987) and P. Corbetta, A. M. L. Parisi and H. M. A. Schadee, *Elezioni in Italia* (Bologna: Il Mulino, 1988).
19. See, for example, G. Pasquino, 'Ora Craxi è al bivio....', *La Repubblica*, 27 June 1989, p. 10; *L'Espresso*, 25 June 1989; and *Panorama*, 25 June 1989.
20. See *L'Unità*, 20 June 1989, p. 5, *Corriere Della Sera*, 21 June 1989, p. 3, and *L'Espresso*, 25 June 1989, pp. 9–11.
21. On the concept of 'internalisation' see Pridham in Lodge (ed.) op. cit.

10 The Netherlands
RUUD KOOLE

INTRODUCTION

The need for democratic control in Europe has increased substantially with the acceptance of the 'Single Act'. 1992 means a shift of powers from national capitals to Brussels. In the Netherlands the original enthusiasm for 'Europe 1992' has gradually made room for a more balanced appreciation. If national sovereignty in some fields is superseded by the power of the Commission and the Council of Ministers, then democratic control by a powerful European Parliament is necessary. The EP's weak powers, however, create a 'democratic gap' in Europe. For the EP elections this is a handicap in mobilising the voters. The difficult EP campaign was hampered even more by the fall of the Dutch cabinet in May. In fact, the campaign was hardly visible.

THE ELECTORAL SYSTEM

The competition for the 25 Dutch EP seats is regulated by a special law (*wet op de Europese Verkiezingen*), but it does not deviate essentially from the electoral system of proportional representation for the Dutch Second Chamber (150 seats). The Netherlands forms one national constituency. The voter casts a single preferential vote for any candidate on one of the ordered lists presented by the parties. In practice, however, more than 90 per cent cast their vote for the first person on a party list. There are two reasons for this. First, the head of the list is the best-known to the electorate. Second, preference votes (i.e. votes not cast for the number-one candidate) are very unlikely to affect the outcome, since a candidate needs a very large number of preference votes (50 per cent of the votes are needed to obtain one seat) to get elected ahead of candidates placed higher on the list. Parties not already represented in the EP have to pay a deposit to participate in the elections. The deposit is forfeited if the party list does not attract at least three-quarters of the votes needed to win one seat. The electoral threshold is as high as the number of votes needed to obtain one seat (4 per cent of the popular vote). All

Dutchmen resident in the Netherlands or in another EC state who have reached the age of 18 are entitled to vote. From 1984 onwards, Dutch residents abroad are able to vote by post. The number of the latter, however, does not have an important impact on the final results.

THE 1979 AND 1984 ELECTIONS IN RETROSPECT

In the first direct elections on 7 June 1979 the 4 per cent electoral threshold affected the number of parties represented in the EP. Only the three major parties (PvdA, CDA and VVD) and D'66 managed to win seats, whereas in the national parliament seven more parties were represented. In 1984 the smaller parties of the left and of the right had learned the lesson of 1979. The orthodox Calvinist parties presented a common list as did the smaller left-wing parties. The result was that both common lists were represented in the EP. D'66, however, failed to win a seat. Hence, from 1984 to 1989 the three major parties and the two occasional groupings were entitled to send delegates to Strasbourg. EP elections reveal little about the national strength of political parties. The difference in turnout is such that the results of the European elections do not really reflect the power relations between national political parties. Whereas about 85 per cent of eligible voters turn out for national elections, only 58.1 per cent did so at the European elections in 1979 and 50.9 per cent in 1984.

DUTCH MEPs

Once elected, Dutch MEPs organise themselves along the lines of the EP's political groups: the Social-Democrats (PvdA) are members of the Socialist Group, the Christian Democrats (CDA) of the Group of the European People's Party, the Liberals (VVD) of the Liberal and Democratic Group, and the representatives of the common list of the smaller left-wing parties are members of the Rainbow Group (in 1989 these parties used the label 'rainbow' to present their common list). The representative of the common list of the smaller orthodox Calvinist parties did not attach himself to one of the EP's established political groups since this specific political orientation does not have its counterparts outside Holland. D'66, which was not represented from 1984 to 1989, decided to work for the creation of a Progressive Liberal Group, together with parties like the Danish Venstre and the Spanish CDS.

There is no reliable roll-call analysis available for Dutch MEPs. Nevertheless, a general impression exists that each Dutch national contingent operates unanimously with the political groups. The Dutch public is hardly aware of what policies they advocate. Even within their parties, MEPs are largely ignored, although lip-service is paid to 'the very important work' they do. Apart from perhaps the leader of the Dutch social democrat MEPs, Piet Dankert, MEPs do not really belong to the high ranks of their respective parties.

CANDIDATE SELECTION FOR THE 1989 ELECTIONS

The first step in EP elections is taken by political parties, when they start the process of formulating the electoral platforms and lists of candidates. As with national elections, voters do not determine candidates, only the number of seats for each party. It is the selectorate within the parties that determines who will be eligible. Because the recruitment of political personnel is a monopoly of political parties, the nomination process within these parties forms the key arena of intra-party conflict. Factionalism does not exist, but regional party bodies and categorical groups (especially women's groups) intervene in the process, in which the national party leadership tries to safeguard a balanced composition of the future parliamentary party. Because of the importance of candidate selection, the nomination processes usually get considerable attention from the media. In the 1989 EP elections, most attention was given to quarrels over the nomination of certain candidates. The formulation of the platforms and even the campaign for the elections itself did not attract much media attention.

The smaller left-wing parties, PSP, PPR, CPN, and some other political groupings, decided to present a common list, as they already had done in 1984. They labelled their list 'Rainbow' (*Regenboog*), to correspond with the name of their EP political group. Before 1989 these parties had presented themselves as the Green Progressive Accord (*Groen Progressief Akkoord*). The new name was adopted after long discussions within the various parties. The PSP especially had problems with a name that mentioned only the green colour. Did such a name not mean that socialism (the red colour) played a minor role? The label 'Rainbow' solved the problem, although one of the minor political partners (the Green Party in the Netherlands, *Groene Partij Nederland*) was disappointed about the disappearance of the term 'green'. The nomination of candidates also created serious problems. If the Rainbow list won just one seat, the situation was rather simple. The incumbent PPR candidate Herman Verbeek, the head of the list, would give up his seat after two-and-a-half years in favour of Nel van Dijk (CPN). But what if the list won two seats, as it had done in 1984? During protracted negotiations it was proposed that Verbeek and Van Dijk would occupy the two seats during the first half of the parliamentary period. Mr Hontelez (PSP) and an independent woman were to succeed them during the second half. In this way there would always be a woman representative. This proposal proved to be in vain. In the end, the fourth place on the list was occupied by a man from a tiny progressive Christian party, the EVP. But since all parties were in favour of an equal representation of men and women during the whole parliamentary period, this implied that Mrs Van Dijk would be entitled to keep her seat during the whole period.

Neither the name, nor the common list could satisfy all the wishes of each party. Only the fact that no party could win a seat on its own prevented the parties from breaking up the difficult negotiations. It was commonly assumed, therefore, that the new common Rainbow list was only a pragmatic result of *ad hoc* cooperation. Surprisingly, however, the smaller left-wing parties suddenly decided to have a common list (Green Left – *Groen Links*) for the national elections in September 1989 too. They did so just before the EP elections were held. Although hard to prove, it is possible that cooperation at the European level may have stimulated the process of cooperation at the national level.

The smaller orthodox Calvinist parties, SGP, GPV and RPF, decided again to present a common list for the EP elections. The agreement they had made for the 1984 elections proved useful again. The only representative of the list between 1984 and 1989, Van der Waal (SGP), headed the list. According to the agreement, the second and third placed candidates on the list changed places. The second place went to a candidate from the GPV (Van Middelkoop) and the third to a member of the RPF (Van Dam). Also the order of the parties on the list's label changed from SGP, GPV and RPF to SGP, RPF, GPV.

Probably the most media attention for the nomination processes was given to D'66. From September to November 1988 members of D'66 could present themselves as possible candidates for the EP elections. The party decided about the order of the list by way of a referendum among its members. Only the head of the list was chosen by the party congress, at which all members are entitled to be present, to speak and to vote. This procedure is unique among Dutch political parties, and is a result of the movement for more participatory democracy in the 1960s. The name of the party, Democraten '66, illustrates this.

Just before November 1988 the diplomat Bertens announced that he was willing to head the list. Bertens' presentation of himself in the media, however, was not very well-perceived by the party. He had created the impression that his place at the top of the list was assured and that the party leadership backed this candidacy. The party, for which democratic procedures are so important, protested. With some difficulty the party leadership managed to convince the protesting members that nothing had been settled yet and that the party would decide. At the end of 1988, after a special meeting at which aspiring candidates presented themselves to the party, the referendum was held. Only 20 per cent participated. Bertens was put in second place, preceded by the vice-chairman of the party, Van den Bos. The latter, who had hesitated to stand also for the national elections, declared that he was willing to 'pull the list', in Dutch parlance. Because Bertens also maintained his willingness to head the list, the party congress had to decide between the candidates. In February 1989 in Bertens' home town, Maastricht, a majority chose Bertens as the flagbearer for the EP elections; Van den Bos was given the second place on the list. So, in the end, the party leadership's favourite candidate had won, albeit not without doubts within the party about the democratic nature of the procedures followed.

Within the Liberal party, the VVD, the nomination process did not cause much of an internal party struggle. Especially after Mrs Larive had said she would not run for the position at the top of the list, the selection process followed *grosso modo* the proposals made by the party leadership. Mrs Larive had a good chance to head the list. But she gave this up for personal reasons and 'in the party's interest'. In March 1989 the party congress appointed Mr De Vries – an incumbent MEP – as the head of the list; Mrs Larive took second place.

Also within the Christian Democratic CDA the selection of candidates was a rather quiet affair. A special committee, presided by the former Minister of Foreign Affairs Schmelzer, drafted an advisory list. This advisory list was adopted by the party executive without alteration. The national party council ratified it as the definitive list of candidates, also without important changes. The work of the special committee, therefore, proved to be decisive. This committee had held separate interviews with about thirty aspiring candidates. Its goal was to draft a balanced list with respect to age, region, sex, specialism, and so on. It also put new candidates in about a third of winnable places, in order to guarantee continuity in the future. Mr Penders headed the list.

The Labour Party (PvdA) also started the nomination procedure with an advisory list, drafted by an 'independent' commission. Within this commission there was some discussion about who was to head the list, Mr Dankert or Mrs d'Ancona, both incumbent MEPs. Both were considered apt for the job. The first position on the list, however, went to Dankert, because of his success in the 1984 elections and his renown as a former EP president. The definitive list order was decided upon at a special party council in March 1989. The first four places on the list were confirmed. The next five places, that still were considered to be winnable places, were subject to discussion. The party council changed the order of these places. In particular, the fifth on the advisory list, Mrs Goedmakers, encountered much criticism and was put in ninth place, which by then was still considered to be a safe place. Thus, the influence of the regional party bodies that send their delegates to the national party council was considerable.

Some other political groupings drafted lists of candidates, although they had little chance of winning a seat. The Socialist Party (SP), a small radical socialist party with electoral strongholds in some cities, presented a list of 30 candidates. A tiny political party with the inspiring name God With Us (*God Met Ons*) traditionally participated in the elections, without having the slightest chance of getting a seat. A new party, the Initiative for European Democracy (IDE), claimed to be the only genuine 'European party'. The party is organised on a European basis and had a more or less liberal leaning. Because the EP elections are held according to national rules, the IDE had to adapt itself to specific national electoral stipulations. In the Netherlands, therefore, they presented a list with the names of over 30 candidates.

The last party mentioned on the ballot paper was the common list of a political grouping around Mr Janmaat (a former MP for the Centre Party) and the Centre Democrats (*Centrumdemocraten*), **who** had split some years before from the same Centre Party. In fact, it was one and the same grouping, reunited after some internal fights. In spite of its name, the Centre Democrats is an extreme right-wing party, comparable with the National Front in France and the Republicans in West Germany. However, they are small by comparison. Janmaat, who is rather well-known in the Netherlands, headed the list.

THE PARTY PLATFORMS

All parties were able to present a special platform for the EP elections. Those parties that belong to an EP political group used the manifesto drafted by the Euro-federation of the parties of their political orientation. Hence, the CDA accepted the platform of the European People's Party, but only after it had successfully tried to alter some conservative stances in more progressive ways (especially with regard to medical technology and to South Africa). The VVD used the European Liberal Democrats (ELD) manifesto. The Dutch liberals had been active in amending the draft manifesto.

The PvdA participated in drafting a common European Socialist platform. The result was very much a compromise. Therefore, the future PvdA MEPs stated that they were willing to defend the European platform, but their political decisions would be guided in the first place by their own Dutch election platform. Other parties presented their own platforms. Remarkably, the three orthodox Calvinist parties, which presented a common list of candidates, did not present one common programme. Instead, three platforms were drafted, which differed, however, only slightly.

All parties mentioned more or less the same issue-areas although the different ideological orientations were present, of course. '1992' and environmental issues were treated at some length. All parties are concerned now about the environment, but – to give just an example – the liberal VVD claims that care for the environment and economic growth can be mutually reinforcing, whereas the other parties are more cautious about economic growth. With respect to the Single Act some parties stressed the need for an integration of the market, whereas others more to the left underlined the need for an adequate European social policy. The small orthodox Calvinist parties traditionally oppose a fully-integrated (Western) Europe. They advocate a confederation instead of a 'unified' Europe. The fact that Calvinists are only a minority in a unified Europe is likely to have inspired this stance.

THE INVISIBLE CAMPAIGN

What can be said about the EP campaign, if there appears to have been none? The billboards offered by the local authorities to the parties (*gratis*) to put their posters on were only partially used. The free time on radio and television given to the parties was used, but the programmes were hardly watched or listened to. The newspapers published series of articles about 'Europe' or 'the candidates', but the campaign never made the front page. The reasons are twofold. First, EP elections are considered by the parties and the public to be of only minor importance. Parties will, of course, never admit this publicly, but if one compares the money spent on a campaign for national elections compared with the one for the Euro-elections, one must conclude that the EP campaign ranks low on the list of priorities (on average, parties spent three times less on the EP campaign than on the last national campaign). Second, and this is perhaps the most important reason, the national political situation dominated the EP campaign more than ever. Six weeks before polling day, the coalition government of VVD and CDA fell. New national elections were announced for 6 September. The coalition broke down because of disagreement over a rather technical question of the tax-deductibility of the costs of transport from home to work by car. The question was discussed within the framework of a broader debate on a National Environment Policy Plan. The parliamentary party of the VVD was against abolishing tax deductibility, as proposed by the Plan. VVD Ministers, however, backed the Plan, albeit not always wholeheartedly. The cabinet crisis was to a large extent also a VVD crisis. After the fall of the cabinet, the VVD was blamed for being the cause of the crisis.

Immediately all media attention focused on the question of which parties would form the next government: the CDA together with the PvdA, or a continuation of the CDA/VVD coalition? In this situation it is not surprising that the very prudently-started European campaign was downgraded completely to a mere tool of the national political game. Candidates for the EP were forced to play this game in order to get at least some attention. So, at party meetings the head of the list for the EP elections gave his or her speech (very often about 'Europe 1992') just before the national leader of the party commented on the national political situation with some dutiful references to the European scene. Media coverage of the meeting, almost always ignored the EP candidate.

Opinion polls indicated that the heads of the lists for the European Parliament were hardly known, not to mention the other candidates. A television debate between the heads of the lists just before the elections was not going to alter this. Very few people watched this rather boring discussion. Other polls predicted a very low turnout. Some parties, therefore, tried to convince voters to go to the poll by saying that the results of the EP elections would be an important indicator for power relations at the national level. Even this proved to be unsuccessful. Never before had so many people stayed at home on election day; a considerable percentage (11 per cent) said they 'had just forgotten that elections were held'. After such an invisible campaign this is not really surprising.

THE RESULTS

The results of the EP elections reflect the absence of public interest. Only 47.2 per cent voted (5 243 911 votes). The official results were made public three days after polling day. Precinct surveys, however, accurately 'predicted' the final results on election night. Opinion polls during the campaign had indicated a big loss for the VVD and a close finish for the PvdA and the CDA. But the final results were less positive for the PvdA, probably because of the very low turnout (see Table 10.1). The CDA made major gains.

VVD losses were expected and went mainly to the CDA. The Rainbow list did very well. To some degree this might be explained by the fact that at the national level the constituent parties had just decided to present a common list at the national elections in September. But it is also probable that some Rainbow voters will vote PvdA (again) then when the real question of power is at stake again. The growth of the smaller orthodox Calvinist parties is accounted for by the loyalty of their electorate: only 14 per cent of their voters at the national elections in 1986 stayed at home. The other lists (including the extreme right-wing Centre Party) did not obtain a seat. And although at the national elections only 0.67 per cent is enough to win a seat, the low turnout prevents us from speculating about their prospects at the national elections.

Table 10.1   European elections in the Netherlands, 1984 and 1989

	1984 %	1989 %	1984 Seats	1989 Seats
Voting turnout	50.5	47.2		
PvdA	33.7	30.7	9	8
CDA	30.0	34.6	8	10
VVD	18.9	13.6	5	3
Rainbow	5.6	7.0	2	2
SGP/GPV/RPF	5.2	5.9	1	1
D'66	2.3	5.9	–	1
Soc. Party	–	0.7	–	–
God With Us	0.5	0.4	–	–
IDE	–	0.4	–	–
Janmaat List/Centre Party	2.5	0.8	–	–

The precinct surveys of the Bureau Interview (*De Volkskrant*, 19 June 1989) give more detailed information about the voters. The PvdA attracted more women than men, and the VVD and especially the Rainbow list more men than women. The sexes were equally divided among the other lists. The CDA and PvdA attracted most of the younger voters. Within the electorate of the Rainbow list the younger voters formed a substantial contingent. Interestingly the CDA picked up many secular votes. Eleven per cent of the non-religious voters voted for the CDA. This had first occurred at the 1986 national elections and, hence, proves to be of structural importance.

CONCLUSION

The 1989 European elections were more than ever overshadowed by the national political situation. The fall of the Dutch cabinet in May and the forthcoming national elections in September absorbed almost all the media attention. The campaign for the EP elections therefore was hardly visible. In the eyes of the voters the EP elections were not even of second order, but were rather 'third-order elections'. Parties and candidates were not able to convince a large majority of the voters of the importance of a new and strong mandate for the EC institution that has to guarantee a certain degree of democratic control within the Community. This is due to a large degree to the national political situation. But also the parties themselves must take some blame. Not willing or able to present electorally attractive candidates and to spend much money and energy on the EP elections, they helped to downgrade the public image of the EP elections. But can the parties really be blamed for this as long as the EP's powers remain as limited as they are now? Without public pressure, however, these powers are unlikely to expand in the near future. Perhaps a 'Democratic Single Act' is needed to bridge the existing democratic gap in Europe.

11 The United Kingdom
MICHAEL BURGESS and
ADRIAN LEE

BACKGROUND

The 1984 EP election in the United Kingdom (UK) occurred almost exactly one year after the national general election of 9 June 1983 which witnessed the return of Margaret Thatcher to office for a second consecutive term. Clearly the second EP election was not a genuine mid-term election and there was therefore some basis for describing it as a 'non-event'.[1] Nonetheless this did not deter the Labour Party's new leader, Neil Kinnock, from construing the EP election as a national referendum on Thatcher's first year of office since 1983. Indeed Kinnock was keen for the Labour Party to perform well in the Euro-election as clear evidence of its recovery after the electoral mauling it experienced twelve months earlier. The SDP–Liberal Alliance also looked forward with optimism to the EP election as a golden opportunity to strengthen its challenge to the longstanding and overwhelming dominance of the Conservative and Labour parties in British electoral politics. It had successfully contested its first general election in 1983 and had won the largest share of the vote achieved by a third party since 1923. Its 26.1 per cent of the vote was just 2.2 per cent behind Labour. Mindful of this progress the Alliance could be forgiven for harbouring high expectations in June 1984.

These Alliance expectations reached dizzy heights on the evening of Thursday 14 June 1984 when the result of the Portsmouth South by-election, held on the same day as the EP election, was declared an SDP victory. An Alliance breakthrough in the Euro-election seemed suddenly to be a distinct possibility. However, the reality proved disappointing. Despite winning 19.5 per cent of the vote the Alliance failed to win a single seat. In its most realistic prospect, the Highlands and Islands, where it had won more votes in 1983 than any other party and where it had a strong candidate in the Liberal MP for Inverness, Russell Johnston, the Alliance was well beaten. It was unable to overcome the double handicap of the Scottish National Party's popular candidate, Winifred Ewing, and a generally miserable performance throughout Scotland. Indeed the four largest falls in the Alliance vote occurred in Scotland, while in Great Britain as a whole it lost a quarter of the vote it had captured in 1983.

The Labour Party's expected recovery was patchy. In total it took 15 seats from the Conservatives, bringing its final tally of seats to 32, and increased its share of the vote from 33 per cent in 1979 to 36.5 per cent in 1984. Despite its somewhat ignominious defeat in the Portsmouth South by-election the Euro-poll clearly showed that Labour was back in competition with the Conservatives for first place rather than with the Alliance for second. The overall swing from Conservative to Labour was 5.5 per cent and the latter's achievement in recapturing first place in London where it recorded a swing of 8.1 per cent and won 41.7 per cent of the vote against 39.8 per cent for the Conservatives was heartening for Kinnock. But Labour's result had to be set in perspective. It looked healthy primarily because it was invariably compared with the débâcle of 1983. By almost any other criterion it was only a modest performance.

Relieved not to have done worse one year into the lifetime of the Government, the Conservatives were clear overall winners. With 45 seats in the EP, their share of the vote had fallen from 50.6 per cent in 1979 to 40.8 per cent in 1984, still 4 per cent ahead of Labour. This enabled the Conservative Party Chairman, John Selwyn Gummer, to claim with some justification that his party had done better than any other governing party in the EC, with a comfortable lead in terms of both seats and votes.

In Northern Ireland, where the 17 Ulster parliamentary constituencies were grouped together to comprise a single multi-member Euro-constituency based upon the Single Transferable Vote (STV) and allocated three EP seats, all three MEPs were re-elected. Ian Paisley for the Democratic and Unionist Party (DUP) increased his share of first-preference votes from 29.8 per cent in 1979 to 33.6 per cent and John Hume for the Social Democratic and Labour Party (SDLP) defeated the Provisional Sinn Fein candidate, Danny Morrison, with a first-preference vote-share of 22.1 per cent compared with 24.6 per cent in 1979. John Taylor's Official Unionist Party (OUP) vote remained stable at 21.5 per cent compared with 21.9 per cent in 1979. With 230 251 first preference votes the size of Ian Paisley's victory was a record in Northern Ireland elections and both he and John Hume could claim significant personal triumphs in 1984.

The nationalist parties in Scotland and Wales could also take some comfort from the EP election compared with their 1983 performance. Plaid Cymru succeeded in pushing its vote up throughout Wales by an average of 4.3 per cent, while the SNP's retention of the Highlands and Islands was matched by an increase in their vote throughout Scotland by an average of 6.9 per cent. On the outer fringes of British electoral politics the Ecology Party signalled its arrival by attracting nearly 71 000 votes, thus quadrupling its share of the vote in the 1983 general election. In total it fielded 17 candidates and obtained 0.6 per cent of the vote with its highest individual result of 4.7 per cent in Hereford and Worcester. Few informed observers would have predicted the remarkable transformation in the party's fortunes during the late 1980s.[2]

Perhaps the most striking feature of the EP election was not the general change in party fortunes but the level of turnout. At 32.4 per cent it was even lower than the turnout of 32.6 per cent in Great Britain in 1979. But there was no consistent evidence that the variation in the change in turnout particularly affected one party more than another. The result of the EP election predictably raised questions about the use of the first-past-the-post electoral system in Great Britain. While the Alliance won no seats with 19.5 per cent of the vote, the SNP obtained one seat with 1.7 per cent of the vote but 17.8 per cent of the total Scottish vote. Both David Steel and David Owen condemned the result as a mockery and an outrage but their protests as usual fell largely upon deaf ears. Overall the disappointing turnout could be ascribed to an assortment of factors influencing voters: the widespread confusion and ignorance about what the EP is and what it does; the invisibility of Euro-issues; the low national profile of most MEPs; the diffidence of the media and most party workers; and the signal lack of controversy usually associated with general elections. Reinforcing these influences was the unfortunate, if unavoidable, timing of the EP election, and the sense that voters had of an election which was not about choosing a government.

The 1984 Euro-election was dominated by national and domestic issues, focusing attention in particular upon the Conservative government's domestic policies and record. As a 'referendum or opinion poll on the popularity of the British parties' the shift to the left was hardly surprising.[3] It remained to be seen whether or not Labour and the Alliance parties could mount an effective and sustained challenge to the Conservative Party's growing belief that it constituted Britain's natural party of government.[4]

During the lifetime of the second elected EP (1984–89) there were two EP by-elections neither of which received much media attention. The first was held in March 1988 in Midlands West after the death of the sitting Labour MEP, Terry Pitt, and resulted in a predictable Labour victory while the second, in Hampshire Central, occasioned by the death of the Conservative MEP, Basil de Ferranti, equally predictably confirmed a Conservative grip on the seat. Held in December 1988, the Hampshire Central by-election recorded a turnout of 14.1 per cent, a figure actually higher than some polls had forecast, and claimed the dubious distinction of setting a new British record for non-voting.

THE NATIONAL POLITICAL CONTEXT

In the years between the two EP elections of 1984 and 1989 the nature of the European debate changed dramatically. The Conservative government was confronted with a range of EC initiatives and proposals designed to accelerate the pace of economic and political integration. Motivated principally by the desire to achieve 'European Union' – an undefined EC commitment stretching back to the Paris summit of October 1972 – both the EP and the Commission intensified their efforts to persuade member state governments to extend EC policies and accept institutional reform.[5] This concentrated pressure for reform reflected a deepseated recognition of the need to strengthen the EC's capacity to meet the new commercial and technological challenges of the late twentieth century. However, the renewed impetus for change also served to highlight the wide divergence of national positions and conceptions of the EC's future. Here the Conservative government and the Prime Minister, Margaret Thatcher, in particular found themselves increasingly embattled as they sought to resist institutional reform, treaty modification and steps towards EMU. Indeed Thatcher's frequently strident attacks upon the statements, intentions and proposals of the new Commission presided over by Jacques Delors from 1985 gradually assumed the characteristics of a personal crusade against European Union.

Thatcher had acquired a reputation in the EC for couching her defence of British interests in distinctly uncompromising tones, especially over the thorny issue of budget grievances. But the Fontainebleau European Council of June 1984 brought to a memorable end the very painful and damaging episode of *juste retour*. From this date the discernible shift in the EC's agenda towards a reinforced internal market, the acceptance of budgetary discipline, the progressive reform of the CAP, the strengthening of cooperation in foreign policy and defence, collaboration in technology and a common approach to trade with Japan conspired to bring the interests of the UK and its major EC partners into temporary harmony. Europe was on the move again and the British government was determined to take the initiative by steadily building up EC-wide support for practical reforms. In particular the drive to speed up the liberalisation of the internal market, so enthusiastically propounded by Lord Cockfield, one of Thatcher's appointees as vice-president of the Commission in 1985, was deemed entirely consistent with strengthening Britain's capacity to pursue its main economic policy objectives. Other, more controversial, EC policies such as British membership of the EMS were, however, conveniently deferred. On such issues the Prime Minister elevated the concept of national interest starkly above EC goals.

The increasingly personalised conflict between Thatcher's limited conception of 'a Europe open for business' and the wider, more constitutionally binding, vision of Europe entertained by several member states (especially Italy, the Benelux and, later, Spain) reached a climax at the Milan European Council of June 1985 where Mrs Thatcher resolutely opposed the proposal for an intergovernmental conference (IGC) to discuss both policy and institutional reform. Suspicious of Commission and EP intentions,[6] she was defeated in a surprise vote in Milan which left the UK, Denmark and Greece in a militant minority. Having opposed the IGC decision, however, the British, Danish and Greek governments could not risk being absent from its deliberations for fear of being marginalised by the decisions likely to be taken by the majority of seven governments. The IGC discussions between September and December 1985 resulted in the Single European Act (SEA) which required unanimous approval by the national parliaments of the Twelve (Spain and Portugal joined the EC on 1 January 1986) and was implemented in July 1987.[7]

What, then, does this short survey of the public debate about Europe's future tell us about the national political context to the 1989 EP election? What role did the British government play in the unfolding of these events so critical to Britain's relationship with the EC? Clearly the political momentum originally generated by the EUT kept institutional reform of some sort on the EC agenda. The

British Prime Minister, dwelling in the fervent language of national sovereignty, had been forced reluctantly to go along with the momentum. Milan had been a bad-tempered affair but the EC (Amendment) Bill, having been guillotined in the House of Commons, finally received formal parliamentary endorsement in November 1986. Despite vocal opposition by the anti-marketeers on the Labour and Conservative backbenches Thatcher was able to present the treaty amendment as a modest reform package which strengthened the EC while simultaneously serving Britain's basic economic and political interests. The British government adopted a minimalist interpretation of the SEA which emphasised its limits rather than its possibilities.

With the exception of the anti-marketeers in the Labour Party at home and in the EP, and an increasingly vocal and disgruntled group of Conservatives at Westminster, the controversies surrounding the SEA debate did not capture the public imagination. The 'quality' press gave widespread coverage of these events and there was conspicuous pressure-group activity, especially concerning those organised interests in business and industry most likely to be affected by the internal market. But in general the debate about the EC's future appeared arcane to the public at large. A considerable reservoir of goodwill existed for the general idea of European unity but this translated confusingly when applied to the EC.

During 1988–89 the question of European Union, for so long derided by British politicians and officials as nothing more than Euro-rhetoric, was suddenly and dramatically catapulted to the forefront of British political debate. The national political context to the 1989 EP election found the Conservative Government and Party in a state of unprecedented public disarray. Thatcher had easily won her third consecutive general election in June 1987 and the 1989 Euro-election coincided with a decade of Conservative government under her premiership. But instead of providing an occasion for celebration the Prime Minister was handed her first clear electoral defeat. How did this happen? Why did the national political context change so significantly?

The background explanation to this is clear and can be attributed to the SEA. This contained commitments which ensured that the momentum towards European Union, once created, would gather pace rather than decline. The SEA was a beginning not an end. Its economic and political implications were and remain far-reaching. This is why the British government's relations with the EC have become increasingly strained since the SEA's ratification. It has to some considerable extent been caught up in the inherent logic of the process of economic and political integration to which it has publicly subscribed by signing the SEA. The public controversy which erupted in September 1988 when the Prime Minister addressed the assembled audience in the College of Europe in Bruges on the subject of Britain and Europe can be regarded as an official rebuttal to the provocative assertions made, perhaps injudiciously, by the Commission President, Jacques Delors, in the EP and at the TUC Conference in Bournemouth earlier in that year. If Delors' claim in the EP that a 'quiet revolution' was taking place as a result of which at least 80 per cent of economic, financial and 'perhaps social legislation'[8] would be directed from the EC in a decade was not throwing down a gauntlet to Thatcher, his open support for EC-wide guarantees on workers' rights, social protection and collective bargaining when he spoke to British trade unionists in Bournemouth certainly was.[9] But the public furore that followed merely underlined the distinctly different conceptions of Europe which were entertained by Thatcher and the majority of her EC partners – differences which were evident during the events surrounding the debate on the SEA in 1985–86.

At home Thatcher's Bruges speech received much publicity. It served to reopen and widen the hitherto soft-pedalled divisions within Conservative ranks. If there had ever been much of a genuine split on Europe within the Conservative Party it had really only existed beween the majority of Conservative MEPs and a doughty group of Westminster Conservatives who were hostile to Brussels. In the post-Bruges atmosphere leading up to the campaign, however, this rift became a veritable chasm. A public row broke out between Sir John Hoskyns, the Director-General of the Institute of Directors, and EP President, Sir Henry Plumb, over allegations of fraud and corrupt practices among MEPs. Hoskyns' headline-grabbing attack (which also stretched to a forecast of doom for Europe's coveted single market) prompted Plumb publicly to resign his membership of the Institute. While this public altercation simmered during March 1989, John Banham, the Director-General of the Confederation of British Industry, defended the 1992 programme and in his Lombard Lecture at the Institute of Chartered Accountants accused Hoskyns of 'whingeing'.

On the issue of British membership of the EMS the well-known differences between the Prime Minister and the Chancellor of the Exchequer, Nigel Lawson, also reached something of a climax in this period. Lawson's support for EMS membership and his determination to prop up sterling by shadowing the Deutsch Mark earned him a prime-ministerial rebuke and led to Conservative unrest as it became clear that at least two Cabinet ministers, Nigel Lawson and Sir Geoffrey Howe, the Foreign Secretary, were lined up against the Prime Minister, Lord Young, the Trade and Industry Secretary, and Professor Alan Walters, Thatcher's economic adviser in Downing Street. Michael Heseltine, the former Secretary of State for Defence, placed himself firmly but discreetly in the 'pro-European' camp, as it came to be seen, when his book, *The Challenge of Europe: Can Britain Win?*, was published in May 1989 and took a favourable line on European Union. Thatcher's Bruges speech was severely criticised again by Lord Plumb in an address to the Royal Institute of International Affairs in the same month and the incessant attacks by Edward Heath on the Prime Minister's renowned sacred cow of national sovereignty combined to present the Conservatives as a weak and divided party.

As the EP election campaign drew closer the discord within the Conservative Party was further fuelled by Thatcher's opposition to the Delors report on EMU, the proposed Social Charter, the Lingua programme, border controls, the harmonisation of VAT and excise duties, and pensioners' privilege cards for old-age benefits. These circumstances delighted both the Social and Liberal Democrat (SLD) and Labour parties which exploited Conservative divisions by presenting themselves as united, pro-European parties. Lord Jenkins and Paddy Ashdown for the SLD and Neil Kinnock and John Smith for Labour each accused the Government of petty obstinacy which damaged Britain's image in Europe and was likely to exclude it from exercising any real influence in the EC. The battle-lines for the campaign were thus firmly drawn from the moment Thatcher had spoken at Bruges in September 1988.

THE CAMPAIGN

Timing and circumstance conspired to ensure that the campaign for the EP election would be far more visible and central to the UK's domestic political process than those of 1979 and 1984. That of 1979 was a lacklustre affair, with the major parties having exhausted their campaigning effort in the general election the month before. 1984, heralded by some as a 'mid-term' election, far from demonstrating a major swing against the party in power nationally merely registered a small recovery by the Labour Party; continued Conservative dominance; and disappointment for the then Alliance.

The 1989 campaign took place in very different circumstances. The timing of the elections ensured that they would be the only UK-wide test of electoral opinion between the general election of 1987 and that due in 1991 or 1992. The opportunity existed for the political parties to treat them as the opening stage of the next general election campaign: the opportunity was grasped by the Labour Party in particular and by political commentators. The Conservatives, on the other hand, embarked on the campaign in an essentially defensive mode, following Labour's recovery in the county council elections in May and their loss in the Vale of Glamorgan by-election on the same day. The SLD, languishing in the opinion polls, could expect little apart from a confirmation of their party's slippage in the county elections. The continuing SDP, led by David Owen, signalled its withdrawal from full-scale electoral campaigning in mid-May, and was to field only a handful of candidates for the EP. The Green Party, in a climate of increasing concern over environmental issues, chose the elections as the venue for its first nationwide electoral challenge. The SNP initiated its campaign on an independent Scotland within Europe platform, seeking to build upon its earlier success in the Glasgow Govan by-election, when it overturned an apparently secure Labour majority. Plaid Cymru contested all four Welsh seats, but its electoral hopes were effectively restricted to displacing the Conservatives in Wales North.

The Conservative defence of the seats held in 1984 opened formally with the publication of the party's European manifesto, which restated the Prime Minister's Bruges vision of Europe, and introduced what was to become the major theme of the Conservative campaign in the closing week, namely, that Labour, unable to win general elections, was seeking to advance the socialist cause via Strasbourg and Brussels. Divisions within the Conservative camp were immediately apparent. Edward Heath, former Prime Minister and long-time opponent of Margaret Thatcher's approach to the EC, attacked the manifesto as that of an individual person rather than of the party, and accused the Prime Minister of misleading the electorate with her depiction of the drift of Europe towards a 'socialist superstate'. In return, Norman Fowler, the Secretary of State for Employment, accused Edward Heath of 'going entirely over the top' and stating that the ex-Premier's views were not those of the

Conservative Party. The opposition were aided in their search for disarray in the Conservative position by the simultaneous and fortuitous publication of Heseltine's book. He argued for the creation of a European Senate drawn from national parliaments, and an additional European ministerial post in the Foreign Office. Overall the book was seen as an attempt to counter Mrs Thatcher's Bruges declaration and to argue for a more emollient and less hostile British attitude to Europe and against Britain's remaining 'aloof'. In terms of more specific policies, the government was signally unable to present a united front. The long-running dispute over Britain's role in relation to the EMS ran throughout the campaign, before an attempt to put it to rest was made by Nigel Lawson three days ahead of polling. If the party's divisions over European issues and the EC's future were to be thrown into greater relief by the campaign, its difficulties on the domestic front were to ensure that its approach to the electorate was almost entirely defensive. The rise in inflation, the balance of payments deficit, rising interest and mortgage rates, coupled with the apparent unpopularity of major legislative measures such as the introduction of the community charge, and the privatisation of electricity and water supply industries, combined to make the presentation of the government's position difficult.

If a party's election campaign is summarised by itself immediately before polling, then the final tone of the Conservative effort can be judged by its closing stages. The Chancellor admitted that interest rate rises were unpopular, and the Prime Minister, in a last attempt to rally Conservative voters, warned that 'Thursday is about Britain's future. In three general elections you voted for our sort of Britain. On Thursday, we need you to vote for our sort of Europe.' The distinctive line was reiterated when she said: 'We haven't rolled back the frontiers of socialism in this country to see them reimposed from Brussels', and averred that 'we did not join Europe to be swallowed up in some bureaucratic conglomerate, where it's Euro-this and Euro-that and forget about being British or French or Italian or Spanish'. The theme was echoed in the party's major poster campaign of the final week. Striking posters with the simple messages 'stay at home on June 15 and you'll live on a diet of Brussels' were widely displayed in marginal and other constituencies, giving rise to considerable criticism by candidates and others within the party after the end of the campaign and even before polling day itself.

The Labour Party's campaign stood in sharp contrast and undoubtedly capitalised on the 'anti-Europe' flavour imparted by the

Conservatives' efforts. Neil Kinnock's leadership, under question as the year opened, was buttressed by the party's steady rise in the opinion polls through the first part of the year, by the outcome of Labour's policy reviews, and, on the electoral level, by victory against the Conservatives in the Vale of Glamorgan by-election and the swift imposition of a Labour candidate on the local party for the Vauxhall by-election. During the campaign, Labour held daily press conferences, both in London and the regions, and was able successfully to play down the faltering challenge from its anti-EC unilateralist left. Labour's campaign was explicitly based on the concept of the EP election as a referendum on ten years of Conservative rule. This strategy appears in retrospect to have been effective in minimising Labour's internal divisions over British membership of the EC and the future development of its institutions, and in assisting the party in presenting the Conservatives as the 'divided' and 'anti-European' party, in remarkable contrast to the position in 1984. In contrast the staged release of elements of the Labour Party's policy review in the months preceding the campaign, coupled with the improvement in the party's fortunes demonstrated by the results of the May county council elections, had led to increased media comment on the growing credibility and 'electability' of Labour. It became increasingly apparent that the equally-discussed 'collapse of the centre' was to be to Labour's benefit.

The SLD, formed in late 1987 and early 1988 after the demise of the former Alliance between the Liberal Party and the Social Democratic Party, had failed to make any by-election breakthroughs since the 1987 general election. The party faced considerable problems in attempting to establish itself under the new leadership of Paddy Ashdown, not least in the face of the confusion occasioned by the continued separate existence of Owen's anti-merger Social Democratic Party. Opinion poll support fell to below 10 per cent after the formation of the SLD, and fell still further from the beginning of 1989. Following its reverses in the county council elections the party's EP campaign did not achieve a high level of visibility, despite its attempts to continue the Liberal tradition as the most 'European' of the political parties. Ironically the only member of the party to achieve significant media coverage was the former leader, David Steel, who stood as a candidate for an Italian seat. In the UK, the party's hopes were limited. On paper only two seats offered the possiblity of providing the party with its first representatives in the directly-elected EP – Cornwall and Plymouth, held by the

Conservatives in 1984 with a majority of 9.2 per cent, and Wales North, a four-way marginal with a Conservative majority of 5.6 per cent over the former Alliance. The SDP did not mount a national campaign, instead fighting only 16 seats also contested by the SLD. Although a formal electoral arrangement was abjured by both party leaders, the SDP unilaterally withdrew its candidates from European constituencies containing Westminster seats held by the SLD.

Fragmentation and decline in the centre left the ground open for a classic two-party contest throughout most of Great Britain, with the challenge of third parties restricted to the peripheries. Labour's planned campaign (coordinated by Bryan Gould, erstwhile leading anti-marketeer), from its opening at the 'Red Rose Rally' in Birmingham in April, stood in sharp contrast to the apparent divisions in the Conservative camp. Many observers, not least within the Conservative Party, considered that the Tory campaign embodied a major strategic error. A negative campaign which concentrated on attacking Labour and encroachments by Brussels on British 'sovereignty' left Labour free to minimise its own divisions and emphasise the benefits of British membership of the EC. In particular, Labour spokesmen were able to stress the benefits allegedly denied to Britain by Mrs Thatcher's resistance to the Social Charter and increased EC involvement in consumer protection and the environment.

THE RESULT

A foreshadowing of the outcome was given by a *Daily Telegraph* Gallup Poll one week before polling.[10] Labour achieved a six-point increase on its performance the previous month to stand at 43.5 per cent; the Conservatives fell four points to 36.5 per cent; the SLD at 8.0 per cent registered a decline of two per cent; and the Social Democrat Party's 3.0 per cent represented a drop of four points on their May position. Barely noticed at the time, the Green Party added 2.5 per cent to stand at 5.5 per cent. Four days later, more comment was occasioned by a subsequent Gallup Poll which found among the 41 per cent who said that they were 'certain to vote' in the EP election preferences divided with Labour standing at 44 per cent, the Conservatives on 29 per cent, and the Green Party at 10 per cent overtaking the SLD which slumped to 5 per cent.[11]

Polling took place on the traditional Thursday but counting did not start until the close of voting in those countries where a Sunday poll was held. Parliamentary by-elections for the London seat of Vauxhall and Glasgow Central, both seats held by Labour in 1987, coincided with the EP election. In the latter case Labour's victory against a strong challenge from the SNP allowed the party some relief. The Vauxhall result perhaps afforded Labour greater satisfaction, with the candidate imposed by the National Executive Committee increasing Labour's percentage majority over the Conservatives.

The results not yet declared, attention concentrated on the BBC's exit poll which predicted an overwhelming Labour victory in the EP election. Putting Labour on 44 per cent and the Conservatives on 32 per cent, it registered a sensational rise for the Green Party to 14 per cent, and a slump by the SLD to a mere 6 per cent. The Labour Party, while acknowledging victory, played down the margin, while the Conservatives, beset by immediate wrangling over the failure of their campaign, attacked the poll findings.

When the result was finally announced it became clear that the poll, while accurately forecasting the movement of opinion in its general pattern, had overestimated the extent of the Labour lead and that of the Conservative loss. Nevertheless the final result demonstrated that Labour had beaten the Conservatives in a nationwide election for the first time since October 1974. The Conservatives, on 34.7 per cent of the national vote, achieved their lowest percentage in any nationwide election in the postwar period.

Between Conservative and Labour, the election produced a virtual mirror-image of the position in the EP election of 1984. The return to two-party politics heralded by so many commentators was not confirmed. The collapse of the SLD vote from the Alliance highs of the early 1980s represented a loss of 13.3 per cent from the EP election of 1984, and of 17.5 per cent from the general election of 1987. The share of the vote obtained by the two major parties remained identical to that in 1987, at 74.8 per cent, less than in the EP election of 1984. The explanation can be found in the subsequential advance of the Green Party from 0.6 per cent of the Great Britain vote in 1984 to a significant 14.9 per cent.

The result in terms of seats won and lost demonstrated the high threshold faced by any minor party without a strongly concentrated regional vote under the simple plurality system. The evenness of the Green performance across the country ensured that it would not gain representation at Strasbourg, just as that of the Alliance had failed in 1979 and 1984. In only 14 seats did the SLD start in second place; only two of these could be considered to be marginal; and in 12 of

Table 11.1   Distribution of seats under regional lists (Great Britain only, excluding Northern Ireland)

	1979 Actual	List	1984 Actual	List	1989 Actual	List
CON.	60	42	45	33	32	26
LAB.	17	28	32	30	45	34
LIB.	0	7	–	–	–	–
ALL.	–	–	0	14	–	–
SLD	–	–	–	–	0	4
SDP	–	–	–	–	0	0
Green	0	0	0	0	0	11
SNP	1	1	1	1	1	2
PC	0	0	0	0	0	0
Other	0	0	0	0	0	0

them it came second to the Conservatives. In no case did the SLD stand second to Labour on the 1984 results. The outcome in terms of seats won and lost was hardly surprising. Labour won 13 seats from the Conservatives, increasing its representation in the EP to 45 seats, and giving it a clear majority of the UK's 81 MEPs. The SNP retained its single seat. In Northern Ireland the order under STV of the three seats registered no change from 1984, with the DUP, the SDLP and the OUP each gaining one. It is conventional to speculate on the distribution of seats between parties if the regional party list system originally proposed in the European Assembly Elections Bill of 1977 had been in operation. For this purpose Table 11.1 compares the actual distribution of seats in the three EP elections with a regional list system operating within the Registrar-General's Standard Regions.[12]

The movement of votes from the position at the general election of 1987 showed a swing of 8.5 per cent from the Conservatives to Labour. This took place on a lower-than-expected increase in turnout. Turnout in fact rose to 37 per cent, only 4 per cent above the 1984 level. In the marginal seats won by Labour, the average turnout was 37.1 per cent. The highest turnout in Great Britain was 46.8 per cent in the highly marginal Wales North constituency. In only twelve constituencies did turnout exceed 40 per cent. London North East was lowest with 27.6 per cent, but at the other end of the country Scotland saw the greatest increases. In Scotland North East, won by Labour, turnout rose by 9.7 per cent whereas in Glasgow, a safe Labour seat, it was up by 10.3 per cent.

Immediate comment on the results centred on two major features. Relatively little account was taken by commentators of the effects of Labour's victory on the UK position in the EC. Media analysts, in the absence of survey evidence, in the main wisely fought shy of reading the election outcome as a direct verdict on the Prime Minister's approach to EC issues. Comment was instead directed at the putative consequences for the next general election, and the quality press swiftly produced projections which predicted a Labour majority of anything from four to twenty-three seats at Westminster. In common with the popular press, the leading national newspapers engaged in exhaustive commentary on the unexpectedly large vote for the Green Party.

A detailed analysis of the results reveals a more complex pattern of shifts in electoral opinion since the EP election of 1984 and the general election of 1987.[13] Despite the significantly lower turnout than at the general election and taking into account the mid-term phenomenon, there is some justification for regarding 1989 as registering important developments.

For Labour, the results showed that it was possible for the party to break out of its heartlands in Scotland and the North to an extent greater than it was able to achieve in 1987. In the Midlands and London its share of the vote rose by 10.5 and 11.0 per cent respectively, giving rise to the observation that at last Labour was gaining support in the region containing the largest number of statistically marginal Conservative Westminster seats. The increase in the Labour vote was regionally diverse: in Scotland and Wales the nationalist parties appear to have benefited most from the anti-Conservative swing. In both countries the change in the Labour vote was restricted, falling by 0.5 per cent in Scotland and rising by 3.8 per cent in Wales. With the squeeze on the Labour vote exerted by the Alliance in 1983 and 1987 and in the EP election of 1984 removed, the party saw its vote in its weakest areas, the South-East and South-West, increase by 8.8 and 7.3 per cent respectively.

While Labour's performance was its best-ever in an EP election, doubt must be cast over the permanence of the party's recovery. Its 40.1 per cent share of the Great Britain vote exactly matched its share in the 1979 general election, and was 0.1 per cent lower than that of October 1974. If a return to two-party politics is taking place, it is notable that in mid-term Labour has not yet been able to increase its share of the vote to that which it achieved (43.9 per cent) when it lost the general election of 1970. In some respects the trends of the late

1970s and early 1980s still appear to be affecting Labour's performance. Its largest increase in the share of the vote over 1987 was in its North-Eastern and Yorkshire heartland (+ 13.6 per cent): the EP election, although registering Labour's return to effective contestation in the Midlands and the South, did not indicate conclusively that the party could win enough marginal seats in these regions to guarantee a parliamentary majority. The 'North/West Britain–South/East Britain divide' was still present: Labour's recovery in South/East Britain was relatively modest. Across the south of England, excluding London, its vote share rose by an average of 8 per cent from its 1987 general election showing of 20.9 per cent.

The Conservative Party could take small comfort from the results. It lost all bar one of the EP seats held in 1984 on majorities of less than 9 per cent. Labour's failure to take London North-West was impressionistically attributed to the party's municipal difficulties in the constituency. In general, Conservative turnout was low. The party's worst result was Cheshire East, which fell to Labour, wiping out a previous Conservative majority of 11.8 per cent. In a number of other constituencies, Conservative majorities were greatly reduced, leaving their MEPs with statistically marginal seats – Bedfordshire South (1.6 per cent majority), Shropshire and Staffordshire (1.2 per cent) and Lancashire Central (3.0 per cent) – in hitherto reasonably safe areas. Regionally, the Conservative decline varied. In Scotland, the SNP pushed the Conservatives into third place. The party was only able to muster 20.9 per cent of the total Scottish vote, and lost both the seats (Scotland South and Scotland North-East) that it had held in 1984. In Wales the Conservatives came a poor second to Labour, losing Wales North, and apparently seeing the Conservative advances of the early 1980s in the Principality wiped out. However, the anti-Conservative swing was insufficient seriously to harm it in the South of England outside London. Indeed, its position was strengthened in a number of constituencies by the collapse of the SLD challenge. In a number of cases, although the Conservative share of the vote fell dramatically, its lead over the nearest challenger either remained virtually the same (e.g. Dorset East and Hampshire West; Wiltshire) or rose (e.g. Somerset and Dorset West). Despite this, the basic shock to the Conservative Party was the fact that it had come an overall second to Labour in a nationwide test of electoral opinion for the first time since 1974, and that its total share of the vote, at 34.7 per cent, was its lowest since 1959.

For the erstwhile Alliance, the EP election was an unmitigated disaster. The only consolation that the SLD could draw was that in council by-elections held on the same day the party achieved 20 per cent of the poll on average, far in excess of their EP election showing of 6.2 per cent nationwide. The best performance was in Cornwall and Plymouth, where a well-known candidate got only 30.4 per cent, 9 per cent down on the 1987 general election. The falls elsewhere were catastrophic, particularly in the areas of the country where the general elections of 1983 and 1987 had seen the then-Alliance replace Labour as the major party of opposition to the Conservatives. The evaporation of this support left the SLD's position on the electoral map of Britain resembling that of the Liberal Party in the 1940s and 1950s, with local pockets of support in the South-West, Wales and Scotland. Even in these areas, its overall support slumped, with the South-West region registering the largest fall with nearly 20 per cent of the 1987 general election vote share being lost. The anti-merger SDP, with 16 candidates, only achieved 0.5 per cent of the vote nationwide.

It is tempting to speculate that the 'third-party vote' simply moved to the Green Party, and that the startling success of the latter was the key to the SLD's catastrophe. In constituency terms, measured against the 1987 general election, the largest falls in the SLD vote share corresponded with the largest increases in the Green vote, almost without exception. Overall, the Green Party, fighting every EP constituency for the first time, won 14.9 per cent of the popular vote. In regional terms a distinct North–South variation in performance could be detected. In Scotland, the poorest Green performance netted only 7.2 per cent overall, whereas in the South-East (excluding London) 20.2 per cent was achieved, just ahead of the South-West, where the party attained 20.1 per cent. This variation gives some credence to the view that another non-Conservative, non-Labour alternative was available to electors in Scotland in the shape of the SNP. In Wales, the Green vote at 11 per cent compared with that in the North of England. The exception to the general level of Green performance in Wales was provided by Wales North. In this case both Plaid Cymru and Labour were vying to take the seat from the Conservatives. Labour succeeded, and the Green vote was the lowest in the Principality at 6.3 per cent. Similarly, the lowest Green vote in the South was in the Cornwall and Plymouth constituency, the only instance in England where the SLD maintained its second place behind the Conservatives.

Although Green spokespersons interpreted their party's

performance as a vote for Green philosophies and policies, the correlation of Green increase and SLD decline indicated that generalised protest voting appeared to operate in favour of the Greens. Heightened awareness of environmental issues undoubtedly assisted the party, but opinion polls following the EP election showed an immediate evaporation of support, with the party dropping back to less than half the level it achieved on 15 June.

The nationalists' fortunes were mixed. The SNP, although displacing the Conservatives to take second place to Labour in Scotland, and retaining its Highlands and Islands seat, was unable to repeat its Glasgow Govan Westminster by-election success. Its 25.6 per cent of the Scottish vote was 4.7 per cent above the Conservative total but 16.3 per cent behind Labour. Its lowest vote was in the two marginal constituencies, Lothians and Scotland South, which Labour took from the Conservatives. The EP election demonstrated that Plaid Cymru's support was, as in previous elections, largely confined to the North and West of Wales. In three of the four Welsh EP constituencies, its vote fell behind that of the Greens.

The nationwide swing from Conservative to Labour was 8.5 per cent, but overall the EP election confirmed the basic pattern of regional diversity in the distribution of party support so clearly seen in the Westminster elections of 1983 and 1987.

CONCLUSION

The 1989 Euro-election had several important short- and long-term consequences. Its most striking short-term impact was on the party-political landscape. The Conservative Party was confused and divided, the SLD and SDP centre ground collapsed and the Labour Party experienced a dramatic revival. In Wales, Plaid Cymru's vote stabilised at 12.9 per cent, while in Scotland the SNP pushed its vote up from 17.8 per cent to 26 per cent. Perhaps the most extraordinary result was that of the Green Party (formerly Ecology Party up until 1985) whose electoral breakthrough from less than one per cent to 14.9 per cent was most telling in the Conservatives' southern heartlands, where they effectively undermined the former second-placed position of the old Alliance. Winning more than 22 per cent of the vote in eight Euro-constituencies and coming second in six Euro-seats, there was an uncanny link between the rise of the Green vote in these areas and the equivalent decline of SLD support.

In Northern Ireland both Ian Paisley (DUP) and John Hume (SDLP) were re-elected together with James Nicholson (OUP) who replaced John Taylor, the latter having decided not to stand. To this extent there was no significant change in Northern Ireland representation at Strasbourg. In an overall drop in support for all of the main candidates, perhaps Paisley's slump from a record 230 251 first-preference votes to 160 110 was the most noteworthy result.

The EP election clearly mattered more to British voters in 1989 than in either 1984 or 1979; turnout rose to 37 per cent. But whether or not this increased turnout was due to the salience of the European debate in British electoral politics, coupled with the Labour Party's determination to deal the Conservative Government a mid-term blow, there was no doubt that the Conservative Party and its leadership suffered the most damaging long-term consequences. Dramatically reduced from 45 to 32 seats, it was not just the loss of 13 MEPs which mattered but their distribution. The EP election demolished Conservative support in Scotland and Wales. With no seats in either nation and little on the horizon to suggest that this will change, the Conservatives look to many north and west of the border like an increasingly alien force, overwhelmingly English-based. Worse still for the Conservative Party may be the severely strained relations between the remaining MEPs seeking membership of the pro-Euro-Union European People's Party and Westminster Conservatives, themselves divided on Europe.

Neither the voting figures nor the overall results constitute a catalogue of doom for the Conservative Government but they may conceivably serve as a signal that both the nature and visibility of the European debate in EP elections have changed significantly in the UK. This is a lesson which all British political parties will have to learn in the 1990s.

NOTES AND REFERENCES

1. D. Butler and P. Jowett, *Party Strategies in Britain: A Study of the 1984 European Elections* (London: Macmillan, 1985), p. 1.
2. For a survey of the Ecology Party's development, see W. Rudig and P. D. Lowe, 'The Withered "Greening" of British Politics: A Study of the Ecology Party', *Political Studies*, XXXIV (1986) pp. 262–84.
3. Butler and Jowett, op. cit., p. 1.
4. For discussion and analysis of the 1984 EP election in the UK, see D.

Hearl, 'The United Kingdom', in J. Lodge (ed.), *Direct Elections to the European Parliament 1984* (London: Macmillan, 1986).

5. See M. Burgess, *Federalism and European Union: Political Ideas, Influences and Strategies in the European Community, 1972–1987* (London: Routledge, 1989).

6. See J. Lodge (ed.), *European Union: The European Community in Search of a Future* (London: Macmillan, 1986).

7. For two different interpretations of this episode, see R. Corbett, 'The 1985 Intergovernmental Conference and the Single European Act', in R. Pryce (ed.), *The Dynamics of European Union*, (London: Croom Helm, 1987) and Burgess, op. cit., pp. 183–94.

8. Delors' speech, 15 June 1988, *OJ* Annex No. 2–366/157.

9. Delors' TUC speech, *Independent*, 9 September 1988.

10. *Daily Telegraph*, 8 June 1989.

11. *Daily Telegraph*, 12 June 1989.

12. J. Curtice, 'An Analysis of the Results', in D. Butler and D. Marquand, *European Elections and British Politics* (London: Longman, 1981), pp. 183–85 and J. Curtice, 'Appendix: an analysis of the results', in D. Butler and P. Jowett, op cit., pp. 158–60.

13. For a discussion of this division relating to the 1987 general election see R. J. Johnston et al., *A Nation Dividing? The Electoral Map of Great Britain, 1979–1987* and J. Curtice and M. Steed, 'Appendix 2: analysis', in D. Butler and D. Kavanagh, *The British General Election of 1987* (London: Macmillan 1988), pp. 319–33.

12 1989: Edging towards 'genuine' Euro-elections?

JULIET LODGE

The 1989 EP elections reinforced the idea of and the tide of change in the EC. Change shows itself in many ways, ranging from turnout, the number of parties contesting the elections, the major changes in the number and make-up of the EP's party groups, to the spirit of optimism that has characterised both the late 1980s and the inaugural address of the new EP President Enrique Barón Crespo in July 1989. This optimism is related directly to the change in what might loosely be termed political will or courage in the EC: the determination to effect change is apparent and was being pursued with a vengeance by the French Council Presidency. An inter-governmental conference (IGC) on economic and monetary union had been called and those in leadership positions in the EC stressed the idea that change was possible as well as desirable. This was an important switch from the days when change was paraded as possibly desirable but probably impossible. Pious lip-service to the notion of change had given way to determination to operationalise it.

In 1989, in sharp contrast to the immediate reactions to the somewhat lower turnout at the 1984 EP election compared to the 1979 results, there was neither talk of 'catastrophe' (the then EC Commission President Thorn's verdict on the 62 per cent turnout) nor was there any evidence of widely-shared pessimism about the EC's future. It is true that when, at the newly-elected EP's first part-session in July, the oldest MEP took the chair, he castigated the 1989 turnout (averaging 58 per cent across the EC) as symptomatic of public indifference and apathy. However, his speech was met with a mass walkout in protest at a member of the extreme right (the French National Front) being able to give the opening address. (The EP's Rules of Procedure are now likely to be changed to ensure that while the oldest MEP presides over the new EP, s/he does so only until the new President is elected.) This aside, the spirit of optimism was much in evidence.

Commenting on this, outgoing EP President Lord Plumb noted that the optimism was, at least, in part due to the SEA and the cooperation procedure which had given the EP an important role in the legislative process. His successor, Enrique Barón Crespo, the first EP President ever to have been elected on the first ballot, immediately set out the policy goals for the future. In keeping with the EP's role as *animateur* of change, he looked beyond 1992 to the next century when he saw European unity becoming a reality through the full participation of EC citizens. His speech took up the enduring themes of the elections and of the EP relating national campaign issues (such as jobs and 1992) to EC legislation.

The over-arching EC framework for the future marks an important psychological shift in perceptions about the relationship between the EC and its institutions and those of the member states. At the practical level, however, it marks the first step towards putting what the EC stands for in concrete terms. Barón Crespo stressed the need for building an EC based on democracy and respect for human rights: two ideals that can be widely applied to all manner of contemporary issues. These span international affairs, East–West relations and EC preoccupations such as the social charter, human rights, economic and social cohesion, the environment and external relations. Each of the party group leaders echoed these concerns. Luigi Colajanni, for the European United Left, argued for the EP assuming the role of constituent assembly for political union as approved by 89.1 per cent of the Italian electorate in the referendum. Giscard d'Estaing, for the Liberals, even suggested that some form of federal union would have to occur during the next century. Progress on matters intrinsic to European Union was called for by a number of other speakers. The recurrent concerns were economic and monetary union, the social dimension to the SEM, and the environment. They were echoed by the EP's debate on the Commission's statement on the Madrid European Council. What the first part-session of the EP with its new MEPs showed was that creating a People's Europe and ensuring that the EP is the voice of the people and the articulator and protector of the public interest are clearly on the agenda.

The EP itself has greater self-esteem and has recognised the need to refine again its own working methods and priorities: making the EP relevant to citizens assumes critical importance. This applies both to the nature of the legislation tackled to its presentation and to the way in which the EP communicates with citizens. Barón Crespo stressed the need to inject greater dynamism into EP debates (that is, at the sessions when the EP can be seen to be performing its 'grand forum' role). This in turn should help to increase media interest in its deliberations, notably in areas where it can affect the ultimate content of draft legislation. It should also help to ensure that the EP receives a better press in future, both in terms of the length and quality of actual press, radio and television coverage.

In addition, the EP's need to increase its credibility as a legislature with the ability to assert democratic controls in the EC is appreciated. While Barón Crespo's speech referred to European Union in the 21st century, he pointed to the usefulness of the minimalist tactic in capitalising on existing achievements. The priorities, therefore, are: exploiting the SEA to develop the EP's role in the EC; increasing the EP's supervisory role over the EC institutions in a spirit of coopera- tion with the Commission and Council; increasing the involvement of national parliaments in EC business; supporting the IGC on eco- nomic and monetary union in the development of the SEM; supporting the social charter, and environmental initiatives, including President Delors' suggestion for a European Environmental Agency. The EP's resolution on the Madrid European Council stressed the need to accord the SEM's social dimension the same importance as its economic dimensions. It also called for the IGC on economic and monetary union to agree on institutional reform and the creation of a Citizens' Europe and a democratic Community in which the EP would have a greater say.

It is significant that responsibility for implementing minimalism at the institutional level has been given to the Institutional Affairs Committee (which historically spearheaded the maximalist strategy through the EUT) which retains responsibility for the question of political union. In this context, the fact that it has been given the new task of drafting a proposal for a uniform electoral procedure for the 1994 EP elections is of particular interest.

Whether and how fast the EP's priorities are translated into EC legislation remains to be seen. However, the degree of overlap and consensus between the EP's majority and the French Council Presidency is noteworthy. This does not necessarily mean that corresponding measures will be taken during France's Presidency but it is symptomatic of a *rapprochement* in thinking between two actors that play a vital role in the legislative process. Equally, this *rapproche- ment* and the inter-institutional consensus over the items that should feature on the short-term policy agenda is in marked contrast to the first two EP elections.

THE 1989 ELECTIONS: DIFFERENT OR PART OF A CONTINUING PATTERN?

The 1989 EP elections were the first to be conducted simultaneously in all twelve member states. More importantly, they were the first to be characterised by concern about a common agenda – the SEM in its many guises. The SEM was the backcloth to the 1989 elections which, in a way, were themselves a necessary distraction from the serious business of ensuring that the SEM legislation be passed preferably by 1993. The EC was committed to this. The Council of Ministers' members differed somewhat in the particular emphasis they placed on certain issues (and the UK fell into the familiar isolated position on critical matters relating to EMU and the social charter). But behind this was action on the EC's future and inter-institutional *rapprochement* over legislative priorities and the content of the SEM legislation. In view of this, it is perhaps surprising that those contesting the elections did not make common cause effectively in arguing over the relative weight that should attach to the SEM's different dimensions. There are two main reasons for this. First, policy priorities are determined largely by the Commission and Council Presidencies (though the EP is gaining influence steadily). EP candidates, therefore, had to avoid creating unrealistic expectations of their capacity to translate either party programmes or electoral promises into legislation within the term of the new EP. Second, there was broad public support both for the principle of greater integration (for example, in defence, foreign and monetary matters) and for common EC standards on matters derived from the SEM's social dimension that affect employees.

While the newly-elected MEPs were to stress the imbalance in realising certain sectors of the SEM without due attention being accorded necessary counterpart sectors (notably the social sector), and while they were insistent upon the need to realise a Citizens' Europe during the EP's next term, the idea of a Citizens' Europe had barely surfaced in the campaign. Even now, it is a rather nebulous phrase, meaning all things to all people: the EP has to flesh it out. The EP has still to realise its own potential both as a legislature and as 'the people's voice'.

One of the paradoxes of the 1989 EP campaign must lie in the fact that while the SEM featured to some degree in the campaigns in all the member states, it did not act as a polarising, unifying or integrative issue. It did not lead to concerted transnational efforts being

Table 12.1   Favourability towards the promotion of common policies by 1992 (percentages)

	Belg.	Dk	FRG	Gr	Sp.	F	Irl	I	L	Nl	P	UK	EC12
Common defence body													
Yes	77	36	66	62	63	80	60	84	80	74	68	71	72
No	12	42	20	14	14	10	19	8	12	13	4	18	14
No reply	11	22	14	24	23	10	21	9	8	14	28	11	14
Common socio-econ. area													
Yes	81	41	77	69	78	85	85	92	83	79	70	70	79
No	10	36	13	9	4	7	3	2	8	8	3	17	9
No reply	9	23	10	23	18	8	12	7	10	14	27	13	12
Single Euro-currency													
Yes	72	27	46	52	61	74	64	77	67	61	52	29	56
No	15	49	40	14	12	14	17	8	21	23	13	58	27
No reply	13	25	14	34	27	12	19	15	12	16	35	14	17
Common foreign policy													
Yes	69	33	65	52	61	63	54	72	68	52	59	41	59
No	16	45	20	18	9	19	19	10	16	24	8	39	20
No reply	15	22	15	30	30	18	27	19	17	24	33	20	20

Source: *Eurobarometer*, No. 30, 1988, p. A28

made by parties of similar persuasions to pursue a coordinated Euro-campaign with a view to mobilising the electorate to vote for a clear socialist vision of the SEM, for example, over a liberal one. Voters certainly chose between different parties contesting the elections but in perhaps only one state (UK) did the result send clear signals in terms of ideologically-inspired choice: green and social issues were to be put high on the agenda for the future, and the parties that the electorate felt had greatest credibility *vis-à-vis* those issues won more votes.

The failure of the transnational federations and their respective manifestos to have much impact on the public and even party-workers, owes much to the continuing intangibility of the federations. Even though the British Labour Party made great play of its membership of and commitment to the CSP, this was a ploy to heighten appreciation of the Conservatives' isolation in the EC. The CSP and other EC Socialist leaders did not feature prominently in Labour's campaign to make common cause with their Socialist allies.

This highlights the reasons behind the federations' weakness. They have to rely on national parties to use the manifestos and campaign material devised in conjunction with them. They lack the equivalence of national parties' membership bases and party infrastructures. National parties themselves also continue to see themselves as uniquely able to judge the tempo, nuances and political mind of their own electorate. None could resist the temptation of using the EP elections as a test of the relative popularity of the government of the day. Inevitably, therefore, national issues took centre-stage. A European veneer was applied when and if this helped to portray the government in a poor light. This tactic was used especially effectively by the British Labour Party with its poster and advertisement campaigns that contrasted a range of British social provisions most unfavourably with their equivalents in the rest of the Twelve.

Even so and even if the idea of EP elections as 'second-order' elections is accepted cautiously, the 1989 EP elections differ in significant respects from the 1979 and 1984 EP elections. Unlike in previous EP elections, it cannot be claimed that there was no awareness of common questions facing the Twelve, or of the prospect of the SEM. Awareness of the SEM and positive assessment of it had grown among the public over the preceding year in all states bar Denmark and Ireland.[1] While the SEM formed the backdrop to the campaign, it was neither hotly nor continuously debated. This was partly because it was a rather nebulous and ill-understood concept and partly because the national parties tended to portray it, if at all in their manifestos, in parochial terms and in terms of more or less EC-level intervention in social or environmental legislation, for example. Mrs Thatcher's protestations at Bruges that the EC and SEM should not become a vehicle for socialism through the backdoor fell on deaf ears. Specific principles for an SEM could be and were raised during the campaigns: equality, fairness, justice, human rights and citizens' rights, for example. As a generalised arena for party conflict the notion of the SEM was too vague, and much of the corresponding legislation had still to be drafted and/or debated.

It is partly because the EC itself had defined the future agenda in terms of realising the SEM that the question of the EC's future direction was not, or hardly at all, at issue in most member states. The concept of the SEM, no matter how vague, had somehow helped to instil the sense of the EC's permanence and increasing vigour in the minds of elites, those contesting the elections and the public. Mainstream political parties had also dropped the question of

Table 12.2   Advantages of the Single Common European Market by 1992 (autumn 1988)

Question: 'The coming into being of the Single Common European Market in 1992 will mean the free circulation of persons, goods and property within the European Community countries. Some people think this will be mostly an advantage, others think it will be a disadvantage. Can you tell me, for each aspect of this Single Common European Market which I am going to mention, whether you personally think it will be an advantage or a disadvantage?'

EC12	Advantage	Disadvantage	Don't know
The opportunity for any citizen of a country within the European Community to go and live without limitation in any country of the Community for instance to retire there or to study there	80	12	9
The ability to make payments without complication within the whole European Community	80	7	14
The possibility to take any amount of money with you when you travel to other countries of the European Community	79	10	11
The possibility to buy in one's own country any product lawfully sold in other countries of the European Community	79	10	10
The opportunity for any citizen of a country within the European Community to go and work in any other country of the European Community	77	14	8
The possibility to open a bank account in any country of the European Community	73	13	14
The possibility to buy land or property throughout the Community	72	15	13
Bringing closer together the rates of VAT (Value-added tax) applied in the various countries of the Community so that products are sold under similar cost conditions	65	17	18
Elimination of custom controls when crossing frontiers between countries inside the European Community	64	26	10
The possibility for a contractor from another country to be in charge of public works (for instance, building a bridge or a road) in our country if his offer is cheaper at the same level of quality	55	31	14

Source: *Eurobarometer*, No. 30, 1988, p. A15

secession from the EC with a resulting semblance of consensus over the desirability of EC membership. Equally importantly, the EP's own sense of its value to the EC was underpinned by its impact on legislation through the cooperation procedure. This was important in terms of its self-esteem and of the extent of soul-searching over its democratic credentials.

TURNOUT AND DEMOCRATIC LEGITIMACY

In contrast to the first-ever and second EP elections, there was very little comment or anxiety over the turnout level for the 1989 election. A small fall in turnout was not seen as a major blow to the EP's democratic legitimacy and credentials. Nor was the prospect of a small increase seen as itself justifying the EP's continuing quest for greater power. Instead, the EP seems to have legitimised itself in its own eyes by virtue of its legislative competence and the concomitant increase in attention the Commission and Council have to afford it. The EP has augmented its scrutiny and control functions discreetly to good effect. It can now rest its case for greater power on the grand themes of parliamentary liberal democracy and representative government. Thus, the third EP elections seem to have fudged the linkage that has been assumed to exist between the level of turnout and the extent to which an increase in EP legislative power may be justified. A marginally higher or lower turnout *per se* justifies neither an increase nor decrease in the EP's legislative powers.

However, if the EP is seen by the public to affect policy outcomes, then voters' sense of the EP's powers may be such as to convince them that the EP 'matters' and that voting 'counts' because there is 'something at stake'. (This might be assisted by the EP acquiring a greater role in the Commission's appointment.) Turnout might then rise. Indeed, it would not be unreasonable to suggest that turnout at the fourth EP election in 1994 could rise for a quite unconnected reason: the uniform electoral procedure (see below).

For the time being, however, the elected EP's legislative competence is seen as a hallmark of its legitimacy. In future, instead of arguing that its direct election alone enhances its democratic legitimacy and the justness of its quest for greater legislative authority, the EP could argue that its legislative competence is constrained by arbitrary limits placed on its legislative role. It could justify a quest for further legislative power by suggesting and demonstrating that these arbitrary limits impair its ability to act in the public interest on behalf of those who elected it. The socio-economic and political climate and expectations of continued change may very well prove advantageous in that a socialist-green majority theoretically obtains in the EP; social and green issues seem to be high on the short- to medium-term legislative agenda; and public awareness of whether or not states match up to an EC average seems to be growing. Voters may not be happy with social and environmental provisions below EC *minima* especially if, in the latter's case, the public feels that it is getting a raw deal and being exposed to serious health hazards outlawed elsewhere in the EC.

There could be real mileage to be had in the EP exploiting these highly visible, highly salient, enduring, emotive, unifying and integrative common concerns. The fact that many environmental, health and safety as well as social issues are not transient questions gives the EP the chance to capitalise on sudden surges in public awareness of its activities. It also gives it the chance to show that it can follow up issues in a coherent and consistent manner; to show that it has the public interest at heart, and that it can act accordingly. The EP's ability to follow up and deliver on highly salient, visible and intelligible public issues may help to boost turnout at the 1994 EP election.

TURNOUT AND PUBLIC AWARENESS OF THE EP

In the past, some correlation has been assumed to exist between the level of public awareness of the EP and the intentions of respondents to use their Euro-votes.[2] By the autumn of 1988, for the first time in three years, over half the respondents (53 per cent) reported having recently seen or heard something about the EP. This figure was significantly higher than at the corresponding time before the 1984 EP elections. The slight fall in overall turnout in 1989 compared to 1984 has to be explained. Only in Ireland, Greece, the FRG and UK was turnout higher than in 1984. In the UK a 5 per cent rise was noted, in the FRG 6 per cent, in Greece one per cent but in Ireland 19 per cent. The suspicion that in Ireland something was at stake, in the sense of getting Labour back into the EP (and even a Workers' Party MEP), may have added a Euro-element to the campaign and mobilised the voters. The simultaneous general elections in Luxembourg and Greece did not have this effect.

Given the dominance of national issues and the 'nationalisation' of Euro-issues like the SEM in the campaigns, it must also be assumed that, except in Italy where there was the referendum on European Union which recorded a higher turnout (89 per cent) than for the EP election itself, voters were mobilised around national issues. In the UK, the Labour Party's success probably owes something to Labour convincing those who actually voted that something was 'at stake' and that the result would signal clearly to the government that Thatcherite visions for the UK and EC were unacceptable. However, the Labour campaign did not boost turnout significantly. The swings in turnout levels within individual states compared to the preceding EP election do not necessarily clarify whether, and if so what, EC issues motivated voters to go to the poll. Nor do they necessarily reflect much in terms of public perceptions of and aspirations for the EP.

While it may be obvious that someone who is unaware of the EP's existence or the polling day may be unlikely *ceteris paribus* to go and vote, and while it may be assumed that awareness of the EP correlates to a degree with turnout, previous *Eurobarometer* polls have found that negative impressions of the EP's role, power and ability to influence policy outcomes have deterred voting among some of the electorate (e.g. in the Netherlands in 1984). In the EC as a whole 49 per cent of respondents had a favourable impression of the EP, with the figure rising to over 50 per cent only in France, Greece, Ireland and Italy.[3] 55 per cent assessed the EP's role in the EC as very important or important and this figure only fell to under half in Germany and the Netherlands – two countries reputed to have a more sophisticated electorate in terms of EC awareness and understanding.

Support for the EP being given a greater role was 44 per cent across the Twelve. (Only the UK was equally divided over a greater or unchanged role at 30 per cent each and 20 per cent felt it should have a lesser role. With a 20 per cent 'no reply' rate, the UK response suggests a high degree of ignorance.) 61 per cent of Italians and 57 per cent of Greeks favoured the EP being afforded a greater role in the EC. Over 89 per cent of Italians voted in the referendum accordingly. Across the EC, 25 per cent felt the EP's role should be the same. This figure rose to 44 per cent and 41 per cent in Luxembourg and Denmark respectively.

The level of turnout at EP elections has also been assumed to correlate with favourability towards the EC. On average in autumn 1988, 69 per cent of respondents saw EC membership as a 'good thing'. This fell to 40 per cent in Denmark, 50 per cent in the UK and 64 per cent in the FRG. 67 per cent across the EC feel that their country has benefited from being in the EC – ranging from 88 per cent of Portuguese to 33 per cent of Spaniards. Spain alone lacks a majority convinced of the benefits of membership.

What these statistics show is an underlying consensus over EC membership and a positive feeling for things European. Opinion polls that probe issues of concern to the public also show support for greater integration and for the EC taking action in a number of spheres that have traditionally been seen as the preserve of domestic governments (see Table 12.1).

Considerable variation from the general pattern is observable only where there is anxiety that EC standards may mean lower standards than those already in force in the state concerned (e.g. Denmark in matters of health and safety regulations in the workplace and other matters relating to working conditions and the work environment). Danish anxiety is particularly acute in respect of collective agreements and the introduction of new technology in the workplace. Even the question of collective agreements elicits a 51 per cent favourable response rate in the UK; that is, almost 20 per cent higher than in Denmark but ten per cent lower than in Greece and fifteen per cent lower than in the rest (see Table 12.3). In general, the suggestion is

Table 12.3   Advantages of the Single Market for working people (percentages)

	Belg.	Dk	FRG	Gr	Sp.	F	Irl	I	L	Nl	P	UK	EC12
Quals	86	72	77	74	77	87	87	89	83	80	71	80	82
Health Safety	87	69	78	78	84	91	92	91	90	81	76	86	85
Work	72	54	62	62	71	72	84	75	72	61	69	74	70
IT	75	47	69	63	66	79	81	80	71	71	69	70	72
Coll. bargain	71	32	70	60	67	73	67	73	65	65	67	51	66
Company Law	72	54	68	64	69	76	81	79	70	66	69	70	72

Key:
Quals – mutual recognition of equivalent qualifications obtained in other EC states.
Health & Safety – equality of health, safety and hygiene in the workplace.
Work – flexibility in working conditions (pay, hours, recruitment, dismissal).
IT – agreement between unions and employers at EC-level over the introduction of technology in the workplace.
Coll. bargain – EC-level-negotiated collective agreements for different sectors of the economy.
Company Law – a European law to apply the same rules for worker-participation to companies throughout the EC.

Source: Adapted from *Eurobarometer*, No. 30, 1988, p. A19.

that providing EC policies are an improvement on existing provisions, they can be expected to secure the support of working people
(though not necessarily, of course, of the business sector and
government).

It would be misleading to draw too-optimistic inferences from this
rather impressionistic data. How then can the lower turnout in the
1989 EP election be explained? Once more, the answer seems to lie
with the political parties, the nature of the campaigns in the member
states and the possibility that the public has not yet been shown that
something tangible in terms of immediate political outcomes really is
at stake in an EP election. There is no governmental outcome or
contest comparable to major national elections. As yet, drama has
been largely absent from EP elections. The turnover in MEPs has
settled at around 50 per cent at both elections and only if a highly
charismatic and well-known politician (often a former high-profile
national politician) fails to secure re-election is there much media
comment. Even then, the political colour and make-up of a Euro-
government is not at stake. Nor has the ideological make-up of the
EP's majority seemed to be of consequence until recently. Even then,
the supposition that a red–green majority will make a difference and
affect policy outcomes in visible, intelligible and tangible ways for
individuals has to be proved. Moreover, the 260 votes needed for
amendments under the cooperation procedure place a premium on
EPP–Socialist cooperation.

THE EP GROUPS

Immediately after the elections, attention certainly focused on the
numerical strength of a red–green alliance in the EP. The Socialist
Group included MEPs from every member state and their number
was up from 165 to 180 seats, largely thanks to UK Labour Party
gains from the Conservatives. With 46 MEPs, the Labour contingent
was easily the largest national contingent both within the Socialist
Group and within the EP itself. The fact that Labour Party leader
Neil Kinnock chose to increase his presence at Strasbourg also signified
his intention to try to keep the fissiparous tendencies within the Labour
contingent under some control. A Group of the Greens in the EP was
formed with MEPs from Belgium, Greece, Spain, France, Italy, the
Netherlands and Portugal, and it secured, with 30 seats, only two
seats less than the British Conservatives. The Rainbow Group (with

Table 12.4   Strength of the party groups

	Belg.	Dk	FRG	Gr	S	F	Irl	I	L	Nl	P	UK	EC12
SOC	8	4	31	9	27	22	1	14	2	8	8	46	180
EPP	7	2	32	10	16	6	4	27	3	10	3	1	121
LDR	4	3	4	–	6	13	2	3	1	4	9	–	49
ED	–	2	–	–	–	–	–	–	–	–	–	32	34
Greens	3	–	8	–	1	8	–	7	–	2	1	–	30
EUL	–	1	–	1	4	–	–	22	–	–	–	–	28
EDA	–	–	–	1	1	13	6	–	–	–	–	–	21
ER	1	–	6	–	–	10	–	–	–	–	–	–	17
LU	–	–	–	3	–	7	1	–	–	–	3	–	14
RBW	1	4	–	–	2	1	1	3	–	–	–	1	13
IND	–	–	–	–	3	1	–	5	–	1	–	1	11
Total	24	16	81	24	60	81	15	81	6	25	24	81	518

Abbreviations: SOC – Socialists; EPP – Group of the European People's Party; LDR – Liberal Democratic and Reformist Group; ED – European Democratic Group; Greens – Group of the Greens in the EP; EUL – European United Left; EDA – European Democratic Alliance; ER – Technical Group of the European Right; LU – Left Unity; RBW – Rainbow; IND – Non-attached.

its green credentials and 13 seats spread across seven states) also secured official party status. The Conservatives sought 'allied' status with the EPP whose size was boosted by 16 *Partido Popular* MEPs. The *Partido Popular* had decided to leave the European Democratic Group before the elections. The policy-divisions between the Italian and French Communists were given concrete expression when the 22 pro-integrationist, progressive PCI MEPs formed the European United Left Group with one Dane, one Greek and four Spanish MEPs. The seven PCF MEPs joined forces with three Greeks, three Portuguese and one Irish MEP to form the Left Unity Group.

The new EP embraced new groups[4] but neither the conservative EDs and the centrist EPP could together command the 260 votes needed to secure an absolute majority for amendments under the cooperation procedure. The red–green alliance, though better placed, was also in the position of having to seek support from other groups (notably the EPP) and among the twelve independent MEPs to muster the 260 votes. This means that while cleavages may be more sharply defined and while the EP's majority will certainly try to secure legislation in line with the ideals and aspirations of Social Europe – People's Europe, this cannot be a foregone conclusion. Moreover, there are signs that the Commission has a countervailing centre–right tendency anxious to subdue Mr Delors. However, early signs were that the Socialist group was going to be a formidable force in the EP owing to its greater cohesion (partly facilitated by the more pro-EC tendency within the British Labour contingent) and to strong leadership.

The new EP's composition has changed in other respects. The number of women MEPs has risen slightly from 69 in the 410-strong 1979 EP (of nine member states) to 75 in 1984 and 96 in 1989. Only one woman is chairperson (or co-chairperson) of a political group – the Greens. Two are EP Vice-Presidents. Three women secured chairpersonships of the standing committees, whose membership ranged from 25 (Committee on Petitions) to 56 members (Political Affairs Committee). A handful of women were elected as vice-chairs of the various committees. MEPs are by background increasingly white-collar, with just under one-fifth (101) drawn from the education sector (though Greece prohibits University professors from becoming MEPs). Only 20 have an agricultural background (marking the lower priority the EC accords the CAP, perhaps). There are 35 ex-Ministers from national governments. Two Prime Ministers were elected (Jacques Santer, Luxembourg and Giulio Andreotti, Italy) but immediately resigned their seats to others on their party's list. Several former MEPs have entered national government and have confirmed the trend that membership of the elected EP (unlike its appointed predecessor) can expedite national career advancement for an individual. This suggests that the experience gained in the EP is perceived as an asset 'back home' and must, therefore, boost the EP's image and self-esteem even if it means the loss of experienced MEPs to national politics. This is not necessarily a bad thing if EP-socialisation brings pro-integrationist attitudes into the national arena. In other words, there is a poly-centric EC parliamentary elite evolving which will not only help to bring EC-level politics into the national political, and especially parliamentary arena, but which will have a spillover effect in terms of contacts with other agencies that also are coming increasingly to 'think EC' and act with an eye on the EC rather than only the nation-state as a primary parameter. However, there can be little doubt that the Europeanness of MEPs would be boosted in the minds of the electorate if all MEPs were elected on a uniform basis. The psychological importance of this should not be underestimated. Nor may it be assumed that existing electoral discrepancies are trivial.

A UNIFORM ELECTORAL PROCEDURE?

The Greens' carefully staged introduction of eleven seats into the EP in July 1989 to indicate the number of seats denied the Green party that polled the most votes in any member state, highlighted once again the significant distortion in the representativeness of each member state's national contingent of MEPs arising out of the member states adopting different electoral procedures (all variants on PR except in Britain). The resultant discrepancies in the relative strength of the EP's party groups and in the numerical strength of national contingents within them arise mainly because the UK rejects PR for Britain, but also because extreme PR in other states gives EP seats to candidates with less than one per cent of the vote.

It may also be the case that the fact that EP elections seem devoid of governmental consequences for the voters (as there is no linkage between the elections, for example, and the taking of office by a Commission that reflects the EP's majority) may also mean that voters see 'little point' in voting or that they use EP elections to vote 'wildly' for a party they would not support in a national contest for fear of 'wasting' their vote. Since the elections do not directly affect a political party's prospects of holding office (at the EC-level), a linkage between the party's campaign and ensuing policy is at best tenuous in spite of the transnational manifestos such as the CSP's 'For a Europe of Unity, Prosperity and Solidarity'. National parties are free to make as much or as little use of these as they wish. Ideally, the national and transnational priorities coincide, at least in broad terms. On the campaign trail, broad guidelines have to be interpreted parochially. No matter how 'European' national parties pretend to be, they cannot resist the temptation to persuade voters to use their votes as interim verdicts on national governments and/or pressing domestic issues. For an EP campaign to be fought on EC issues, there would have to be consensus among the parties that parochial domestic politics would be left out. This could further distort the reality of how EC legislation directly affects individuals, and lead to the trivialisation of major issues. Even so, this does not mean that an EP campaign fought on EC issues (presented in terms relevant to each member state) is a non-starter.

In seeking an electorally meaningful campaign, national parties turn EP elections into contests about the conservation or overthrow of national governments whenever possible. This begs the question of whether change is possible and even probable in this area of EC affairs too. A qualified yes must be the answer. The linkage between the EP and the Commission is important and the EP's quest for a role in the Commission's appointment might eventually convey the impression of a logical connection existing between the election of the EP and the ideological composition and priorities of the Commission. This would become more pronounced if EP elections and the terms of office of the Commission coincided. However, any change along these lines must be set in longer-term perspective.

During the life of the third elected EP, the EP's electoral priority must be the introduction of a uniform electoral procedure (UEP) for the next EP elections. This is one of the most important preconditions of change after the cooperation procedure and the EP's colonisation of a Brussels seat for itself. Indeed, elections under a uniform procedure to an EP based in the city of the EC's 'seat of government' would be likely to render the elections more visible and intelligible to voters.

A uniform electoral procedure would not transform the elections or turnout overnight but it may have a significant impact on the conduct and content of EP campaigns in the member states. This tendency might be quite pronounced where parties and even states tried to secure the 'Euro' high ground in proving their Euro-credentials to the voters. Only then would a record of achievement become genuinely important to sitting-MEPs and their parties. Such a record would certainly have to go beyond the mere recital of how much money the MEP concerned had secured from the structural funds, for example, for the state in question. The EP's party groups may well try to distinguish their record from that of their rivals. They would almost certainly be obliged to tell the voters in advance with which party groups they would be willing to form 'winning' alliances after the elections.

There is a good deal more to the concept of a uniform electoral procedure than the simple stipulation that EP elections must be conducted throughout the Twelve (or more) member states according to a prescribed form of PR. The uniform electoral procedure might be rigid in its prescriptions or, at least in the first instance, sufficiently flexible to allow member states a good deal of freedom in interpreting its provisions. It seems unlikely, therefore, that the EP's Institutional Affairs Committee would advocate a procedure that ignored the allocation of fixed numbers of seats according to existing national boundaries, even though there are significant discrepancies between the 'cost' of each seat among states of unequal population size. The 'cost' varies, for example, from 62 000 voters per seat in Luxembourg at one extreme to 756 976 in the FRG.

More pertinently, the 'withering-away' of national boundaries within the Single European Market logically should have a political counterpart with the EC being treated as one community possibly subdivided into electoral regions. Some would be uni-national. Others could cross state boundaries. The implications for a host of electoral matters would be legion. Even if regard to political expedience and the politics of the possible rules out such far-reaching change, there would be nothing to stop a group of MEPs (an Intergroup possibly) from adopting a maximalist tactic in respect of a uniform electoral procedure to ensure the adoption of a minimalist package.

The main priority must be to ensure that the UK is not permitted any longer to distort the EP party groups' strength by using an electoral system that does not come close to representing the proportion of votes cast for a party and the number of EP seats won. If necessary, the isolationist tactic so successfully pursued in respect of the SEA should be employed again. Failing the adoption of a uniform electoral procedure, the member states should simply agree among themselves to run their EP elections according to PR (possibly as outlined by the EP's Seitlinger report), and preferably according to an agreed PR formula on a single day. However, the electoral traditions of the Twelve vary greatly. It is instructive briefly to outline some of the more important differences.

COMMON ELECTIONS?

Before commenting on the discrepancies, it must be recalled that under the terms of Article 21 of the 1951 Treaty of Paris and Article 138 of the Rome Treaty, the EP's election by a uniform procedure is prescribed. Not until 1976 did the Council of Ministers agree to permit the EP's direct election. Even then, Article 7(2) of the Act of 20 September 1976 on the direct election of members of the European Parliament (termed Assembly) provided for such elections according to national provisions pending the entry into force of a uniform electoral procedure. The task of drafting a UEP is assigned by the Rome Treaty to the EP. After the 1979 elections, it adopted on 10 March 1982 the Seitlinger report which prescribed PR in multi-member constituencies consisting of 3–15 seats apiece. This formula allowed, for example, a member state (like Ireland) to constitute itself as five constituencies or a single national constituency. On 24 May 1983, the Council of Ministers rejected this formula. The 1984 elections therefore were conducted according to national electoral regulations, as were those in 1989.

The EP had not kept up the pressure on the UEP, partly because its main preoccupation was with its legislative role. Moreover, while its Political Affairs Committee had adopted on 28 February 1985 the Bocklet report on a UEP, this was not presented to a plenary within the second legislature's term. The reasons for this lapse include insufficient pressure, the anticipated obstacles this might have posed for the accession of Spain and Portugal, and the added political difficulty this would have injected into the debate about European Union and the Intergovernmental Conference. The UK could, and did, try to divert attention from more serious concerns (like the Intergovernmental Conference and SEA process) by focusing on the *minutiae* of a UEP which it would veto no matter what. The EP was, therefore, justified in avoiding the pitfalls this presented. It cannot, however, afford to do so again.

There are sound reasons relating to the SEM for pursuing a UEP. In exercising a basic democratic right conferred on them by the Rome Treaty and confirmed as one of the SEM's intrinsic four freedoms (freedom of movement between member states) individuals can simultaneously forfeit both their Euro-franchise and the right to vote in and contest local elections in their new state of residence. The Commission, after years of EP pressure, recognised this incongruity and drafted a directive on extending voting rights to nationals resident in any EC state. However, this throws the absence of Council agreement on a UEP into sharp relief. It is highly unlikely that the Council will act on the UEP drafted by the EP unless it is pressurised into so doing. On grounds of citizens' democratic rights alone, the EP has a case against the Council. At a time when realising a People's Europe has a fairly high profile, Council inaction might be seen as cynical disregard for the people's rights. EP pressure in favour of a UEP can also be justified in terms of MEPs' self-interest.

So far, the only elements of commonality and uniformity in the EP elections are provided firstly, by the fact that direct elections are held at all; secondly, by 18 being set as the age of voter-eligibility; and thirdly, by the list of posts that the 1976 Act ruled as being incompatible with being an MEP. Broadly speaking, these include being: a minister or secretary of state; an EC Commissioner; or a member or administrator of an EC institution or body that administers or guides the EC's structural funds. Member states have added unilaterally other varying incompatibilities. Some ruled out the dual mandate from 1979, others are considering it only now in a bid to ensure that MEPs attend the EP. Some MEPs have attended only about half the EP's sessions. In general, there has been a fall in the number of dual-mandated MEPs.

Electoral system

Most states use the D'Hondt system of PR (Denmark, Belgium, FRG (the Hare-Niemeyer variant), Spain, France, Luxembourg, Netherlands and Portugal).

Election day

Most vote on Sunday. The inability to agree on a single day eventually led to a compromise to vote on two days within a four-day period. Thus, Spain, Ireland, Denmark, the Netherlands and the UK voted on Thursday, 15 June and the rest on the following Sunday. The polls open and close at different times and counting may not begin in any state until the last polling booth has closed on Sunday.

Voting

Voting is compulsory in Belgium, Greece and Luxembourg, and considered a 'civic duty' in Italy where non-voting is legally noted.

Voter eligibility

All Twelve allow 18-year-old national residents to vote. Most states restrict the right to vote to national residents. Some make provisions for expatriates (and in France's case overseas territories) to vote at embassies or consular offices (e.g. Spain which also permits postal voting). Others only give this entitlement to their nationals in other EC states. (For instance, Denmark, Portugal, Italy. The latter allows expatriates to vote only if they return to Italy. Greeks abroad similarly have either to return to Greece or to a consulate in an EC state.) Non-residents may qualify for postal ballots in the state of which they are a national (e.g. the Netherlands and Luxembourg). The UK provisions are not automatic, however. Thus, an EP vote is restricted to national non-residents who meet certain criteria: they must have lived in the UK and have been on the electoral roll during the preceding five years; they must also actively request an EP vote. Unlike national parliamentary elections, members of the House of Lords may have an EP vote. Not until the 1989 elections did the UK enfranchise its EC officials; Irish non-residents are disenfranchised but, in the UK, may vote.

Some states permit other EC national residents to vote for candidates in their 'adopted' state of residence (e.g. Ireland) and usually after a minimum qualifying period of residence of at least three years and/or if they are disenfranchised by their 'home' state (e.g. the Netherlands). Belgium allows British and Irish citizens to vote for Belgians under these conditions. The FRG extends the EP vote to its nationals in other EC states, and abroad if they satisfy a minimum residence requirement of ten years and are on the German electoral register.

Candidate eligibility

A few allow 18-year-old national residents to contest the elections (the FRG, Spain and Portugal). Most raise this, usually to 21 (Greece, Ireland, Luxembourg and UK, for example). It is 23 in France and 25 in Italy. Italy alone allows other EC nationals to contest the elections on the same basis as Italians.

Opinion polls

Opinion polls and forecasts are prohibited often by law in some states and sometimes by custom (for television at least, e.g. in Greece) for stipulated periods before the ballot. This restriction ranges from one month in Belgium and Luxembourg (30 days in Italy) to five days in Spain and seven in France to the day of the vote in the FRG. In Denmark, Ireland and the Netherlands there are no restrictions. Portugal imposes a total ban throughout the campaign which begins officially 12 days before the ballot.

Campaign period

The official campaign period may be limited (e.g. to 40 days before the ballot in Belgium). In the UK the campaign officially began on 18 May; in Spain on 25 May; in France on 3 June. The Netherlands,

Greece, the FRG and Ireland have no official period, while in Luxembourg the parties are supposed to determine it themselves. In Italy the official campaign opens 30 days before the ballot.

Media air-time

There is no common pattern to the amount of air-time EP candidates and parties have. Some states make formal provisions. Portugal gives all parties presenting lists air-time. In the Netherlands, this is regulated by government; in Greece by the High Court; in Denmark, the FRG and Ireland by the press and television authorities and the parties. In Belgium, air-time is apportioned according to parties' strength. Spain restricts radio and television time to parties represented in the EP and national parliament. France divides two hours between groups represented in the National Assembly or Senate and allots a further 30 minutes to the rest. Media coverage is also complicated by whether or not political advertising is allowed.

Campaign funding

There is little comparability across the Twelve regarding campaign expenditure by the parties. The UK, for instance, does not provide state funding for the campaign. Expenses are supposed to be limited to £2000 per candidate and up to 3 pence per voter. By contrast, Portuguese parties (responsible for funding the campaign) may not spend more than fifteen times the minimum monthly salary on each candidate's campaign (approx. 181 ECUs). In Belgium, expenditure is supposed to be limited by inter-party accord. In Luxembourg, parties polling a minimum of five per cent of the vote are reimbursed the postal costs for one mailing of election material. France similarly reimburses certain electoral expenses to those polling a minimum of five per cent (with due regard to the March 1988 law on financial transparency). In Spain, state funding is limited to 15 000 ECUs per seat won and 70 pesetas per vote. Greece distributes funds between the parties. The FRG funds election expenses according to the strength of the parties and providing the party list has won at least 0.5 per cent of the vote. This runs to about 5 DM per voter.

Actual expenditure varies greatly and additional costs are incurred if candidates have to make a deposit. In France, a refundable deposit of 100 000FF per list is required and is refunded to those winning at least five per cent of the vote. In Ireland a £1000 deposit is refundable if a candidate wins one-third of the vote necessary for election. In the Netherlands, those not already represented in the EP have to deposit 18 000 florins. In the UK, a deposit is required from each candidate.

Candidates

The rules regarding the nomination of candidates deviate significantly from state to state. In the UK, each has to be supported by 30 voters. In Portugal lists have to be deposited with the Constitutional Tribunal. In the Netherlands, each list must be supported by at least 25 voters' signatures and no list may have more than 40 candidates. In Luxembourg lists must be supported either by 25 voters or by an MP or MEP. Italian parties may only present lists if they have already won a seat at the preceding EP election. Individual candidates may contest the election if they are supported by 30 000 signatures. In Spain, parties, coalitions, federations and groups of voters can put up lists if signed by 15 000 voters or 50 elected representatives. In Greece, lists are restricted to a maximum of 24 names and have to be presented by political parties. In the FRG, if a party has neither 5 MPs in the *Bundestag* nor *Landtag*, they have to get 4000 signatures in order to present a federal list or 2000 for a *Land* list. Transnational European federations are allowed to put up lists in their own right. Danish parties may put up a list by right if they have won seats in a preceding EP or *Folketing* election. Other party lists need to secure the support of a number of voters equal to two per cent of the valid vote at the preceding national elections. Belgian lists or candidates need the signature of at least five national representatives or 5000 voters (1000 in the case of candidates in a single constituency).

From the above, it is clear that there are wide discrepancies in the electoral rules governing EP elections in each member state. Even so, some member states made special provisions to introduce more flexibility into their EP electoral procedure. France, for instance, introduced PR in a single ballot, and the FRG permitted parties to put up federal or regional lists to ensure that smaller parties would not find insurmountable obstacles to securing seats in the EP. If these electoral laws are to be changed again, the question must be posed as to what function a UEP would serve. It can be argued that the Euro-vote constitutes one of the first and most basic political rights enjoyed by EC citizens.[5] It is the most readily understood expression of democracy in the EC and the precondition to the EP being able credibly to assert the legitimacy of its case to effect democratic accountability by decisionmakers in the EC. This can no longer simply be construed as an extension of EP scrutiny and control *vis-à-vis* the Commission and the Council.

The cooperation procedure, by augmenting the EP's influence over the content of legislative outputs, must also have implications for the EP's accountability to the voters. This brings us full-circle. Whereas in national elections, voters can indicate their relative satisfaction with the performance of MPs and governments by voting a government out of office and a rival or alternative into office, this sequence does not hold for EP elections. Consequently, there is a temptation to construe the level of turnout as an indicator of relative satisfaction levels. This is not necessarily a useful indicator, and not only because voting is compulsory in some states (Belgium, Luxembourg and Greece) but not in others. However, it may be argued that this is the only indicator available so long as there is a disjunction, in the minds of the electorate at least, between what the EP does and what the parties that contest the elections (until now primarily the national parties) purport to stand for.

National parties can, at present, make promises that have no chance of being implemented at EC-level, for a number of reasons. Firstly, they have no power to ensure that MEPs, who exercise an independent mandate, pursue policies outlined by their national parties. Secondly, even if a national contingent of MEPs from a particular party were to adhere to national party guidelines, there would be no guarantee that they could muster an EP majority behind them. Thirdly, if such a contingent were to act in this way, then decisionmaking within the EP itself would become seriously blocked. Fourthly, the right of legislative initiative still rests almost exclusively with the Commission. Fifthly, neither national parties nor the EC party federations can ensure that EP party groups attempt to implement their Euro-election manifestos. As a result, it is tempting for the federations to put forward somewhat anodyne manifestos that enjoy the broad support of their constituent parties but that do not have very clear short-term operational consequences. Nevertheless, MEPs as members of EP party groups are affected by the cooperation procedure and do share a conception of what political priorities are desirable. A legislative record will inevitably be built by the EP groups between now and 1994. The nature of the EP's party groups as well as their interrelationship and interdependence must be affected. Their role in EP elections (as yet rather distant or non-existent) must change, though it is highly unlikely that in the short term they would have a decisive role in the selection of candidates to contest the elections or even in the campaign's management within individual member states. Organisationally, institutionally and financially they are too diffuse and weak for this. Moreover, citizens cannot 'join' parties outside the EP that correspond to the EP's party groups. (This is theoretically possible in the case of the EPP group's federation but it is not always easy. British Conservatives seeking a backdoor means of EPP membership were denied this route.) EP party groups and, therefore, MEPs as members of such groups, lack a network of party recruits and workers to campaign on their group's behalf. In a sense, they are non-participatory and fluid, and their relationship with national parties varies greatly from one group to another. But all have to rely electorally on national parties who jealously guard their party bases and demand at least a modicum of national party loyalty from their MEPs. Some national parties make interpenetration of national party and EP party elites very difficult. None has much of an incentive to see the EP groups strengthened as this would increase MEPs' already considerable autonomy, augment the possibility of EC party hierarchies developing in a federal manner and reduce MEPs' limited dependence and possibly concomitant responsiveness to the national parties. Voters' party loyalties, therefore, are indirect and 'mediated' by national parties. However, change must again be the order of the day. The catalyst of change again being the cooperation procedure, and the agent the UEP.

The EP has recognised the desirability of greater cooperation and exchange between itself and national parliaments be they in the form of information, documents, joint working parties, observer status for their respective Members and administrators on appropriate committees, or closer working links and cooperative strategies designed to ensure that governments do indeed implement directives in the intended spirit. A negative corollary to a clearly positive development might, however, be national parliamentary parties trying to qualify 'their' MEPs' independent mandate. What is necessary is accommodation between the two sets of party elites. EP elections, together with the cooperation procedure and the continuing expansion of integration and European Union, have implications for the organisation and management of interaction between the EP and national parliaments and, crucially, between EP party groups and national parties that have not been well appreciated yet. If the EP is successful in stimulating interest in a uniform electoral procedure (for EP elections *per se* rather than simply some basic principles governing entitlement to vote in local and municipal elections) and if it manages to get a rudimentary UEP accepted for the 1994 elections, there will be far-reaching consequences for all concerned. It must not be forgotten that the franchise, particularly a Euro-franchise, marks an important stage in European integration and the development of a decentralised federal European Union. The franchise itself is already linked to concepts of citizenship (whether based on the criteria of nationality and/or residence), freedom of movement, individual rights under EC law, immigration, and individuals' entitlements to equal treatment as EC citizens in each member state.

A Euro-franchise that could be exercised according to a set of uniform electoral provisions (such as the criteria regarding candidate and voter eligibility, PR and a single day for the elections) would have a psychological impact on individuals. Concerning the consequences for the evolution of the EC's party system, it would necessarily stimulate greater interaction between the various levels of party organisation. It would affect the management of the existing complexities and diffuseness of decisionmaking power within EP party groups. It would also affect the nature of party cooperation (necessary to asserting the EP's will against that of the Council) and party competition. Within the EP, voting alliances are essential and made possible by cooperation between MEPs who are opponents in the national arena.

Above all, a Euro-vote exercised under the terms of a uniform electoral procedure would be a potent expression of the dual nature of EC citizenship. The pursuit of the UEP will not take place in a political vacuum but as part of the overall movement towards a People's Europe. Combined with the way in which the EP exercises both its legislative authority as the elected chamber of a *de facto* bicameral legislature, ideally having a single seat in Brussels,[6] and its role as voice of the people and conscience of the EC, this should energise and consolidate the system-transformative trend in the EC during the 1990s.

NOTES AND REFERENCES

1. *Eurobarometer*, 30, December 1988, 11.
2. Ibid.
3. Ibid.
4. For background to the groups' formation in 1979, see G. and P. Pridham, *Transnational Party Co-operation and European Integration* (London: Allen & Unwin, 1981).

5. See C. Sasse et al., *The European Parliament: Towards a Uniform Electoral Procedure* (Florence: EUI, 1981).
6. See V. Herman and J. Lodge, *The European Parliament and the European Community* (London: Macmillan, 1978).

Index